MATER DEI LIBRARY
M/ 330.904 BRET
Brett, E. A
World economy since the war : the politi

0 1165 8436

The World Economy since the War

D1584916

Also by E. A. Brett

Colonialism and Underdevelopment in East Africa

International Money and Capitalist Crisis

The World Economy since the War

The Politics of Uneven Development

E. A. Brett

MACMILLAN
EDUCATION

© E.A.Brett 1985

All rights reserved. No reproduction, copy or transmission
of this publication may be made without written permission.

No paragraph of this publication may be reproduced, copied
or transmitted save with written permission or in accordance
with the provisions of the Copyright Act 1956 (as amended),
or under the terms of any licence permitting limited copying
issued by the Copyright Licensing Agency, 33 – 4 Alfred Place,
London WC1E 7DP.

Any person who does any unauthorised act in relation to
this publication may be liable to criminal prosecution and
civil claims for damages.

First published 1985
Reprinted 1986, 1988

Published by
MACMILLAN EDUCATION LTD
Houndmills, Basingstoke, Hampshire RG21 2XS
and London
Companies and representatives
throughout the world

Printed in Hong Kong

British Library Cataloguing in Publication Data
Brett, E.A.
The world economy since The War: the
politics of uneven development.
1. Economic history—1945-   2. Economic
development
I. Title
330.9'04   HC59
ISBN 0-333-37199-2
ISBN 0-333-37200-X Pbk

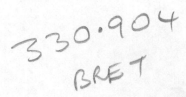

FOR JULIE

*In the hope that Adam, Katie and Adi
may have a future*

Contents

Preface

This book attempts to provide a general assessment of the political implications of the present crisis in the world economy. It should be looked at alongside my earlier *International Money and Capitalist Crisis* (London, 1983) since it depends upon some of the theoretical arguments presented there, but it is intended to broaden the scope of those arguments and develop the empirical material required to substantiate them. However, to ensure that this volume can also stand alone, some of the general issues treated there are also covered here, hopefully in a more accessible form with the most complex technicalities removed. It, too, excludes any consideration of the problem of East–West relations and the internal structure of the socialist bloc, but covers a number of areas (the role of multinationals, the decline of the British economy, and the international dimension of the development problem) which could not be treated adequately there because of its focus on monetary problems.

Although the book will probably serve primarily as a textbook, the problems that it addresses are not of purely academic concern. International instability and recession are having the most devastating effects upon the welfare and future prospects of all of us, and are therefore the subject of intense and necessarily highly partisan debate. This book attempts to present this debate without doing serious injustice to any of the views involved, even where its final conclusion has been to reject them. But it does not aspire to an apolitical academic detachment, but is intended to counter the liberal view of the functioning of the capitalist international system which now dominates orthodox political science and economics and sustains the efforts at reform being organised by the establishment. Having reviewed the evidence as dispassionately as possible, it therefore concludes by asserting the validity of a socialist vision which stands in direct opposition to the atomistic views of liberal orthodoxy. And although it rests heavily upon the Marxist critique of that view, much of the analysis does not depend upon a Marxist fundamentalism, but should be equally acceptable to those who are prepared to go no further than radical variants of Keynesianism. It is therefore intended as both a political and an academic intervention in the devout hope that the two are not inherently incompatible. After all, *The Wealth of Nations* was written to provide a rational resolution of the major political controversy of the day, that between Whigs and Tories in Scotland, but is nevertheless still used as a text in even the most respectable universities.

Many people have contributed to the development of the argument and the final text – the former emerged out of general discussions with Andy Pople, Mike Hall and Steve Gilliatt, the latter has been greatly improved through comments from Steven Kennedy, Andrew Gamble, Susan Cunningham and Robert Wade. I am also particularly grateful to Jeremy Beale for producing the index, and to Helen Warner for typing the original manuscript. Responsibility for the errors and omissions is, needless to say, entirely my own.

Brighton   E. A. Brett

Acknowledgement. The author and publishers are grateful to the Department of Applied Economics, University of Cambridge, for permission to reproduce data from *The British Economy, Key Statistics, 1900–66*.

Introduction: Understanding the International Crisis

At the end of the Second World War the main concern of American policy was 'to avoid drifting from the peace table into a period of chaotic competition, monetary disorders, depressions, political disruptions and finally new wars within as well as among nations'.[1] To avoid this the Americans could now see that conditions would have to be created after the war which would ensure that 'the war-torn and impoverished nations' in the rest of the world would not be driven back into 'the pre-war pattern of every country for itself, of inevitable depression, of possible widespread economic chaos, with the weaker countries succumbing first under the law of the jungle that characterised international economic practices of the pre-war decade'.[2] International co-operation and the guarantee of a return to prosperity for the weak as well as the strong had finally been recognised as an essential precondition for the economic and physical survival of the capitalist world. In the words of Harry Dexter White, the American architect of the International Monetary Fund (IMF) and the World Bank (more properly to be known as the International Bank for Reconstruction and Development (IBRD), but here the more common usage will be preferred):

> A breach must be made and widened in the outmoded and disastrous economic policy of each-country-for-itself-and-the-devil-take-the-weakest. Just as the failure to develop an effective League of Nations has made possible two devastating wars within one generation, so the absence of a high degree of economic collaboration among leading nations will, during the coming decade, inevitably result in economic warfare that will be but a prelude and instigator of military warfare on an even vaster scale.[3]

Confronted with the devastation of two world wars and the threat of a third, the capitalist system was finally prevailed upon to modify the system of national and international competition that had prevailed in the 1930s. Then international monetary and trading arrangements had been based upon the operation of relatively autarchic economic blocs based around the old imperial system dominated by the Americans, the British, the French and the Japanese; domestic economic policy upon the neoclassical commitment to balanced budgets and the rule of market forces. After the war the national principle came to be challenged through the creation of a number of international agreements which established the basis for a substantial degree of multilateralism, though without making a frontal attack on the principle of national sovereignty itself. Domestically the 'interventionist state', in the industrial countries at least, accepted a commitment to economic management designed to sustain full employment, economic growth and adequate welfare services. A new era appeared to have dawned, completed with the decolonisation of the Third World and the consequent elimination of the old imperial system which Lenin had taken to be a necessary element in the structure of monopoly capitalism.

Writing towards the end of the First World War, Lenin had argued that the growth of monopoly capitalism on a global scale, and the corresponding ability and necessity to plan production, meant that private economic and property relations now constituted 'a shell which no longer fits its contents, a shell which must inevitably decay', and eventually be removed.[4] In 1945 his prediction still stood as an immediate and imminent threat to the capitalist system itself, a threat clearly grasped by White, and one made more real by communist expansion and consolidation in Eastern Europe and China during the next five years. Yet ten years later these dangers appeared to have been triumphantly overcome. Economies had been rebuilt, employment restored, growth had become continuous and an international framework for the progressive liberalisation of trade and capital flows had been created under firm capitalist control. The 'end of ideology' was at hand, and a leading economic theorist could assert, with little likelihood of contradiction, that 'the overwhelming majority of economists in the Western world agrees, [that] the chance that [deep and protracted slumps in the industrial countries] will happen is practically nil'.[5]

In the context of the most dynamic and extensive period of growth the world has ever seen, such optimism was inevitable, but we can now see that it was built upon insecure foundations. We *have* now drifted into a period which corresponds with uncanny accuracy to White's worst fears set out at the start of the chapter. Monetary disorder and depression have led to an intensification of begger-thy-neighbour competition, to the further impoverishment of the poorest peoples in the poorest countries, and to a corresponding increase in political disruption and wars within as well as among nations. And if this *should* lead to a third world war as White feared, it could be the last.

These conditions now clearly add up to a crisis for the system itself – that is to say, a situation in which stability can only be restored through structural changes in a pattern of relationships where conflict has become so intense that breakdown is inevitable. Urgent and radical action is obviously essential if immediate and intensifying suffering is to be alleviated and unimaginable dangers averted, yet this will only serve its purpose if it is based upon a clear understanding of why these problems have arisen and what can realistically be done about them. Much sophisticated intellectual effort is being devoted to the production of these solutions, yet few are convinced by the prescriptions offered by the orthodox economists and policy-makers. Each promise that a further tightening of belts and loosening of controls over market forces will shortly be followed by a new upturn and return to full employment is followed by another failure. Growth stagnates, employment declines, inequalities increase, monetary arrangements collapse, and financial agreements between creditors and debtors are increasingly undermined by bankruptcies on a global scale. These are clearly the outward manifestations of a weakness in the system which is so deep-seated that it will require what Margaret de Vries, official historian to the IMF, calls 'structural solutions' which must ensure that the rest of this century is 'clearly going to be very different from anything that had gone before'.[6]

This combination of political and economic deterioration and intellectual incoherence has left many people confused and disheartened. Some things are reasonably clear: that these problems arise out of a global deterioration which cannot be dealt with on a purely national scale; that some countries and classes are in a much stronger position to influence and benefit from events than others;

that much of the responsibility for what is happening lies with the multinational corporations (MNCs) and banks which dominate the world economy, and not with the governments and international agencies that are usually held to be responsible for them; and that any solution will necessarily involve a very substantial alteration in the balance of power and wealth both between countries and within them. But without further development, this knowledge can merely serve to increase confusion rather than reduce it, since it does little more than indicate the complexity of the problems to be solved, rather than provide clear guidance as to how to do so. What is the connection between international and national political control implied in the relationships between governments and agencies like the IMF, the World Bank and the EEC? How far is the fate of the poorest people in the poorest countries determined by decisions taken in Washington, Bonn or Tokyo rather than in their own capital cities? To what extent does the continuous expansion in the 'global reach' of the MNCs intensify or ameliorate the problem of economic deterioration and loss of political control? Can a major transfer of wealth and power take place without precipitating conflicts so intense that the survival of humanity itself will be put at risk? Clearly these issues are so complex that no individual can hope to comprehend them fully, let alone satisfactorily resolve them. At the same time the dangers they identify are so urgent that we must all make every possible attempt to do so if we are to secure a bearable future for ourselves and our children. This book is an attempt to provide a non-technical introduction to the problems of understanding the current economic and political crisis for readers looking for an alternative to the orthodox views put forward by neoclassical economics and functionalist political science.

What, then, will this involve? We know that our inability to solve our own problems rests in part at least upon the fact that hostile external forces constantly undermine the policies adopted to restore employment and welfare services. We know that things were very different a few years ago when an international prosperity served to improve the opportunities available in all countries through a continuous expansion in external markets and the supply of capital and new ideas and equipment. We know, too, that MNCs have constantly expanded their control over production and distribution on a global scale, and are now increasingly blamed for the general deterioration by radicals because their political autonomy and need to maximise international profits means that they can and must act in ways which undermine the changes that the national and international authorities must make in order to restore stability to the system. Finally, we know that different schools of political and economic theory look at the world from entirely different perspectives, are concerned to achieve very different goals, and prescribe very different remedies for its problems.

Now any explanation for the crisis must necessarily take account of all these elements, elements which include the political and the economic, the national and the international, the historic and the contemporary, and must consider them within an intellectual framework which, while not ignoring the significance of all the major theories that have been used to explain them, nevertheless attempts to do so in a consistent and convincing way. Attempting to make all of these links in a single work runs against the most powerful intellectual tendencies within capitalism, which has usually concerned itself 'with objects that arise either from the process of studying phenomena in isolation, or from the division of labour and specialisation in the different disciplines'.[7] Given that the crisis is a fundamental one arising out of the mutual dislocation of the various elements in the system, an adequate understanding of it will only be reached if we can deal with it at the most general level, that is to say by producing a 'single, unified – dialectical and historical – science of the evolution of society as a totality'.[8]

Starting from this conception of the totality implies the need to postulate the nature of the real relationships between the various elements listed above, since it is only thus that we can demonstrate how and why the system has developed as it has. Ideally it would involve a historical account of the development of the international economy since the war, incorporating a clear formulation of the relationships that have prevailed during its various phases – of how national and international agencies have interacted with each other, with the power of national and international capital and with the political and economic pressures generated by the working class. Since all these elements constitute a seamless web in the real world, our concern should be to provide an equally integrated and unified account of our intellectual representation of it. Yet such an attempt would be neither possible nor useful, since, as Marx points out, to move from a 'chaotic' to an ordered view of reality we have to discover 'through analysis' the 'small number of determinate, abstract, general relations' that allow us to understand the world 'as a rich totality of many determinations and relations'.[9] This suggests that our historical account can only be developed in the context of an examination of the theoretical formulations required to reduce the chaos of immediate appearances to a coherent grasp of the totality as a process of development.

This work will therefore begin with an attempt to outline the essential theoretical presuppositions that have served to order the historical data which are then presented in the second part of the book. No qualitative distinction is being made here between 'theory' and 'reality', only a recognition of the need to consolidate and clarify the conceptual apparatus that has served as the basis for the selection and interpretation of the 'facts' which follow. Thus the next chapter attempts to identify the political and economic relationships and structures which must be sustained if the world market is to operate and evolve as an integrated and unified whole, while Chapter 2 deals with the varieties of orthodox, reformist and Marxist theories that are currently used by competing elements in the class struggle as the means of understanding it.

In these chapters the attempt will be made to develop the key conceptual assumptions that will serve to give the book its structure. Firstly, that the nature of the dynamic forces inherent in the evolution of the capitalist production process has as Marx predicted, 'universalised competition' despite attempts by nation states to resist this through protection and, by so doing, created 'the modern world market . . . and the centralisation of capital' and thus 'produced world history for the first time, insofar as it made all civilised nations and every individual member of them dependent for the satisfaction of their wants on the whole world'.[10]

The second assumption is that this means that economic and political science can no longer be written from a perspective which places the major emphasis on the autonomy of the self-sufficient nation state. Neither 'closed economy' nor 'sovereign state system' exists in a world in which economic interdependence is universal and the capacity of national governments to plan policies is a function of their ability to control overwhelmingly powerful external forces which are decisively mediated by the activities of offical and private international agencies like the IMF and the commercial banks.

The third conceptual assumption is that the successful functioning of this world system – its capacity to survive and expand as an open and integrated whole – depends upon its ability to guarantee that the development of the productive forces within it takes place on an *even*, not an *uneven*, basis. To the extent that even development occurs, the political and economic relationships between countries, and more especially the productive forces within them, will be seen to be mutually beneficial and international integration will get positive political support. To the extent that development in one area is far more rapid than in another, and, most especially, where it is seen to take place there at expense of some other area, relations will be viewed as contradictory and pressures for disengagement will intensify.

Fourthly, while orthodox economic and political theory treats the relations between capitalist producers and countries as inherently reciprocal, provided that market competition is not interfered with, a more realistic understanding of the operation of the system sees it as a profoundly ambiguous one dominated by the tendency towards an intensifying centralisation and concentration of productive forces. Hence the dominant feature of the evolution of the world economy is a process of *combined and uneven development* which guarantees that massive gains in productive capacity will occur, but will be associated with an increasingly unequal distribution of the benefits which they bring.

The third and fourth of these propositions suggest a clear contradiction between necessity and possibility: while an open and integrated world economy can only survive on the basis of even development, the actual process of international capitalist development constantly pushes in the opposite direction. The concentration and centralisation of capital constantly pushes more and more productive capital into already developed regions, and into the hands of established multinational corporations. Although a few new centres of production and firms can emerge, the tendency constantly reinforces the relative weakness of the other elements in the system. *This contradiction is the most important feature of the development of the world economy in the post-war period and provides us with the key required to understand the way in which it has been organised and why that organisation has failed.* It will also serve as the fundamental organising principle determining the choice of subject matter and structure of the rest of the book.

Having used the first and second chapters to identify the theoretical implications, both political and economic, of the problem of combined and uneven development, Chapter 3 and 4 will be concerned to look at the nature of the public and private structures which evolved at the international level in relation to it. Here we must consider the compromises between the interests of the strongest and of the weaker countries required to establish the leading international economic agencies (the International Monetary Fund, the World Bank and the General Agreement on Tariffs and Trade–GATT), and the relationship between the private economic power of the system of multinational corporate capitalism and the policy requirements of the nation states that have come to depend on them for capital, jobs and new technology. The dominant objective in these four chapters will be to show how the major concern has been to create an open and integrated world system based on the 'maintenance of a voluntary rule-based order'[11] sustained by free exchange between economic agents and the decentralised management of a balance of power system by a society of autonomous sovereign states. This will involve an examination of the conditions that have made it possible for both states and firms to continue to participate in a system from which the gains have been very unequal, and hence with the essentially *political* problem posed by the need to create a unified structure out of a decentralised system which has no overriding authority exercising a monopoly of physical coercion.

Yet to pose the problem and necessity for order and organisation is not to resolve it, as the world's economic decision-makers have discovered to their cost over the past fifteen years. Thus, while the first part of the book is primarily concerned with the theories and structures created to stabilise and integrate the world economy, the second will look at their successes and more especially their failures in practice. This will involve a largely historical account of what would seem to be the key features of the development of that economy over the past decades, an account which will focus on the central problems generated by the process of uneven development.

From a political point of view the success of a voluntary order depends mainly upon its ability to provide real and visible benefits to the weak, since it can be assumed that the strong will be satisfied with their capacity to look after their own needs within it. Thus, according to Hager:

there is an incompatibility between the extraordinary performance of one or more members in a system and the maintenance of a voluntary rule-based order. The strong tend to believe that a system which allows others the freedom to emulate them is the best of all possible worlds. In the real world, however, the weak have to be bribed or forced to continue playing a game they lose . . .

Rules are the essence of . . . international organisation. They create equality, but they also assume equality to exist. Much of the Western political development since the eighteenth century and of the international community since 1944 can be explained by this central tension: the conflict between the need to impose a single standard on a heterogeneous population as the precondition for minimal justice and stability on the one hand, and the perceived need by groups in society or nation states to offset the de facto unequal results produced by common standards.[12]

Hence our main concern in what follows will be with the fate of the major deficit countries in the system, with a much less central treatment of that of the surplus countries which will be provided mainly to show how their success related to and was ultimately threatened by the weakness of the former. Here again, limitations of space will only allow us to focus on the major problem areas – the role of the USA, initially as the dominant surplus country, but later as a chronic deficit producer; the UK, a deficit country by the end of the war and in chronic deficit thereafter, yet still attempting to provide the system as a whole with the financial resources only available to a great power; and, finally, the Third World as a whole which, as 'late industrialisers', could be expected to confront a chronic shortage of capital, a 'development deficit', and thus to require continuous access to external resources if they were to achieve their minimal economic objectives. The balance of the relevant chapters is dictated more by pragmatic than theoretical considerations – the problem of the US deficit has been extensively considered in the literature and can therefore be treated only in outline here; the complex interaction between domestic and external, political and economic considerations in British development has been seriously neglected and is covered in what some might consider excessive detail as a result; finally, the experience of the

Third World has become increasingly diverse and subjected to a correspondingly diverse range of theoretical interpretations so that it has been impossible to contain an account of the relationship between developmental objectives and the external system within the scope of a normal chapter. In conclusion, two very general questions will be raised: on the one hand the mechanisms through which the system of public and private power have come together to respond to the problem of uneven development through the recycling of resources to deficit countries through the private banking system; and on the other the long-term political implications of the evident inability of the present structures to provide an adequate solution to the problems that now confront it, which can no longer be circumvented, and which threaten to push the system back to lower levels of organisation and, in all probability, of productivity as well.

Thus, since the purpose of the whole work will have been to demonstrate why the maintenance of an open and integrated world economy is incompatible with the uncontrolled operation of international capitalist competition, the fundamental purpose of the final chapter will be to identify the necessity for and the political implications of a transition to a much higher level of conscious control over production than has existed hitherto; that is to say, to deal with the necessity for and possibility of a transition from the present atomistic system to a socialist internationalism.

PART I

The Theory and Structure of International Economic Organisation

1

A Political Theory for the World Market

Covenants being but words and breath, have no force to oblige,
contain, constrain, or protect any man, but what it has from the
public sword.

T. Hobbes, *Leviathan*

The differing interests of producers and consumers may come
into collision with each other; and although a fair balance between them on the whole may be brought about automatically,
still their adjustment also requires a control which stands above
both and is consciously undertaken.

G. Hegel, *Hegel's Philosophy of Right*

The world economy appears to us at first sight as a multitude of
unregulated exchanges between individuals; an exchange based on
the laws of supply and demand which depend in the last analysis
upon the free expression of individual needs and creativities in a
situation of general scarcity.[1] These are what we call 'economic'
activities, and apparently clearly distinguishable from those which
are oriented towards the need to maintain order in society and
which relate in the last analysis to the nature of the state which is
defined by its monopoly of the powers of physical coercion.[2] These
apparently distinct latter activities are characterised as 'political'
and are predominantly oriented towards national governments
since it is they that have the exclusive juridical right to enforce
contracts. At the international level politics is then seen not as
existing in its own right, but as a function of a global *system* whose
development is viewed as the outcome of the interactions between

the autonomous nation states of which it is composed.[3] Our common-sense observations of the relationship between these economic and political, national and international variables, which powerfully condition our approach to public affairs, are then given scientific status and development in the orthodox disciplines of economics, political science and international relations.

Yet looked at more closely, we can see that this individualistic and atomised conception of the world economy is a very misleading one. As Marx pointed out, and as the more sophisticated bourgeois theorists like Hobbes have always understood, the existence of the detached individual standing outside social control is an illusion: 'The human being is in the most literal sense a political animal, not merely a gregarious animal, but an animal which can inviduate itself only in the midst of society'.[4] The ability of individuals to exchange freely with each other requires the consolidation of a system of property relations whose conditions can only be effectively enforced by the state. And this requires much more than the mere enforcement of the outcome of voluntary agreements; it involves the creation of an environment whose structure will determine the possibility of exchange itself and the terms on which it will be carried on, factors which will decisively affect the opportunities available to the individual actors involved and will be almost entirely outside the control of their particular wills.[5] Equally important (and increasingly clear with the emergence of the welfare and interventionist state) the possibility that property rights will be voluntarily respected (the existence, in other words, of a *legitimated* social order) will depend upon the existence of political arrangements which ensure that the distribution of resources between classes and regions in society is seen to be equitable and bearable by both rich and poor. Where this does not exist, individual rights will be constantly invaded and an increasing proportion of social resources will have to be devoted to the unproductive provision of coercion required to maintain public order.

Now the implications of these requirements have been more or less adequately recognised in relation to the nation state, where an unbroken theoretical tradition stretching from Hobbes to Poulantzas has been concerned to specify the political conditions that must be established if capitalism is to function as a hegemonic system of social organisation. This tradition began with pure liberalism oriented towards the elimination of *direct* state control over the actions of individual entrepreneurs, and was then transformed, from the latter part of the nineteenth century onwards, into social democracy concerned to specify an interventionist role for the state designed to overcome competitive capitalism's tendency to economic crisis and to allow the working class to be incorporated within it as an active political force. This political transition corresponded directly to the economic transition from competitive to monopoly capitalism, and was finally consolidated through the creation of the redistributive welfare state, in the industrial countries at least, after the Second World War. The enormous stability of the economic structures in these countries during the post-war period cannot be separated in any way from the regulative and redistributive activities of this social democratic structure, which has to be seen as the most developed framework yet created for the stabilisation of capitalist social relations.

Given that monopoly capitalism not only created the need for a fundamental restructuring of social and political relations within nation states, but has also created the world market involving complex and continuous exchanges across boundaries, we have now to consider the adequacy of the political structures created at the level to regulate them. For as long as exchanges *within* states greatly outweigh those *between* them, it is possible to treat the problem of international political control as subordinate to that at the national level. Politics is seen as the outcome of the struggle between *national* classes, and the structure of international economic relations becomes a function of the external agreements and treaties entered into by their national governments on their behalf. International relations can then be seen as an essentially atomistic interaction between a set of autonomous and at least formally equal sovereign national entities. In its most developed form this interaction can then be said to constitute these entities into 'a society of states' when the consciousness of common interests and values induces them to 'conceive themselves to be bound by a common set of rules in their relations with one another, and share the working of common institutions'. These rules would include respect for 'one another's claims to independence, that they should honour agreements into which they enter, and that they should be subject to certain limitations in exercising force against one another', the institutions would include 'the procedures of international law, the machinery of diplomacy and general international organisation, the customs and conventions of war',[6] and the regulation of economic interaction.

But the actuality of international relations has never actually corresponded to this orthodox formulation, which ignores the reality of imperialism as the basis of a structure of international political organisation. Yet capitalistic expansion has been associated from the beginning with the direct and forcible subordination of 'savage' peoples to the political control of those nations where it first took root, thus creating an international power structure based not on free interaction but on Hegel's assertion that 'the civilised nation is conscious that the rights of barbarians are unequal to its own and treats their autonomy as only a formality'.[7] It was because the great majority of the world's peoples were looked on as barbarians and therefore not autonomous members of the community of nations that it was possible to assume that international relations could be managed through a relatively unstructured system of alliances and treaties entered into between a small number of dominant industrial countries until well after the Second World War. Global 'financial management' was provided for in this system by the City of London, and 'a world-wide money market and monetary system were kept in being, and equilibrium and discipline maintained by a carefully regulated flow of international investment, the main source of which was the British investing public'.[8]

Thus a political structure for the management of international political and economic relations did exist which overcame the potential conflicts of interest between less and more developed regions through force organised around the colonial system, and which attempted to regulate the relationships between industrial countries through the maintenance of a 'balance of power'.[9] Although the elements of an international political and economic order could be sustained on the basis of this combination of control and atomistic interaction, two world wars and two depressions between 1914 and 1944 demonstrated that voluntary agreement and competition alone was an inadequate mechanism for regulating the relations between states, even when the views of the populations of most of the Third World were entirely excluded from view.

After the war even this latter possibility became increasingly difficult to sustain as increasingly violent and coherent nationalistic resistance from colonial peoples forced a recognition of their right to join the society of independent states and thus to raise at the international level the necessity of a global economic order that would take account of their inequality and need for development. As the number of at least formally independent countries expanded, the volume of international economic exchanges also began to grow far more rapidly than domestic production. Thus between 1959 and 1971, for example, 'the volume of manufacturing trade tripled, while the volume of manufacturing output only doubled'.[10] To sustain a structure of increasingly dense economic interaction between a rapidly expanding society of states without a reversion to the wars and depressions of the three decades prior to 1944, a structure of organisation and management would be required that was far more extensive, egalitarian and flexible than had prevailed during those years, a structure which would inevitably impose real limits on the sovereign economic rights of its constituent parts.

To understand the nature of this structure and of the limits on national sovereignty which the structure which was eventually created imposed, is to understand the *political* dimension of the post-war economic order, an order which, in our view, is now so organised that no nation state, not even the most powerful, can develop its own domestic or foreign economic policies on the basis of a purely self-regarding choice of the full range of options potentially available to it. An attempt to solve a balance of payments problem, for example, by imposing direct controls over the national currency, closing the border to imported goods and expropriating the assets of non-co-operative private producers, would infringe a wide range of treaty obligations organised through the international organisations and produce potentially devastating retaliation from the international community of countries and multinational firms.

To argue that these agreements with other countries have been voluntarily entered into and that the power of private capital is formally subordinate to that of the sovereign state is surely no counter to the claim that both nevertheless impose real and far-reaching limits on the freedom of action of governments as they attempt to resolve the most fundamental economic problems. These limitations certainly exclude many of the policy options that have been considered to be essential for effective economic management in the past (for example in the 1930s and 1940s) and therefore imply *de facto* reductions in purely national autonomy which are no less real for the fact that they leave the ultimate power of the state to ignore them intact in purely juridical terms. As Bull himself concedes, 'an independent political community which merely claims a right to sovereignty (or is judged by others to have such a right), but cannot assert this right in practice, is not a state properly so-called'.[11] Even Keynes, in his proposals for what was eventually to become the IMF, while attempting to defend the autonomy of national economic policy-making, conceded that 'a greater readiness to accept supranational arrangements must be required in the post-war world', and, more especially, that countries must be invited 'to abandon that licence to promote indiscipline, disorder and bad-neighbourliness which, to the general disadvantage, they have been free to exercise hitherto'.[12]

Thus, when we observe national governments debating the most sensitive of national policy issues with the IMF, issues concerning the rate of wages, of profits and the level and distribution of social services, and then signing letters of intent which constitute firm political obligations, we are merely confronting the reality of this loss of sovereignty in its most obvious and visible form. Lying beneath this ultimate intrusion is a complex structure of political and economic interaction and obligation which has bound the community of states into a far tighter unity than ever before and which can no longer be understood through the use of the old categories which presuppose the separation between the national and the international, the political and the economic. Since this is not a generally accepted view, an attempt will be made to justify and clarify it in the rest of this chapter before going on to deal with its implications in the rest of the book.

The world economy, although it functions on the basis of an atomised system of market exchanges, does not regulate itself, but can only function effectively for as long as the conditions are maintained which allow those exchanges that take place between individuals across borders to be sustained in a stable and equitable way. Appearances to the contrary, this requirement imposes important political and economic constraints on the behaviour of the supposedly 'sovereign' countries involved, and, in a highly integrated international economic *system* of the kind that exists at present, the creation of political or at least quasi-political institutions at the global level to organise and enforce them on behalf of what can then be appropriately called the 'community' of nations.

We can therefore begin to understand the political pre-conditions for the existence of a world economy by looking more closely at what the conditions required for stable exchanges necessarily involved.

What fundamentally distinguishes international from domestic exchanges is that they take place between citizens subjected to the control of different governments whose juridical statuses are therefore potentially distinct. The condition for stable exchange inside a country identified by Hobbes is that the acts of each citizen are regulated by covenants which, without the sanction provided by 'the public sword' are 'but words, and of no strength to secure a man at all'.[13] The partial illusion of the non-existence of an international state derives from the fact that there is no global authority which disposes of this capacity to *enforce* contracts, and which can therefore guarantee that they will be fully honoured on both sides. Should an individual in one country repudiate an agreement entered into with another, or, more likely, should the government of one country decide to repudiate externally held property rights within its own territory, then there is no global authority to which the aggrieved party can appeal. In the last analysis, therefore, there is no fully enforceable system of international law for the settlement of disputes arising between individuals and/or countries across boundaries. Thus the Castro regime in Cuba and the Allende regime in Chile could appropriate American assets and their *legal* right to do so not be effectively challenged. It is at this level, and in relation to this fundamental problem, that we can identify what Murray has called 'the problem of territorial non-coincidence' between the way in which the world is organised politically and the way in which it functions economically.[14]

Yet when we come to look at the actual functioning of international economic relations, we find that this absence of an ultimate political authority with full coercive powers counts for relatively little in the day-to-day running of the world economy. What we do find is that the obligations and functions that Murray identifies are almost always sustained through a multitude of mechanisms, many of which he identifies and all of which, taken together, add up to what he calls a 'permanent form of integrated cooperation, a *de facto* international state body'.[15] Given that he has set out the components of this structure so clearly, it will only be necessary here to identify some of them very briefly. They include the establishment of an agreed and stable monetary mechanism,[16] a set of regulations governing trade, and the transfer of capital and technology, and the mutual enforcement of contractual and property rights to ensure that labour discipline is sustained, debts are paid, profits remitted and the ownership of capital assets guaranteed. Beyond these essentially *regulative* functions we can also identify a more problematic *distributional* political function performed by national states when they intervene to ensure that inequalities do not grow to the point where they threaten the integrity of the community. Although this function is not performed on anything like the same scale at the international level, with consequences which will provide a major focus for this book, they nevertheless are taken account of, in however inadequate a way, in the arguments and structures which link the maintenance of global stability with the need for effective mechanisms for the transfer of real resources from rich countries to poor.

In the post-war period this structure of international regulation and even of redistribution has existed as an integrated, permanent and formalised multilateral structure, and not merely as a set of contingent agreements negotiated by a number of otherwise atomised nation states. Membership of the relevant agencies involves acceptance of a set of general principles (a commitment to economic liberalisation) embodied in 'Articles of Agreement', adherence to agreed decision-making procedures, and a willingness to be bound by properly reached agreements which can be enforced through the withholding of privileges or, in the last resort, explusion for non-compliance.[17] To the extent that these obligations are accepted and the costs of non-compliance are seen to outweigh the advantages of co-operation, a *de facto* structure does exist with the capacity to subordinate national governments to its requirements. Membership effectively excludes the adoption of a wide range of policy options normally thought to be the prerogative of sovereign governments, and therefore predisposes them to solve domestic economic problems in a manner which sustains the existing structure of international economic exchange, rather than undermines it. This is clearly evident in IMF interventions. The 1983 agreement by the French government to adopt an 'austerity' programme (thus repudiating many of its electoral commitments) as the price for agreements which would sustain the integrity of the European Monetary System was simply another example of the same process at work. Clearly this suggests a situation in which the *de facto* powers of supposedly non-political international agencies carry far more real weight than the legally unchallengeable *de jure* powers of supposedly sovereign nation states.

Of course, these open and constitutionally agreed powers of international economic enforcement are greatly reinforced when considered in relation to the complementary structures of international military control co-ordinated through the NATO alliance with the USA in the pre-eminent place. Here we have the most powerful agency of all for the enforcement of capitalist contracts – military alliance commanding not only the overt military might required to support compliant governments in the suppression of socialist opposition, but also a developed structure of covert security services capable of destabilising hostile regimes and ensuring that power reverts to more 'responsible' hands. Thus the CIA organised the return of American oil-wells in Iran in the early 1950s by reinstating the Shah, and the overthrow of Allende in Chile, while Cuba only escaped the same fate through its integration into the global network created by the Soviet Union. The significance of these arrangements is clearly understood by leading American policy-makers, if not by their political scientists, as the following statement from a former Secretary of Commerce makes clear:

It is impossible to over-estimate the extent to which private American ventures overseas benefit from our commitments, tangible and intangible, to furnish economic assistance to those in need and to defend the frontiers of freedom ... in fact if we were to contemplate abandoning those frontiers and withholding our assistance ... I wonder not whether the opportunities for private American enterprise would wither – I wonder only how long it would take.[18]

A decisive shift has therefore already taken place towards the creation of an international political system based upon a recognition of Mandel's assertion that:

Economic programming within the nation state is incompatible in the long run with multinational fusion of capital. The first will either force back the second, especially in periods of crisis or recession, or the second will have to create an international form of programming congruent with itself.[19]

Thus we can see that a developed structure of international economic regulation and control has come into existence which can and does impose severe limits over the freedom of action of national governments in relation to the most sensitive aspects of domestic policy. No realistic evaluation of the political options open either to particular classes in particular countries, or to the development of the world economy as a whole, can therefore be made which fails to take full account of the implications of this fact.

This is not to say, however, that this structure is capable of performing the functions required of it if the stable evolution of the system over the long term is to be guaranteed. On the contrary, perhaps the central message of this book is that its development, a response to the uncontrolled, uneven and intensely competitive development of monopoly capitalism, has never achieved the levels that would have to be reached if it were to succeed in doing this. More especially, it is to anticipate subsequent argument that it is insufficiently developed to provide the 'anti-cyclical economic policy' on an international level required to bring us out of the recession by organising a vast transfer of resources from strong to weak areas in the world economy.[20]

Before we can look at the conditions that would have to be met to overcome these weaknesses, however, two fundamental points must be made. Firstly, although a *de facto* structure of international political organisation has developed during the post-war period, the fact that it has not eliminated the 'territorial non-coincidence' of political and economic power at the juridical level does put serious obstacles in the path of any effective international intervention to deal with particular crises. Weak nation states can follow policies that will directly or indirectly involve them in partial or wholesale repudiation of their external obligations (for example, a heavily indebted and technically bankrupt Argentina going to war to reclaim the Malvinas/Falkland islands), while strong ones can refuse to make the resource transfers required to enable the former to deal with their problems. Equally important, the political structures through which these problems are dealt with do not provide for full representation of all the most important interests involved in them, and therefore do not serve adequately to legitimate the resulting solutions from a political point of view. Thus, when a non-democratic institution like the IMF must enforce unpalatable policy decisions on elected national governments, it always confronts political problems of the most intractable kind.[21]

Secondly, and more fundamentally, to the extent that overall control of the system depends upon the unmediated international extension of the national power of one or more dominant countries over all the rest (that is to say, upon imperialism rather than upon an equal exercise of constitutionally agreed power relations), then stability will depend on the extent to which the actual structure of imperial power is itself unified and stable. Now Mandel has brilliantly outlined the various possibilities that exist with respect to the possible developments in the relations between the dominant imperial powers during the coming phase.[22] Here he concludes that the most likely outcome will be an 'intensification of inter-imperialist rivalry' leading to 'an intensification of inter-imperialist contradictions'.[23] In these circumstances, although every effort will be made to reach effective and binding international agreements to allow expansion to continue on the basis of general collaboration, the underlying conflicts of interest will constantly undermine them. In our view the increasing tendency towards instability within the key political structures of the international economic system can be traced directly to the relative decline in American predominance which became decisive at the end of the 1960s and which has given way to a period in which no single power can provide the economic, political and military backing for stability, together with the increased internationalisation and inter-penetration of private capital through the development of the MNC at the global level. This has undermined the authority of the national government, without producing any equivalent political structure to control the crisis tendencies in the system at the international level.

The tendencies towards disintegration identified by Mandel writing in the early 1970s have now greatly intensified, thus fully confirming his original hypothesis. Yet we have also to recognise that the fact of global integration remains fundamental, and that the process of internationalisation has continued unabated despite the increasingly problematic environment within which it has now to operate. This means that the structures that have been created to allow this process to continue are proving very resilient. Before we can consider further the factors which are clearly inhibiting recovery, we have therefore to look more closely at those that have made it possible to create the degree of unity which actually still exists.

The international political system is, as we have seen, made up of a set of juridically independent nation states, each of which retains the monopoly of physical force within it own boundaries. While it is true that this monopoly can be subverted through the use of covert intervention by foreign powers, for the most part national autonomy must be respected. This means that the maintenance of a generalised commitment to respect the decisions arrived at by international agencies required that the most influential political elements in all of them must remain convinced that they gain more than they lose by doing so. Political goodwill of this kind cannot be imposed by force except in limited and very unsatisfactory ways, so that institutional stability must depend directly upon a close correlation between the internationalisation of economic activities and the benefits accruing to the dominant class interests in the various countries involved. Here we must be careful to note that this condition must be met, not in relation to the principle of international organisation *per se*, but in relation to the specific forms which these organisations have taken in the post-war period.

Subsequent chapters will be concerned to demonstrate that the agencies we will be concerned with here (mainly the IMF, World Bank and GATT) were built upon a fundamental commitment to liberalisation; a specific ideological orientation, strongly contested by the weaker countries, arising out of the dominant position of the USA in the world at the time. The need to incorporate all of the countries into the system ensured that the *laissez-faire* principle was not imposed wholesale, but it was generally accepted as the *fundamental principle of organisation* for the system as a whole, as a look at the introductory articles of agreement of any of the agencies concerned will quickly show.[24] Thus what we have to consider is the conditions that have to be met if a system based mainly on a commitment to free trade is to be able to survive as an open, integrated and dynamic whole.

This question is clearly a political one, since it relates to the maintenance of the consent required to sustain an overall system of social organisation required to enable individual interactions to take place on a stable basis. But when we look at what has to be achieved to secure that consent, it is clear that we immediately enter what is usually considered to be the economic sphere, since it clearly depends on the ability of the dominant elements in the countries concerned to benefit materially more from entering into these interactions than they would do from abstaining from them. Indeed, examined thus, we can see that the problem goes even deeper than this, and cannot be construed at the level of ideology alone. Exchanges between individuals in different countries depend on the ability of those in one to earn sufficient currency in the other by exporting goods to them, to be able to pay for the imports which they wish to obtain in return. And this, whatever the preferences of those involved, can only be achieved if the *productive capacity of the one country is sufficiently developed* to allow it to do this. Thus we can see that in this area, as in many others, an adequate political theory of the development of the system as a whole depends in the last analysis upon a command over the conditions that determine the basic relationships and structures established at the level of production. This proposition can be clarified by looking at it more closely in relation to the maintenance of stable relationships with respect to international money and trade.

Technically speaking, the problem of sustaining stable international economic relations can be expressed as one of maintaining a long-term balance of payments equilibrium between the various countries in the system. Since the currency of one country will not normally be directly exchangeable for goods in another,[25] purchasers of imports will require access to appropriate supplies of foreign exchange if they are to be able to make their purchases, and these will only be available to them if domestic producers have already earned the currency abroad or if it has been possible to borrow it. Since loans will eventually have to be repaid with interest earned through the sale of goods and services, we can see that the demand for a balance of payments equilibrium is no more than a demand that a particular country should consume no more than it produces by earning as much from exports at it spends on imports over the long term.

Now where market competition prevails, the state of the balance of payments in any country will depend upon the outcome of a multitude of individual transactions between local and overseas producers which will depend upon private calculations of profit and loss, and will not be under the direct control of governments. What will in fact determine the overall tendency is the relative strengths and weaknesses of the economies concerned. Where a national economy contains a large number of powerful firms, it will have no difficulty in earning all the foreign exchange it needs; where industry is backward and agriculture underdeveloped, however, deficits will be very likely, and a constant tendency to borrow or to reduce domestic consumption will emerge as a result. Since excessive imports will also have the effect of undermining the economic viability of domestic firms producing for the domestic market, the effects of this weakness will not merely affect external economic relations, but the stability of the domestic economic system as well. An inability to compete with international firms means not only the loss of export markets, but also that of domestic markets through 'import penetration' and a corresponding increase in unemployment unless competitiveness can be restored.

Thus where a situation of real inequality exists between the productive powers of the various countries in any system (that is to say, one of *uneven development*) we can see that the maintenance of balance of payments stability will be extraordinarily difficult. Indeed, where deficits have persisted to the point where foreign exchange reserves and the capacity to borrow have been exhausted, governmental intervention will be essential to restore the balance. Devaluation of the currency, controls over imports or general policies designed to reduce domestic consumption and increase exports will have to be introduced to enable the country to meet its external obligations. Thus, *where we have an open trading system and a competitive market economy, all aspects of domestic and external economic policy come to depend directly upon the relative competitiveness of domestic producers on the world stage.* In strong (surplus) countries this condition allows them to increase living standards much more rapidly than they could do otherwise, and will not be experienced as a negative constraint upon domestic autonomy. In weak (deficit) countries, however, it will lead to constant deflationary pressures and will be bound to generate political hostility to the form of economic organisation which allows them to develop. Equally important, it will force the government into interventionist measures designed to overcome the external balance, which may well interfere with the free trade principle and therefore destroy the integration and openness of the system as a whole and with it the liberal principle of mutual equality of access to each other's markets on which it is based.

Thus we can see that a general tendency towards *even development* is an essential *political* pre-condition for the maintenance of an integrated international economic system based upon the *laissez-faire* principles that are now deeply embedded in the constitutional arrangements of the key international economic agencies. This does not mean that each country in the system must have equal economic powers; what it does require is that the conditions under which exchanges are taking place are sufficiently equalised that each can gain from trading with the other on a liberal basis and that a stable balance of payments equilibrium can be maintained between the two over the long term. When we move from a situation involving only two countries to one involving many, we can see that the same condition must apply: each country must be able to sustain equal exchanges with all of the others over time if it is to remain a fully integrated member of the system as a whole. Where a powerful tendency develops for one or more countries to move into more or less permanent deficit (that is to say for the disequilibrium to become *structural*) the possibility of sustaining the existing system of political and economic agreements on which integration was based will be fundamentally threatened.

To avoid some serious misunderstandings two very important points must be emphasised here. Firstly, the necessity for even development is a pre-condition for countries to benefit mutually from a situation of *free* trade and not from trade *per se*. All weak and underdeveloped countries (barring perhaps the very first) have become developed through trade, usually by exchanging unprocessed raw materials which they *could* produce for new methods and technology from more developed areas which they could not.[26] But where the underlying inequality is too great to allow this process to operate on the basis of free exchange, it can only function successfully where trade is *planned*; in other words where the weaker country in particular uses state power to ensure that imports are limited to those commodities that are essential for further economic development, and potentially disruptive goods are forcibly excluded. Thus, and secondly, we have to note that the existence of free trade as the basis for international organisation is an entirely exceptional condition, one that has been more nearly approached in the post-war period than in any other, but one which has yet to be fully realised. As Emmanual notes, 'the normal practice of the world ... has been and still remains protectionism',[27] despite the importance attached to free trade in the neoclassical textbooks and the constitutions of the international agencies.

Yet from the point of view of capitalist international economic organisation, the long-term commitment to liberalisation is nevertheless a fundamental objective, since it is this that enables each firm to produce and sell wherever it best can and thus maximise its profits on a global basis. It is when this condition obtains, so the argument runs, that competition becomes the main determinant of where productive facilities are to be located, extra-economic interference in the market mechanism is minimised and the 'maximisation of world income'[28] must result. It is because economic policy at the international level is motivated by the desire to establish free international competition as the basic mechanism for the allocation of global resources that we have therefore to evaluate its possibility of success in relation to the conditions that would have to be sustained for free trade rather than planned trade to serve in this way. Given what has been said already, therefore, we are justified in asserting that the post-war history of the development of the world market can only be effectively understood through an analysis which relates the evolution of its political superstructure to its economic infrastructure through the related conceptions of even and uneven development, conceptions which recognise the importance of the sphere of circulation and exchange, but which place the greatest emphasis on production itself.

The significance of this approach is that it provides us with the theoretical insights required to sustain a historical materialist approach to the analysis of the political evolution of the world economy and to distance ourselves from the ahistorical and abstract orientation of neoclassical theory. What it tells us is that the creation of a liberal structure of economic integration cannot simply be postulated on the abstract analysis of a set of trade equations which demonstrate a necessary tendency towards mutual gains from trade, supposing that a certain set of assumptions about the real world is made. Instead it asserts that the possibilities of reciprocal interaction must depend in the first instance on the extent to which the real competitive power of particular national economies complement each other at any point in time and, more importantly, on the extent to which their relative rates of growth are tending to sustain, increase or diminish existing degrees of equality or inequality. In the real world we know that levels of development are enormously unequal, and that *relative* levels of productive capacity are constantly changing as a result of very unequal rates of growth. Out of this mass of complex, confused and often contradictory tendencies we have therefore to decide whether we can discern any overall trajectory with respect to the system as a whole. Having done this we have then to show how these tendencies have influenced the functioning of the system as a system – how far they have contributed to its integration by strengthening the desire and the capacity to co-operate by benefiting both weak and strong (and preferably the former more than the latter), or have intensified tendencies towards crisis by benefiting the former at the expense of the latter.

This analysis should have served to reinforce the general theoretical assertion made at the end of the Introduction, and to have clarified the nature of the relation between the theoretical and historical chapters outlined there. But we cannot yet move on to the substantive issues, because the argument has so far only been posed in the most general and contingent fashion. To say that an open economy can only evolve in association with a general tendency towards even as opposed to uneven development is to say nothing about whether one tendency or the other is to be expected, or why this should be so. Yet these are not matters that are simply open to conjecture, but problems that have been subjected to close and rigorous examination by theorists of every shade of opinion from the most orthodox to the most radical. Their views have decisively conditioned the political debate that has always ranged around these issues and, indeed, the structure of the political institutions established to deal with the actual economic activities which they relate to. Before we can look at our history, therefore, we must look at the history of the economic thought that has provided us with the intellectual apparatus through which to interpret it.

2
Economic Theories of the World Market

The previous chapter was in effect an attempt to demonstrate that the successful political integration of an international economy based on *laissez faire* would depend upon the ability to sustain a process of even growth in the development of the productive capacities of the various countries which composed it. This condition could be expected to hold most comprehensively where actual levels of social and economic development were relatively equal, and interactions between the countries concerned tended to maintain that equality, preferably by demonstrably contributing to the growing prosperity of all of them. In this case real losses of welfare would stem from any reversion to autarchy, and political support for integration would be overwhelming. Where, however, substantial inequalities actually existed between countries (the real situation in the post-war world) then this condition requires that people in the weak countries have good reason to believe that trade liberalisation and economic integration would induce a developmental process that would benefit them at least as much and preferably more than those in the strong. A situation in which all benefited from trade, but the strong more than the weak, might suffice, but would very probably create problems in the long run. The effect of a continuous growth in the relative strength of the producers in the strong country would always threaten that they might soon begin to overwhelm the weaker producers over the border and drive them out of business, thus causing the latter to demand the break-up of the union. What we now have to consider, therefore, is whether we can realistically expect these conditions to hold on theoretical grounds.

When we come to look at the most influential bodies of international trade theory from this point of view, we are immediately struck by two things, Firstly, that all of them do in fact address this problem directly, since they are concerned, in the last analysis, to establish the extent to which, and the conditions under which, particular forms of international economic interaction tend to maximise not merely the welfare of the strong,˙but that of all the participants in the system. Secondly, however, there is no agreement on the extent to which an uncontrolled *laissez-faire* regime will in fact lead to this desired outcome, but rather fundamental differences of view. At one extreme we have orthodox ('neo classical' or 'new classical') theories which assert that this is likely to be the case; at the other we have Marxist theory, which claims that free trade will necessarily lead to uneven development and international disintegration unless planning is introduced. Between these extremes we have Keynesian and protectionist theories, which concede that *laissez-faire* will lead to unevenness and breakdown unless corrective action is taken to stop this in certain circumstances, but which nevertheless consider that free competition remains the best method of organisation provided that these tendencies can be controlled through limited state intervention.

Before examining each of these bodies of theory here, it is important to note that their claims are not merely a matter of abstract intellectual significance, but are of direct relevance to the political class struggles that have conditioned the historical development of the capitalist world economy. Each of these theories has been used by particular classes in that struggle as a means of understanding their own relationship to it and of legitimating the special claims that they have been making for particular policies from the national and international state system. Indeed, as will become clear in the next chapter, the very structure of the international economic system itself has been decisively conditioned by this thinking, the leading agencies being fundamentally conditioned by orthodox views, but also being forced to make certain significant concessions to Keynesian and protectionist thought. Thus no adequate history of their development can leave out of account an understanding of the intellectual basis on which they were built.

Free market theory

Liberal free market theory asserts that global welfare will be maximised if all individuals are allowed to buy, sell and invest as and where they choose and thus no obstacles are put in their way by the existence of national boundaries. Here 'economic' interaction is entirely separated from direct political control, and the role of the state (which is certainly not defined) is confined to the important but nevertheless secondary maintenance of the conditions which allow competition between individuals for resources to continue on a stable and equitable basis. The theory in fact contains two main elements: a set of arguments demonstrating that trade will maximise welfare in a stable fashion, and another set laying out the conditions that must be brought into existence to enable this to occur. Let us begin with the first of these.

Why should countries trade with each other on a reciprocal basis? Prior to classical theory it was widely believed that national welfare could be increased by trade, but that this should take the form of minimising imports and maximising exports, thus ensuring a continuous increase in the national ownership of gold and silver. This body of theory, known as mercantilism, therefore excluded the possibility of free and equal exchange and in fact was closely associated with the direct use of military force as an instrument of external economic relations. Clearly no 'community' of nations could evolve in this situation.

At the end of the eighteenth and in the first half of the nineteenth centuries, however, these arguments were fundamentally undermined by the free trade theories put forward by the classical political economists, the most important of whom were Adam Smith, David Hume and David Ricardo. They denied that any nation could enrich itself at the expense of another for any extended period, and argued that they could only benefit through an even exchange in which the productive powers of each grew in parallel, thus constantly increasing the size of the markets and the cheapness of the commodities that they provided to each other. Thus Smith claimed in the *Wealth of Nations*, first published in 1776, that a nation received only a very limited benefit from the importation of gold and silver, but that all nations received two benefits from foreign trade in that 'it carries out that surplus part of the produce of their land and labour for which there is no demand among them, and brings back in return for it something else for which there is a demand'.[1]

At about the same time, David Hume wrote a seminal essay, 'On the balance of trade', in which he demolished the mercantilist case for the accumulation of precious metals by showing that it would be virtually impossible for any country to do this over the long term.[2] Here he claimed that if two countries traded with each other and one was in constant surplus and the other in deficit, the flow of money (or 'specie', hence this process is often referred to as the 'specie-flow mechanism') out of the latter into the former would continually increase the demand for goods there, and the profits available to the capitalist class. This would increase the demand for labour and thus push up wages and also the price of the raw materials which they used. This, in turn, would push up the prices of goods in this economy and make its products less competitive in the markets of the deficit country, and in its own markets in competition with the imports from the country. Its surplus would soon turn into a deficit, and the gold and silver accumulated in the past would flow out. The opposite effects would be felt in the deficit country. There the failure to sell competitively would put the least efficient producers out of business and lead to unemployment and falling wages. Those producers who remained in business would now be able to produce more cheaply, just as their overseas competitors were having to cope with increasing costs. They would soon find that their exports could increase to the former surplus country, thus evening out the earlier imbalance. When Hume wrote there was a relatively limited transfer of capital from one country to another; now it is argued that these changes would also be accompanied by a large flow of capital out of the surplus into the deficit country in search of cheaper places to invest and produce, thus strengthening the relatively crude mechanisms which he was describing.

This argument would appear reasonably convincing with respect to two countries in which relative costs were fairly equal, but not where one was consistently more expensive than the other. With relatively equal costs most producers in both countries might be expected to feel reasonably confident about their ability to deal with foreign competition, and thus allow protective barriers to be reduced, but where most of the producers in one country faced higher costs of production than those in the other, they could be expected to oppose this and insist on their governments raising barriers to trade.

In the early nineteenth century Ricardo dealt with this problem by developing the theory of comparative advantage, which demonstrated that two countries could benefit from the specialisation in particular lines of production that would result from trade even where the costs of production for all of the producers were initially higher in one country than in the other.[3] He did this through a famous example in which he compared the effects of the introduction of trade in two commodities between England and Portugal, where each of them was producing both commodities and the costs of both were higher in England than in Portugal. Here he assumed that there was full employment in each country before trade was begun, that there would be no technical innovations in either industry after trade occurred, and that transport and other difficulties could be excluded. He also assumed, probably quite realistically, that although both commodities cost more to produce in England, the relative costs of producing each would differ, and it was from the exploitation of this difference in relative (or comparative) costs that the advantages stemming from trade come. Thus if wine required 120 and cloth 100 units of labour to produce in England, and 80 as opposed to 90 units to produce in Portugal, it would still benefit both countries for them to specialise in the commodity they produced most cheaply and to buy most of what they required of the other commodity from the other country. Thus in this case it would benefit Portugal to increase its output of wine and export it to England, where it would find a large market because it only cost 80 units to produce in Portugal, but 120 to produce in England. But with full employment and no technological improvements in the wine industry in Portugal, it would have to attract workers away from the cloth industry in order to be able to meet the increased demand. This industry would find its costs increasing (with rising wages) and its output declining, and the only way in which the larger number of higher paid workers in the wine industry would be able to satisfy their need for cloth would be by importing some of what they needed from England, despite the higher prices that they would have to pay. Meanwhile in England, the first effect of Portuguese imports would be to create unemployment in the wine industry, but the increase in demand for cloth from abroad would soon create increased employment in that sector, and the workers would soon move from the one to the other. Consumers in both countries would now be buying from the most efficient producers in each country, and everyone's welfare would be maximised.

Since then these formulations have been developed into a general equilibrium trade theory which demonstrates that, where countries have differing endowments of productive assets ('factors'), each will tend to export 'those products which use more intensively the country's plentiful factors'.[4] Where free trade exists, this will also have the effect of equalising prices throughout the world. This view, the so-called H-O-S model (after its founders, Heckscher, Ohlin and Samuelson), therefore implies a powerful tendency towards even development and mutual benefit from trade, provided that full employment prevails, since international competition can be expected to maximise efficiency and consumer choice while breaking down the barriers between nations.[5]

The crucial full employment element is introduced as an assumption in all of the foregoing theories, but it does rest, in turn, upon one of the most central equations in classical economics, generally dealt with under the heading of 'Say's law'. Full employment requires that the supply of, and demand for, goods must balance at the point which provides sufficient employment for the whole population, and that consumer spending must be sufficient to cover all the costs of production. Say, a nineteenth-century French economist, argued that this condition must automatically prevail under free market conditions, since the costs of producing goods would automatically reappear as demand for them, as the money paid out in wages, costs of equipment and raw materials, profits, interest and rent would have to be spent by those who received it. Thus supply necessarily creates its own demand and everything produced would be sold provided that money was not hoarded.[6]

Where full employment did not prevail for any reason (the most likely being that excessive wages had reduced profits) this would tend to force down wages and restore profits. This would then encourage investment, leading to an increase in employment which would continue until full employment was reached. At this point wages would be expected to rise relative to profits, thus bankrupting the least efficient producers, temporarily increasing unemployment, and allowing the cycle to be repeated, but this time at a higher level of efficiency since new investment would now make use of the most efficient technology. A long-run, though cyclical, tendency to both full employment and growth could therefore be assured.[7]

Finally, it is important to note that Say's law assumed that there is good reason to believe that the money received by individuals and firms *will* be spent immediately and not hoarded. Both individuals and firms will not wish to spend everything they receive on immediate consumption, and will therefore save a proportion of it. If these savings were not spent there would be a lack of demand, a fall in output and the emergence of unemployment. Orthodox theorists deal with this problem by arguing that these savings will be invested rather than hoarded and therefore spent just as surely as if they had been spent immediately on consumer goods, as a result of the operation of banks and other credit institutions. Almost all savings are now kept in banks, and these have to lend this out at interest in order to finance their own operations; they can, indeed, even lend out more than they borrow, thus compensating for the effect of the action of those people who fail to deposit their money in this way. Investors who borrow in this way will then spend the money on wages, materials and rent, and thus restore the level of effective demand to the point where it guarantees full employment.

The combination of all of these arguments therefore suggests that the capitalist system based upon *laissez faire* internally and free trade externally will provide a stable basis for a process of long-term even development with full employment. Any failures in this process are then attributed to the effect of 'external' interventions in the market mechanism which disrupt the tendencies towards balance already described. Thus if the British wine producers respond to the increase in cheap Portuguese imports by imposing import controls, not only will British consumers suffer, but Portuguese exporters will not be able to absorb extra labour from the Portuguese cloth industry, and the relatively more efficient British cloth industry will be unable to expand and absorb labour from the inefficient British wine industry as a result. Where the government or unions respond to rising unemployment and falling wages by trying to force capitalists to pay more than they can afford, they will reduce the rate of profit and make it impossible for new investment to take place and thus for the upswing to begin again. In this view unemployment is the result of the voluntary choice by workers to insist on wages which make it impossible to employ all of them, and can only be remedied by a willingness to allow unemployment to rise high enough to make them change their minds – the view now being put into affect by monetarist governments all over the world.

Now we have already noted that this *laissez-faire* or non-interventionist view of the system also incorporates a view of how the government should act in order to guarantee the smoothest possible operation of the national and international market mechanism. Here we therefore arrive at the area of 'policy theory', which is to be derived from the 'pure theory' outlined above and which sets out the principles on which governments should operate their domestic and foreign economic policy in order to ensure that the benefits to be derived from free trade are secured. Here we must look at four issues: the nature of the regulations governing the movement of goods and credit across borders; the organisation of money to make it possible for payments for them to be made; the provision of credit for countries that are in deficit; and the nature of the domestic policies that have to be adopted in order to move out of deficit into surplus.

Relatively little needs to be said about the first of these. The free trade principle presupposes the establishment of regulations governing trade which provide foreign producers with access to domestic markets on terms as nearly equal to those of domestic producers as possible. It also presupposes the lowest possible level of tariff and non-tariff barriers to trade and the application of all of the protection enjoyed under the law by domestic producers to foreign ones. To the extent that barriers do exist, these should be operated in such a way that they do not discriminate between overseas producers in order to ensure that the only basis on which consumers make their choice is the relative quality and cheapness of the goods concerned. If the arguments outlined above are accepted as to the inherently *even* nature of the economic development that will occur with free trade, then no serious objection can be made against these recommendations, since there will be an automatic tendency for the balance of payments between the two countries to remain in equilibrium, and for full employment to be maintained as well.

Once direct political controls on trade have been lifted, it is essential that monetary arrangements be made which enable it to take place in a stable and equitable way, and which are not manipulated by governments to give their country competitive advantages on the international market as they certainly can be. In the early days of international trade, goods had ultimately to be paid for in gold, and it was therefore based on a form of money which had the same intrinsic value on both sides of the border (gold, unlike paper money, has no nationality), and which could not be made more or less valuable, more or less acceptable through the actions of governments. But in the modern world of paper and credit money, with most transactions being paid for through banks' shifting credits from one company's accounts to those of another, it is governments that are directly responsible for maintaining the arrangements which guarantee the stability and openness of the international payments system. Because a central bank can simply *print* additional money and the government can issue it to whomever it chooses, the internal and the external value of the currency has become a directly political matter (as the term 'monetarism' as a description of a particular body of policy theory suggests). The implications of a government's powers in this regard are very significant and complex, and must be exposed by looking at two points in particular – the convertibility of currencies and the nature of the exchange rate system.[8]

A particular currency will normally only be legal tender (money which *has* to be accepted in exchange for goods or services) in its country of origin. It can only be used for payments elsewhere if it can be converted into the national currency and spent there. Since governments have the power to control the use of all currencies, they can choose whether to allow individuals to convert the domestic currency into and out of foreign currencies whenever they wished to do so, or to retain the right to allow this to take place only with official permission. A convertible currency, then, is one which can be so converted at will; a non-convertible one can only be converted on the basis of conditions imposed by the government. Between the extremes of full as opposed to non-convertibility lie many variations: Britain, for example, established convertibility for the payment of goods and services at the end of the 1950s, but only allowed it for the export of money for capital investment at the end of the 1970s.

The importance of this decision is, of course, substantial, since the existence of a non-convertible currency makes it possible for any government to control all foreign transactions directly, by issuing or not issuing the money to pay for them. It is probably more effective than tariff policy in controlling the market at the international level. From a liberal free trade point of view, therefore, the greater the degree of convertibility the better, since this transfers the ability to make decisions about imports and exports from the government to private individuals.

Trade between countries involves payments which will involve the conversion of money from one currency to another and back again, and this will involve the people concerned knowing the appropriate *ratio* at which to make the exchange. If, as a British trader, I buy a thousand pairs of shoes in the USA for $1,000, I first have to change my pounds into dollars in order to pay for them, and then obtain enough pounds from selling them in England to make a profit. Clearly the rate of exchange prevailing when I change my money will have a decisive influence on how much I make or lose. If the exchange rate is £1 = $4 (as it was in 1945), then I will have to sell the shoes for £250 to cover their cost; if it is £1 = $2 (as it was in 1981) then I will need to sell them for twice as much. My decision as to whether or not to go through with the deal will then depend upon the price of comparable British shoes, so it is clear that the lower the exchange rate, the higher domestic prices can rise before they cease to be competitive with imports. Thus a government cannot only control trade through the monetary system directly by non-convertibility, but it can also do so somewhat less directly in cases where it can manipulate the rate of exchange. A fall in the exchange rate (a 'devaluation') will have the same effect on foreign imports as an equivalent increase in tariffs, so that monetary policy is just as directly involved in protectionism as tariff policy.

Here again governments can organise their exchange on the basis of two alternative principles. They can either allow the exchange rate to move freely up or down in response to the relationship between the supply of and demand for foreign currencies, thus using a 'flexible' or 'floating' exchange rate system, or they can attempt to keep it stable within very small limits, thus using a 'fixed' rate system. The leading capitalist economies now use something close to the former method (though some degree of 'managed floating' still prevails), but they attempted to maintain fixed rates until 1973 when the system broke down for reasons that will be considered in Chapter 5. Here there is some dispute between orthodox theorists which needs to be outlined briefly.

With floating exchange rates a currency's value will fall or be 'devalued' when the country concerned remains in a balance of payments deficit for any length of time. It will rise or 'revalue' if it remains in surplus. The effect of devaluation will be to make imports more expensive and exports cheaper in foreign markets, and this will tend to reduce the deficit; a revaluation will have the opposite effect. Thus many orthodox theorists argue that allowing flexible exchange rates will lead to an automatic tendency for the balance of payments to move into equilibrium without direct governmental intervention, so that it is probably fair to say that this system is the one which conforms most directly to their general philosophy.[9]

Where *even* development exists it can be seen that it will be possible to associate *flexible* with *stable* exchange rates, since there will be no continuing deficits or surpluses to cause them to fluctuate. But where countries are at different levels of development, the possibility of structural imbalances can never be ruled out, and it is possible that flexibility will lead to extreme fluctuations which will make trade very risky and difficult. This will also create the possibility for larger profits to be made by speculation, which will also have the effect of increasing the fluctuations and inflicting heavy losses on traders and on producers. (If I were to exchange £1 for $4 and the exchange rate fell to £1 = $2 next day, I could then change my $4 dollars back into £2 and make a profit of 100%.) Thus, at the end of the war when immense inequalities existed in the international economy, there was a strong feeling that countries should attempt to make a firm commitment to the maintenance of stability by trying to establish fixed rates. At that stage it was possible for this to be supported through direct action, since most currencies (apart from the US dollar and Swiss franc) were non-convertible, and governments could ration foreign exchange in order to stop exchange rate fluctuations from taking place. The other great fear among orthodox theorists was that governments would actually manipulate exchange rates for 'competitive balance of payments purposes' (as they had done between the wars), notably by using currency depreciation as a substitute for tariffs. This, of course, would be impossible under fixed rates, and this was probably the most important argument used by those who supported this system against the flexible rate system, despite the fact that it did involve a higher level of direct governmental intervention than the latter.[10]

Here again, the assumption that fixed rates could be maintained was based on the arguments already set out demonstrating that trade between two countries would normally tend towards even development and balance of payments equilibrium. Since this seemed to prove that any country that adopted 'responsible' economic policies would 'naturally' tend to move into equilibrium, there would be little difficulty in maintaining the commitment to fixed rates. If governments did manage to do this (and the reasons why they failed to do so and moved over to flexible rates will be considered later) then all traders could operate in a framework of complete stability and would be able to conduct their business secure in the knowledge that their profits would not be affected by arbitrary changes in the exchange rate which they could neither control nor anticipate.

It is important to note here that no system will ever be characterised by complete fixity or by perfect floating. Under the fixed rate system the possibility always existed that deficits or surpluses would continue for so long that governments would be forced to re- or devalue whether they wished to do so or not. The actual system in operation did allow for adjustments to be made in certain circumstances (hence it was called the 'adjustable peg system'), although these were very rare among the main currencies between 1945 and 1971. Again, since it is ultimately the central bank which maintains the level of the exchange rate by buying and selling the currencies in its foreign exchange reserves, it is bound to make decisions about the exact level at which it wishes the rate to be maintained and to intervene on the market by buying or selling in order to influence that price when it moved out of line. The difference between the fixed and floating rate system therefore mainly lies in the extent to which private traders are free to trade directly in currencies, and in the strength of the obligation on the central bank to maintain the existing rate when selling or buying pressures threaten to modify it. The present system is in fact usually referred to as 'managed floating' and is one in which central banks are expected to try to maintain stable rates, but are allowed to permit them to rise or fall when the balance of payments situation makes it difficult to do this.

Thus whether rates are fixed or not, the central bank will always have to take some degree of direct responsibility for controlling its movements. This will then necessarily involve it in the third issue set out earlier, that of international credit policy. The exchange rate will tend to fall when the balance of payments is in deficit and the bank is losing its reserves as a result, and to rise when it is in a surplus and accumulating them. It will only be able to defend the existing rate when a deficit exists for as long as it has enough foreign exchange to meet the demand for it at the existing price, and will therefore be tempted to borrow to do this, especially if it has reason to believe that the balance of payments situation is likely to improve in the near future. A surplus country, on the other hand, will find its reserves increasing and will wish to obtain interest on the money it is holding by lending it to someone willing and able to do so. Thus central banks are usually actively involved in borrowing from and lending to each other, and this gives them the power to maintain rates for longer than they would be able to do otherwise.

From an orthodox point of view the use of credit to defend an appropriate exchange rate is a perfectly legitimate procedure, and an immense quantity of official and private credit is available for the purpose through mechanisms which will be outlined later.[11] The two strongest reasons for borrowing rather than allowing the exchange rate to change would be to cope with what was expected to be a short-term deficit (for example, a harvest failure) or with an attempt by speculation to push the rate down by selling currency in large amounts to make a subsequent profit. Here the availability of credit would enable the government to avoid having to impose other more direct controls over money or trade, or would enable it to defeat the speculators. On the other hand these theorists would consider it to be wrong to borrow in order to defend an 'overvalued' exchange rate (one which made imports more competitive than domestic products) and would recommend instead a devaluation and domestic economic policies (an 'adjustment' programme) designed to make home production more competitive. What, then, are the principles on which such policies should be based?

If the balance of payments is in deficit, a country will eventually be forced to establish a surplus in order to stop the drain on its reserves or to meet the costs of its debts. This will require either a reduction in imports or an increase in exports, or some combination of both. This could be done by direct governmental intervention through protection of the home market or subsidies to exporters, but these policies are rejected by orthodox theorists for the reasons outlined already. Thus less direct methods have to be used to achieve either, but more usually both, of these objectives.

A balance of payments deficit means that a country is consuming more than it is producing, and this, since international trade is based on competitive market principles, must be because domestically

produced goods are too expensive or inefficient to compete effectively with foreign ones at home and abroad. The gap can only be
closed by reducing consumption or by increasing output without
any increase in costs, thus making domestic goods more competitive
with foreign ones. The politics designed to achieve these ends are
called 'adjustment policies', since they are intended to adjust the
levels of economic activity and consumption at home to the ability
to earn foreign exchange abroad.[12]

Domestic consumption can be cut through reductions in wages, in
public services, or in the luxury consumption of the wealthy. The
first thing any government facing a deficit is likely to do is cut one or
more of these forms of spending, since it is always quicker to cut
consumption than to increase output. This will involve the imposition of *deflationary* pressures on the level of economic activity, that
is to say a *reduction* in the level of activity, since this will reduce the
demand for both domestically produced and foreign goods. Unless
exports increase, therefore, there must be an increase in unemployment, which will have the effect of reducing consumption even
further. Cuts in public services can be made directly by governments, since they are responsible for the level of both taxation and
spending, though it will often be *politically* difficult to secure cuts of
the necessary size. Wages can be attacked either directly, by enforcing legally binding policies of wage restraint, or indirectly by
allowing unemployment to increase and thus weakening the worker's bargaining power. The latter solution is more compatible with
orthodox theory than the former, since it involves little direct
control over wages, and leaves the actual setting of wages to the laws
of supply and demand ('free collective bargaining'). Thus, where
wages are rising too rapidly and excessive imports are being drawn
in, monetarist theory will assert that unemployment is too low, and
call for an increase to the 'natural' rate of unemployment, which is
the level high enough to bring wages into line with those needed to
make domestic industry competitive with that overseas.

These policies will ease the balance of payments problem through
what is called 'import compression': a transfer of productive resources from domestic to export production combined with an
increase in efficiency and reduction in costs is what will be required
to solve it through an 'export-led boom'. Here both a reduction in
costs and an increase in the rate of profit will be required, the latter
being a necessary result of the former. Costs can be reduced by

reducing any of the bills which capitalists have to pay (wages, taxes, interest, rent, cost of machinery and raw materials), or by better organisation of the workforce, or through the introduction of better machinery. The cost of rent and of materials and machinery is likely to be difficult to modify, but we can see that the policies adopted to cut demand will also have a direct effect on cutting costs, as they will reduce wages and taxes and most probably bring down interest rates as well, since these are often kept high as a result of government borrowing to pay for services that cannot be paid for out of taxation. Better organisation of the workforce, however, will require additional action in terms of improvements in management and changes in labour practices, neither of which are usually easy to achieve.

The introduction of better machinery through greater capital investment is sometimes put forward as a way of improving efficiency without having to incur the unpopularity which will be the inevitable result of the package of policies outlined so far. But the possibility of doing this cannot be separated from these measures in a capitalist economy, since investment in new machinery must come directly out of *profits*, and profits can only be increased through a reduction in wages, taxes and interest rates when foreign competition makes it impossible to raise prices. Once these policies have been adopted and have had the required effect, profits will go up. Orthodox theorists argue that competition will force the capitalist class to invest the bulk of their increased income in new productive capacity rather than spend it on personal luxury consumption. This increase in investment will then have the effect of lowering costs further, increasing profits and encouraging still further investment. In the first instance the new output produced by these investments will mainly be exported, thus solving the balance of payments problems, but once this dynamic process is under way, more and more workers will be drawn back into the production process, unemployment will go down, wages will recover, and the deflationary situation will give way to a period of growth and prosperity in conditions of balance of payments stability.

Here the effects of this policy have been set out in the most favourable light, and some of the criticisms of this optimism will be given in the rest of the chapter. What we can see from this argument, however, is that the possibility of this positive solution to the problem of the deficit countries must depend on an ability to increase exports in order to offset the deflationary effects they must have upon the home market. This possibility is usually taken for granted by the politicians who advocate these policies, but it will only exist in specific circumstances if there is to be a solution to the problems of the deficit countries as a whole, and not simply one for a few who are able to be outstandingly successful. The deficit countries will only be able to *expand* their way out of their problems if the surplus countries in the system are willing and able to adopt the policies that will enable them to do this, since one deficit country cannot increase its exports to another without making that country's situation worse. Here we meet the problem of *even development* once again, and can see that orthodox theory would expect this not to pose any serious problems because of the arguments advanced by Hume that were outlined above. Thus there would be even more reason to expect it to be achieved when it became an objective of adjustment policy, but only where surplus countries were willing and able to allow imports to expand to the point where their surpluses disappeared and they were forced to spend the reserves they had accumulated. Where this occurs, the adjustment process will be 'symmetrical', with surpluses and deficits being equalised out in a harmonious way. We have therefore to consider why they should be willing to do this, and what they should do to ensure that a symmetrical result is obtained.

A country which runs a continuous balance of payments surplus will accumulate money in its foreign exchange reserves as payment for the extra goods it has exported: paper tokens in exchange for real resources. It can invest these resources abroad and earn interest on them, but unless it then spends this interest on imports this, too, will accumulate as yet further paper tokens and not add directly to the welfare of any of its citizens. For as long as this is going on they might just as well be 'shipping goods to mid-ocean and dumping them there',[13] and one can only imagine it continuing indefinitely in a society in which everyone was addicted to work for its own sake and had no desire to be paid in real goods and services for what they produced. Further, for one country to run a permanent surplus, at least one other must remain in deficit, so that the only way in which the process could continue would be if the former was to be willing to supply the latter with the credit that we have seen they would need to enable their goods to be bought. Thus we can see that an attempt to run a permanent surplus is based on the entirely irrational assumption that one country should not only provide another with a portion of its consumption, but also with the money that it uses to purchase it with.

There seems to be no rational reason to suppose that any country should wish to remain in surplus for any longer than it needs to in order to accumulate sufficient reserves to provide it with an adequate defence against the possibility of having to adopt undesirable policies in order to deal with short-term losses on its export markets. In a rational world all of them should therefore be perfectly willing to adopt the policies required to eliminate their surpluses once this objective had been achieved. These policies would, of course, be of exactly the opposite kind to those recommended for deficit countries. Thus they would wish to increase imports and reduce exports, and could do this by allowing domestic consumption to rise above the level of domestic production. They should increase public spending, allow wages and luxury consumption to rise, and show less concern for efficiency by allowing these increases to be taken out of profits rather than be achieved through increases in efficiency and investment. With rising costs and falling profits in the surplus countries, producers in deficit countries would now be able to compete very effectively on their markets, especially since they would have been working to reduce costs and increase profits at the same time. Capital would tend to flow out of surplus into deficit countries, thus speeding up the process and allowing the latter to move out of recession into boom with very little difficulty. Symmetrical adjustment, even development and rapid growth with full employment in an open and unified trading and monetary system, would be the happy result.

When we put all of these recommendations derived from orthodox theory together we find that we have a developed and sophisticated set of explanations which seem to provide us with a guarantee of freedom of choice and permanent prosperity if only all of the countries in the system would do what so clearly lies in their own best interests. This does not imply that none of them will ever adopt certain kinds of policies of a protectionist kind in order to achieve short-term national gains at the expense of the the unity of the system as a whole, but since the benefits of not doing so seem so self-evident, it would seem a small price to pay. Thus, since there are no fundamental conflicts of interest in the system when viewed in this way, *the problems of securing an effective international agreement to guarantee its operation would seem to hang mainly upon the existence of the political willingness required to set aside short-term national interests in order to create the framework for international co-operation, and upon the technical competence of those given the task of devising the practical mechanisms through which it is to operate.*

These policies are, in fact, those broadly accepted by the conservative and centrist governments that have dominated both developed and less developed countries in the 1970s, and are the basis on which the leading international economic agencies have been functioning since their inception. Yet the existence of the crisis and the evident growth of uneven development associated with it suggests that they are not working in the way that they should, and we have now to ask why. In the rest of this chapter we shall look at some of the more powerful theoretical criticisms of these views to provide us with the basis for the criticisms of the practical workings of the institutions themselves to be developed in the rest of the book. We can therefore start with Keynesianism, the least radical, but most influential, of these.

International Keynesianism

J. M. Keynes was active and influential from the end of the First World War till his death in 1946, and produced a body of writing which attempted to challenge the orthodox explanation for unemployment and their recommendations on policy. He is mainly known for his work on domestic economic policy (and particularly for *The General Theory of Employment, Interest and Money*, first published in 1936), but he was employed by the British Treasury during the war and was responsible for writing the policy paper which the British used in the negotiations for the setting up of the International Monetary Fund.[14] Here he applied the implications of his theory of a single economy to the problem of maintaining full employment in the world economy, and set out very clearly the substance of many arguments put forward subsequently by potential reformers of the international economic system.

Before we can look at what he had to say about the global system, however, it will be necessary to summarise briefly his criticisms of the orthodox view that supply and demand would always remain in balance within the domestic economy.

We have already seen that this view was based on Say's law – the assumption that 'supply creates its own demand' since all the money spent to produce goods will automatically be used to buy them once they come on to the market. Keynes, however, claimed that in a modern, relatively wealthy country, individuals, firms and public authorities would have a strong propensity to save a substantial proportion of their incomes. If the propensity was strong enough, the level of savings might well exceed the amount of money which entrepreneurs were willing to invest, and savings would lead to *hoarding* and thus to a reduction in the level of demand for goods below that required to absorb all of the output of existing firms. These firms would then be forced to reduce their output and lay off workers, and this would lead to yet further reductions in demand, in output and thus to a continuous deepening of the recession. These conditions would lead to falling wages, as orthodox theorists argued, but instead of restoring the equilibrium by reducing costs, this would simply further reduce demand and discourage capitalists from investing, despite the reduction.[15]

In Keynes's view the only way in which the problem of unemployment could be overcome was by inducing the capitalist class to increase its level of new investment, thus putting people back to work and restoring demand to the level required to maintain full employment. But whereas orthodox theory assumed that this could only be ensured by reducing costs and especially wages, he argued that it depended mainly on persuading the capitalists that there would be a sufficient growth in demand to guarantee them a market in the future when their investments had borne fruit. He argued that capitalists made their investment decisions on the basis of their *expectations about the future level of demand,* so that their 'propensity to invest' (a function of their optimism or 'animal spirits') would only be high if they saw some reason to suggest that it would expand, but that this would disappear if they thought that it was declining. Where government policy was designed to cut wages and services, it would demonstrate clearly that demand would go down, thus reducing business optimism and producing exactly the opposite effect than had been intended. By inducing pessimism rather than optimism, investment would collapse and no level of wages would be low enough to induce a new period of expansion. Money would remain unused in the banks, forming the 'hoards' that orthodox theory felt could not exist, machines would stand idle and workers would rot on the dole where they would be very likely to lose their faith in a system which could allow productive resources to go unused in the midst of poverty and want.

Keynes therefore argued that the classical application of the market mechanism to the solution of this problem would be counter-productive, since no *individual* capitalist could take the risk of investing during a depression unless he was certain that a sufficiently large number of others would do the same. He could not sell the additional goods he had produced to his own workers and suppliers, and would therefore only be able to get rid of them, without stealing markets from existing producers, if other capitalists were increasing demand by taking on more labour and buying more machinery and raw materials. But he also saw that it would be very difficult for the capitalist class to arrange this concerted investment process without outside assistance, since they all *competed* with each other as individuals on the market. Any new producer would be seen as a threat by those whose markets were already being threatened by the recession. The only solution lay in intervention by the only authority which stood outside the capitalist class itself and acted on behalf of all of them – the capitalist state with its capacity to raise taxes and borrow money and thereby raise the level of demand to the point where capitalists would be able to invest with security and, by so doing, expand it even further (through the 'multiplier effect') until full employment was achieved. Once full employment had been reached, the government would have to reverse its policies and act in much the way that orthodox theory recommended, by reducing spending and wages, since otherwise the level of demand would exceed the economy's capacity to increase production and prices would have to rise. Hence the Keynesian policy is not one of permanently increasing public spending, but one of 'fine tuning', in which it is increased when unemployment appears, but decreased when over-full employment leads to wage and other price increases rising in an inflationary way.

The problem with Keynesian policies is that they can be defeated by overseas interventions if they are applied in just one or a few countries. If one country increases wages and public spending while another is decreasing them, costs will rise in the first, decline in the second and lead to a growth in exports from the one to the other. This will absorb the increase in demand in the first country without creating any additional employment there unless it adopts protectionist measures, thus destroying the unity of the system. Keynes himself was a protectionist in the early 1930s,[16] and his most influential modern followers have also adopted this view, as we shall see. But in the early 1940s he came to the conclusion that these difficulties could be overcome if only a form of economic intervention could be organised on a global scale to ensure that production and demand could be allowed to develop evenly throughout the system. How would this work?

When countries trade with each other, those that are in surplus are *saving* resources; those in deficit are *spending* them. If one or more countries stay in permanent surplus and fail to lend their savings to the others, then they will effectively be hoarding money on a global scale and reducing the demand for goods and services in the system as a whole, with very deflationary results. Keynes felt that the USA had in fact done this during the inter-war period when it had been in permanent surplus (by 1947, in fact, 70 per cent of the world's gold and foreign exchange reserves were held by the Americans), thus making it virtually impossible for any of the other countries in the system to expand their way out of the recession and producing an 'asymmetrical' adjustment process and the international recession. When this occurred he felt that the first victims would be the deficit countries, but they would soon be followed by the surplus countries, since the latter would soon find that they could not maintain their exports on these declining markets and would be faced with growing unemployment as a result.

Keynes therefore argued that the solution to this problem would be an international agency capable of performing a role analogous to that of the national state at the domestic level. The savings of the surplus countries should be lent on a large scale to the deficit countries, not just for short-term balance of payments purposes, as orthodox theorists believed, but for long-term developmental purposes. This agency should play a role virtually identical to that of a national bank, using the savings of those who did not wish to spend their money for the benefit of those who did, and thereby maintaining the level of demand required to guarantee the full utilisation of labour and other resources throughout the system. He therefore put all his emphasis on the *credit* element in the policy programme, but wanted it greatly expanded to the point where no deficit country would ever have to cut its economic activities back to a less than full employment level in order to deal with a balance of payments problem. In 1944 Keynes himself put these proposals forward on behalf of Britain, then a country which expected to remain in deficit for some time to come,[17] at the Bretton Woods conference called to set up the IMF and it can be seen how this was certainly a way of looking at the problem which could be expected to appeal to such countries, since it would spare them from the serious difficulties that always followed the attempt to adopt more orthodox policies in a rigorous way. But Keynes also felt that it would be acceptable to the surplus countries as well, since it would provide them with a means of using resources which would otherwise stand idle, and simultaneously guarantee them expanding markets overseas which would otherwise be lost through import compression or protectionism.

In conclusion, it is important to note that this policy did not imply any fundamental attack on the rights of the capitalist class to control production by their companies either in its domestic or its international variants. In its least controversial form, Keynesianism simply meant that the authorities would manipulate the level of credit, of taxation and of public spending to ensure that the 'right' level of demand be maintained to ensure full employment. If there was no other interference with the market mechanism then the success or failure of particular countries or firms would still be the outcome of competition and not the result of governmental planning or interference. Free trade, convertible currencies and stable exchange rates determined by the level of supply and demand would still prevail and would be even more secure than before, since the tendency towards even development would be backed by governments' ability to use international credits to supplement the automatic market mechanisms. In fact Keynesianism came to be much more influential at the domestic than the international level, where orthodox views were much better entrenched, though it has always exerted a powerful influence over the various attempts made since the 1940s to reform the system, as we shall see.[18] But long before Keynes, another body of theory critical of orthodox free trade theory had emerged, and it is to this, in its modern guise, that we must now turn.

Protectionism and import substitution

Free trade has always been the economic theory most favoured by the strongest capitalists in the strongest countries. The weak have always taken a much less enthusiastic view, since they were always more likely to find that their markets would be taken away from them by the more efficient foreign producers unless the state intervened to erect protective barriers behind which they would shelter. Thus, although free trade has always been the orthodox view among most economists, protection has always been the favoured policy among most of the governments of relatively weak and unsuccessful countries. In the nineteenth and early twentieth centuries, only Britain, then the leading industrial country, was firmly committed to free trade; Europe and the USA were firmly protectionist. The USA was only converted at the end of the Second World War, and was followed by the remainder of the industrial countries in the 1960s, but most of the Third World is still committed to the use of direct controls to promote the industrial development they consider to be essential for their 'modernisation'. Indeed, as the recession deepens, protectionist demands are intensifying in the advanced countries themselves, especially in the less successful of them like Britain. Let us now consider the case for protectionism, starting with the problem of less developed countries, and then examining the less successful advanced countries.

The central argument for protection in less developed countries (LDCs) stems from the conception of 'infant industries'. With modern production techniques, any established industry will be at an inherent advantage over a backward one using outmoded technology, even where wages are much lower in the latter than in the former country. Since a modern plant is usually capable of very rapid expansion in output, and depends upon being able to operate on a very large scale, there will be a strong tendency for its products to take over the markets of backward countries, thus destroying the industries that exist there, as British textiles destroyed most of the Indian textile industry in the nineteenth century. Since any attempt to set up a local opposition to the existing foreign plant will almost certainly be unable to operate on the same scale, or to achieve the same level of efficiency in the short run, it will be essential to protect them against foreign competition in their infancy and allow them to operate at a higher level of costs until they are established. This will mean that domestic consumers will have to pay more for their purchases, but this will be justified by the increase in employment and wealth which the new investment generates. Once the infant has matured and is operating on the same scale as the foreign firm, then the necessity for protection disappears and the orthodox arguments apply.[19]

This case is greatly strengthened in countries where a large proportion of the population is either unemployed or is working in very backward occupations where they are producing very little. Here using protection to set up industries which will be producing on a higher cost basis than their foreign counterparts will not draw workers away from otherwise useful occupations and increase the competition for labour, but will put people to work who would otherwise have produced very little at all. Here the theorists are not questioning the logic of the orthodox argument where full employment and an existing level of even development exists, but are arguing that their theories do not apply when these conditions (which are usually taken as the normal state of affairs) do not exist. In this situation it becomes the responsibility of the state to bring full employment and even development into existence *before* free trade and a unified international monetary system can be created.

These are probably the strongest arguments used by the protectionists, and they are often accepted by orthodox theorists as the 'second-best' solution to the trade problem where underdevelopment exists. Now most LDCs also depend almost exclusively on the export of raw materials to pay for their imports, and this too is often advanced as a justification for the adoption of protection. It is claimed that the demand for raw materials, and especially for agricultural products, tends to increase more slowly than for industrial goods, so that the prices for the former tend to lag behind those of the latter. Since newly industrialising countries have to import virtually all of their capital equipment, they are therefore likely to face an almost permanent trade gap (or 'development deficit') which requires them to ration their scarce foreign exchange by favouring the import of capital equipment and discouraging that of luxury goods or of simple consumer goods which can be produced locally.[20] If the advanced countries are willing to accept the Keynesian arguments in favour of generous supplies of aid for these countries outlined below, then the need for protection becomes less urgent, but they are bound to remain in some form until the infant industry problem has been overcome and the dependence on raw material production has been substantially reduced.

These arguments therefore lead to a very different set of policies from those based on orthodoxy. Sometimes called 'structuralism' or 'import substituting industrialisation' (ISI), they require that the state takes a leading role in creating the conditions for development by directly controlling the flow and price of imports, and by allocating foreign resources to the creation of the capital base required for industry and taking them away from the purchase of consumer goods. They do not necessarily require that the state actually plays a leading role in the production process itself (though this was the case with many of the social democratic governments which used these policies both in developed and less developed countries) but they certainly require a very much higher degree of intervention to control international trade and domestic investment than orthodox theory considers to be appropriate. These policies were actively followed with considerable success in the war-damaged European and Japanese economies in the 1940s and early 1950s, but much less successfully in a number of very important Third World countries in the 1950s and 1960s. They have been out of fashion for the last decade and a half, but are very likely to be revived again in response to the continuing balance of payments crisis afflicting almost the whole of the Third World.

From the end of the 1950s protectionism was largely rejected in the developed countries in response to the apparent success of the liberalisation of monetary and trading arrangements that was then under way and which was associated with rapid and widespread growth. More recently, however, the recession and the balance of payments difficulties suffered by some of the weaker industrialised countries has led to a revival of these ideas, notably on the left of the political spectrum, but by no means confined to it. Two elements can be found in this case: the development of what can be called the 'geriatric industry argument' on the one hand, and a revival of Keynesianism on the other.

In late capitalism we now have countries with a mature industrial structure that can be said to be suffering from the problems of old age: there has been a failure to invest on a large enough scale, an inability to get rid of outmoded practices, and the continued use of backward technology. The result has been a growing inability to meet the competition stemming from the dynamic growth that has taken place in more adventurous foreign countries where investment is higher and in some cases (though by no means all) wages are much lower.[21] In free market conditions it is only possible to deal with this problem through a substantial reduction in wages – a very unpopular response – since profits will otherwise be too low to allow domestic industries to reinvest on the required scale or to attract foreign investment from outside. The only alternative to a direct attack on wages, therefore, would appear to be the use of trade controls to enable these companies to survive, together with the use of governmental intervention to provide them with the resources that they required and to ensure that they did not exploit their position by increasing prices and failing to make the necessary changes.[22] Here again it is assumed that protection will be a temporary measure that will be removed once competitiveness is restored.

These arguments can be reinforced through the addition of the Keynesian analysis outlined earlier. In these unsuccessful countries the collapse of domestic industry in the face of foreign competition has led to very high levels of unemployment. The orthodox response to this would be a reduction in public spending and wages, but we have seen that this would simply worsen the problem by further reducing demand. The Keynesian response would be to increase public spending to give capitalists an incentive to invest, but where domestic industry was uncompetitive, most of the increased spending power would go on imports, thus worsening the balance of payments and doing nothing to increase domestic investment and reduce unemployment. In this situation Keynesianism can only be effectively practised if it is accompanied by effective controls over imports, since the effects of uncontrolled foreign competition will be to increase the deficit, force the government to borrow from private banks and the IMF, and thus force it to adopt the orthodox policies that they always favour.[23]

We can see that the combination of Keynesian and protectionist critiques of the orthodox theory produces a case for import-substituting industrialisation, which involves a high degree of state intervention in the operation of the market in deficit countries in order to ensure a process of even development in the capitalist system as a whole. These policies do not seek to eliminate capitalism, but to enforce sufficient controls over its operations to ensure that it works in a symmetrical way both internationally and domestically. These are the policies that have been supported by centrist and left reformist governments in the post-war period. They have been in eclipse more recently with the success of monetarism, but are emerging again much more strongly as the crisis intensifies. They are rejected by orthodoxy as incompatible with the rationality of the free market, and they are also criticised by Marxist theory for not recognising that the problems they are concerned to overcome by reformist measures are not the result of short-term difficulties, but are fundamental to the nature of the operation of the capitalist system itself.

Marxism

Marx himself never produced a systematic examination of the operation of the international economy of his time, since he died before starting the fourth volume of *Capital* which was to take up the problem, although he did argue that it was inevitable that the capitalist system would extend itself until it operated on a global scale, thus displacing other less developed forms of economic organisation. But his analysis of the nature of the operation of the capitalist system itself within the framework of a single economy is directly relevant to the arguments that have been presented already, since it challenges many of their basic assumptions and therefore leads to very difficult policy recommendations.[24] Essentially Marxism argues that the nature of the processes of production and distribution under capitalism is such that it leads to an ever-increasing centralisation of production facilities in a smaller and smaller number of hands and places, thus leading to an irresistible tendency towards *uneven* development and crisis. It would not dispute the need for some of the reformist measures outlined above, and would argue that the system has not broken down earlier because these have been widely adopted at critical times, thus overcoming short-term problems, allowing the system to expand for a little longer, but leaving the fundamental underlying problems untouched. In the rest of this section we will therefore set out the 'pure' theory of the capitalist economy as seen from the Marxist viewpoint. We shall then leave the most important of its political and policy implications for the concluding section of the book.

Marx saw the development of the capitalist system as the result of the ability of the individual capitalist to force the workers under his/her direct control to produce a greater quantity of goods than he/she actually paid them for. By selling these goods at a profit (more correctly described as realising 'surplus value') it would be possible to invest in additional capital equipment, thus increasing the productivity of the worker and the amount of surplus value. By repeating the process the enterprise would grow more or less indefinitely, eventually creating the modern multinational corporation operating on a global scale and controlling resources larger than the gross national product of many countries.

This process does not produce a natural tendency towards mutual benefit and equilibrium, but fundamental conflicts of two kinds. Firstly, the struggle to maximise profits means that the capitalist has to attempt constantly to minimise the share taken by the worker as wages. Since the worker has no control over the firm and no *right* to the job he/she holds, this attempt at profit maximisation must lead to a constant struggle over wages and conditions of work. Thus the 'adjustments' needed to overcome a balance of payments crisis in the form of reduced wages and greater efficiency will be experienced by the workers as an attack on their economic and social position and a reinforcement of that of the class that exercises arbitrary economic power over them. Unless the government that attempts to enforce it it is prepared to associate these policies with some increase in the leverage of the working class in the system as a whole (and it is very difficult to see how this can be done without having to make a *political* attack on the position of the capitalist class itself) the adoption of orthodox policies will be associated with conservatism and be rejected by the working class.

Alongside this struggle is another which will have an even more direct effect on the *international* aspect of the problem of balance of payments adjustment and even development. Each capitalist is locked in perpetual conflict with every other who is attempting to produce the same commodities and sell them on the market. Each will attempt to produce and sell more cheaply than the other in order to obtain a larger share of the available consumption and, by so doing, will constantly reduce the profits of those who do not adopt the most modern equipment and impose the most rigorous discipline on their workers. Now the most effective way to do this is usually (though not invariably) to increase the quality of the capital equipment at the disposal of the workforce and thus increase the output of each worker. By exploiting *economies of scale* in this way it will be possible for the capitalist actually to increase the wage rates paid to the workforce, while taking a larger share of the resulting income. Thus, in the 1960s a single worker in the motor industry might have produced about six cars a year; now, with the introduction of robots, one worker can produce up to forty. Provided that the capitalist can sell the very much higher level of output required to justify the worker's job (and this, of course, is based on an outlay of an immense amount of capital, a much larger amount than that required to employ him/her in the 1960s) it is possible both to pay much higher wages and to make a larger profit. In this situation output can go up while employment goes down, a condition which Keynes and orthodox theorists both failed to take into account, but one described by Marx as the 'rising technical composition of capital'.[25] To the extent that this process is taking place, (and the introduction of computer technology suggests that it is accelerating dramatically at the moment), the tendency towards instability and uneven development is likely to be strengthened both domestically and internationally. The latter point can be demonstrated by looking at the implications of rapid technical change with increasing economies of scale for the orthodox arguments presented earlier.

Hume argued that when a country was in surplus with full employment, any attempt to increase production must lead to rising costs and to capital flowing out into other areas where they are lower. If, however, the capitalists in the country are able to exploit technological innovations to produce more goods with fewer workers and lower unit costs, then this effect disappears. Provided that they can sell the additional output required to justify the increased investment (and this will force them to export more, not less, thus worsening their neighbour's balance of payments problem) they will be able to continue to expand until their markets are exhausted. This effect, initiated by *individual* capitalists, will then benefit *all* of the capitalists in the nation concerned, where the government then taxes some portion of the resulting profits and uses them to improve the economic infrastructure of the economy as a whole (communications, education, research, health, law and order, social services), thus further reducing their costs of production (through what are called 'external economies') and giving them an even greater advantage in international trade than before. Thus the strong will grow stronger at the expense of the weak and a process of *combined and uneven development* will result. Some countries will become advanced centres of modern industry with high wages, rapid capital investment and excellent public services; others will become backward raw material producers without the technical capacity to modernise on an autonomous basis or the resources required to maintain the necessary level of investment in economic infrastructure to attract overseas capital on a substantial enough scale. Here we find the explanation of the 'development of underdevelopment' in weaker areas, the exact opposite from the 'catching up' which less developed countries are supposed to experience when they trade on an equal basis with advanced ones.

Ricardo's calculations also collapse in Marx's capitalist world. When Portuguese wine producers expand their output by selling to England, they do not take on more workers, but lay some of them off by using their additional profits to invest in better equipment and labour-saving technology. These workers then move into the Portuguese cloth industry, which meets the additional demand stemming from the wine industry without any increase in costs and thereby excludes the more expensive English producers. This has disastrous effects in England. Wine production declines and unemployment increases. The demand for cloth declines and no exports are possible, so unemployment emerges there as well. Wages fall, but not fast enough to compensate for the technical change occurring in Portugal, financed by the surplus profits gained from the expansion in production induced by the opening up of the English market. The struggle between labour and capital intensifies in England (although it is very likely to be moderated in Portugal, since both labour and capital gain from the increase in investment and productivity) and this is likely to lead to social and political unrest and quite possibly to the necessity for authoritarian forms of government if the capitalist system is to survive.

If these changes are allowed to continue it is clear that Say's law must also soon break down at the international level. The growing Portuguese surplus leads to hoarding of the kind identified by Keynes. Consumption in England must decline as imports are compressed, and Portuguese exports will also have to be reduced. This will lead to a reduction in the demand for Portuguese cloth and workers will start being laid off in both industries. The corresponding decline in demand will increase costs as a result of the loss of economies of scale, and this will also induce a Keynesian reduction in the optimism of entrepreneurs who will stop investing. The crisis will then be further exacerbated if there is a monetarist government in power which applies orthodox remedies and cuts wages and public spending still further for all of the reasons given by Keynes. Unless a government emerges willing to take drastic steps to alter the situation by interfering with the free operation of the market mechanism, which is what produces this tendency towards centralisation and uneven development, the economies of all the countries involved in the system will remain in a state of permanent unemployment and crisis.

The only hope for the system is if the surplus country can be persuaded to reduce the efficiency of its own producers enough to allow expansion in the deficit country and, furthermore, if it does this before its own economy has been driven into recession by the conditions which its very success has created. We have already seen that orthodox theorists claim that it is entirely rational for the surplus country to do this, but even this argument becomes much less secure when it is subjected to close examination on the basis of the Marxist view of the capitalist production process. Portuguese exports to England are actually produced by individual capitalists whose incomes and security depend upon their ability to operate on a scale sufficient to cover their costs and maintain their profits. If they allow their competitiveness to be reduced in order to allow the English to recapture either the domestic or the export market, their own existence will be threatened and with it that of the workforce whose high wages also depend on their access to export markets. Since they are likely to exert considerable influence over their own government, it is difficult to imagine them accepting the orthodox policies which would have the effect of threatening their very survival. They are much more likely to demand and obtain policies designed to keep their industries internationally competitive, as they did in the USA during the 1930s and as the Germans and Japanese are doing now.

Thus we can see that the nature of the constraints within which the individual capitalist *must* operate within capitalism forces him/her to demand policies *that are irrational from the point of view of the capitalist class as a whole*. This has the most serious political implications, since it means that the evident inability to overcome the crisis is not the outcome of a simple failure of will or of technical competence, as orthodox theorists believe, but *of the nature of the system itself*. This is why Marxists argue that a dynamic and *even* process of international development is impossible under the unfettered rule of capitalism, but requires a fundamental restructuring of the way in which it operates at both the domestic and international levels. This implies the need for far more drastic interference with the rights of private owners and with the free market than that recommended by even the more radical reformist theorists considered already. Marxist theorists themselves have always tended to confine their efforts to the demolition of the arguments of their opponents and have generally failed to put forward coherent alternative strategies in their place. This book will not be able to do much better, but it will refrain from even attempting to do so until it has explored the nature of the structures set up within the capitalist system to deal with the international economic problem, and has looked at its recent history.

3

The Post-War Political Settlement

We have realised . . . that politics includes economics, and that the consequences of a world-market are the settlement in common of those matters of common concern which arise from the fact of a world-market. Since, that is to say, matters like the supply of raw materials, or tariffs, or emigration, affect the world as a whole, no State can be a law unto itself in laying down the rules which obtain in relation to them. International control of some kind and degree is postulated wherever a given State-function directly impinges the common life of States.

Harold Laski, *A Grammar of Politics* (London: Allen & Unwin, 1925) p. 587

The ending of the Second World War confronted its survivors with both a challenge and an opportunity: while it should never have been allowed to happen, it had nevertheless demolished an old order and created space on which a new one might be built on more progressive and stable principles. This chapter will be concerned with the steps taken to meet that challenge through the creation of a set of international institutions designed to regulate the matters of common economic concern that were expected to emerge with the re-establishment of a hopefully open and integrated peace-time economy. These institutions have survived remarkably unchanged into the present, so this exercise will essentially be concerned with the creation of the 'social contract' which established the basis on which the post-war economic order has functioned, initially with great success, more recently in conditions of intensifying difficulty.

The preceding chapters have attempted to outline the political and economic preconditions required for the creation of an open and integrated system of economic exchange. If a system is composed of free individual economic agents living in independent sovereign states, then stable exchange must depend upon the unforced willingness of both weak and strong to refrain from actions that would fundamentally threaten the welfare of other members by undermining their productive capacity or by excluding them forcibly from equal access to their markets. These conditions, as we have seen, are both politically and economically incompatible with a structure of economic exchange which produces or reinforces a structure of combined and uneven development, since, although the strong may be happy to remain within its bounds, the weak will soon opt out unless an effective redistributive mechanism exists that is designed to keep them playing a game that they persistently lose. The creation of the Bretton Woods institutions (the IMF and the World Bank) and of GATT can only be properly understood in relation to the way in which their structures were designed to come to terms with this problem, since they emerged directly out of a situation characterised by the most extreme inequalities in economic and military power.

At the end of the war, the USA controlled some 70 per cent of the world's gold and foreign exchange reserves and more than 40 per cent of its industrial output, while Europe and Japan had been devastated by war and the Third World was still locked into colonial servitude and contained less than 1 per cent of the world's industrial capacity. Furthermore, we argued at the end of Chapter 2 that free competition under capitalist conditions is more likely to intensify inequalities than reduce them, so that an attempt to create a liberal international trading system in such conditions would be bound to worsen the inequalities and quickly lead back to the instability and autarchy that prevailed in the 1930s.

Yet by the end of the 1940s the major international institutions had been established on essentially liberal principles, and a period of rapid and relatively even development was to begin. This happy result was the outcome of an immensely complex balancing act managed principally by the USA, and involving a series of compromises in which it used its economic strength to provide short-term inducements to the weaker countries to co-operate, in exchange for a willingness to build a long-term commitment to liberalisation into the structure of the institutions themselves. Thus, the immediate post-war period can only be seen as one involving the practice of protectionism and managed trade while establishing the institutional mechanisms required to sustain a long-term transition to one based on free trade. In Chapter 5 we will show how this transition was successfully managed by the end of the 1950s; here we shall look briefly at the compromises involved in the creation of the structures themselves, using the political debates of the time as a means of evaluating the relative influence of the most important interests and ideas involved.

We can interpret the post-war economic debate as an argument between the USA on the one side representing the interests of the strong surplus countries, and the rest of the world on the other having to deal with the problems of economic reconstruction or underdevelopment. By 1944, the Americans, having built their predominance on a thoroughgoing commitment to protectionism, had been converted to free trade, always the ideology of the strong, and now wished to see the world economy fashioned on the same principles. Yet they also saw themselves as the leading protagonist in the post-war political settlement, and recognised that they could only perform this role effectively if they could establish a widespread agreement on the principles on which it was to be established. In particular, their commitment to liberalisation was associated with, if anything, a more powerful anti-communism dedicated to ensuring that no further expansion of its influence was to take place beyond the limits set by the 'iron curtain' at the end of the war.

For Western Europe, however, (where Britain was still predominant) liberalisation and anti-communism were not the immediate concerns. While Europe desperately needed access to American goods to serve as the basis for reconstruction, its own weakness was such that it could not hope to import them by earning the currency required through exports to the USA. The hard realities of uneven development meant that free competition would lead to the further destruction of the individual countries' already weakened industrial structures and an economic crisis equivalent to that which struck the world shortly after the First World War. In Britain, the new Labour government, although actively anti-communist, incorporated some radical socialist elements, while the Popular Front government in France included communist representation until 1947. These governments, although not prepared for a fundamental break with capitalism, had nevertheless accepted the need for a radical attack on the *laissez-faire* principle in relation to both domestic and foreign economic policy. After a decade and a half of unemployment, crisis and war, they were no longer willing to allow market competition alone to shape their futures. Social democratic planning, based on Keynesian principles and incorporating the use of monetary and tariff controls to regulate exchanges across the border, was now the dominant approach supported by both the working class and many elements in a weakened capitalist class. Any American settlement of the international problem would therefore require an effective compromise with the political and ideological forces represented by this consensus.

The material in the previous chapters must suggest that this compromise was not going to be easily established in a situation characterised by such acute economic and ideological differences. The US view suggested a world governed by a central, regulative agency charged with the maintenance of a system of open competition and empowered to resist attempts by national governments to adopt protectionist policies that would destroy its openness and integration. The view of the deficit countries required an agency capable of guaranteeing the defence of their weaker industries from overseas competition and, even better, some effective redistributive mechanism for providing them with direct financial assistance during the period in which they were building up their industrial capacity. Without these guarantees they would never voluntarily surrender any of the national sovereignty required to consolidate the power of the principle of centralised international co-ordination, yet with them the American ideal of an apolitical self-regulating free trade system would be substantially distorted. Both the strengths and the weaknesses of the institutions that were created at this time can be attributed to the contradictory nature of the attempt to reconcile these differences which the founders had necessarily to make. The implications of the resulting settlement can only be fully grasped by looking more closely at the actual events of the time and their immediate outcome.

The International Monetary Fund

An international credit money system must be based on the ability to resolve five problems:

(1) it must ensure the possibility of one national currency being made available in exchange for another (the convertibility problem);

(2) it must specify the relative values at which they will exchange (the exchange rate problem);

(3) it must provide an internationally acceptable and available monetary unit (the centre currency problem);

(4) it must guarantee the credit required to deal with balance of payments deficits in the short term at least (the financing problem);

(5) it must ensure that the policies adopted to deal with payments imbalances by national governments are never such as to destroy the integrity of the system as a whole (the 'adjustment' problem).

What we have to consider, however, is not merely the fact that these problems were resolved in 1944 at the Bretton Woods conference, but the terms on which they were settled, since, as the discussion in the previous chapter makes clear, it was this that would determine the extent to which it was subsequently to operate on *laissez faire* as opposed to interventionist lines.

From the orthodox liberal point of view, monetary arrangements must function as an entirely neutral mechanism expediting the exchanges between individual producers and consumers in different countries. Currencies must be freely convertible; exchange rates must not be manipulated to gain competitive economic advantages; the centre currency must serve as a stable means of payment, measure of value and store of value; credit must serve to overcome short-term balance of payments deficits before the countries concerned are forced into protectionism; and all the countries in the system must renounce the use of discriminatory policies as the means of overcoming their particular economic difficulties. From an interventionist point of view, however, the position is entirely different. Controlling the allocation and price of foreign exchange is one of the most effective mechanisms for controlling trade; the allocation of international credit as a means of transferring real resources from strong to weak economies becomes a powerful means of guaranteeing to the latter the possibility of rapid development; and the overall orientation of economic policy has a decisive effect on the possibility of the planning of both domestic and international production and exchange.

A serious debate took place before and at Bretton Woods around all of these issues, in which the American view essentially favoured the former solutions, the deficit countries' view the latter. The details will not be presented here, as they have been clearly set out elsewhere.[1] We can, however, set out very briefly the main decisions that were reached in relation to each of them.

At Bretton Woods the Americans were anxious to ensure a rapid transition from the situation of currency control which prevailed throughout most of the world to one of full convertibility. The weaker countries were unwilling to accept this until they had established their ability to compete with American industry on relatively equal terms. In the resulting compromise countries which did not yet feel able to adopt convertibility were allowed to retain monetary controls under Article 14 of the Articles of Agreement under which the Fund is constituted.[2] Those that did, accepted the obligations under Article 8 and were thereafter expected to maintain convertibility indefinitely. Most of the advanced countries accepted convertibility at the end of the 1950s, and a number of LDCs have done so since then. Convertibility here relates to payments for current transactions (the buying and selling of goods and services). Under another Article countries are permitted to maintain controls on the free movement of money for capital investment if they wish to do so.

On exchange rates, the main concern at Bretton Woods was to eliminate the situation that had prevailed in the 1930s when countries manipulated the international value of their currencies in order to secure competitive advantages in international trade. This had involved excessive devaluations and the use of 'dual' exchange rates – that is, rates which either gave special benefits to customers in particular countries, or to the import or export of particular categories of goods. The Bretton Woods agreement therefore outlawed the use of dual exchange rates, and called for the maintenance of fixed rates so far as this was possible. Technically this was organised by fixing the value of the dollar to the price of gold, maintaining a fixed gold price (the US bought all available gold supplies at that price), and then fixing the exchange rates (the 'parities') of all the other currencies in the system to the dollar. In the case of the LDCs the connection to the dollar was often indirect, since they were pegged to the currency of their colonial (or ex-colonial) power, so that their value would vary if that of their leading currency was altered.

'Fixing' currencies in this way meant that countries could not use devaluations to deal with balance of payments deficits in the manner set out in the previous chapter, but would have to put much more emphasis on other kinds of policy instead. But it was recognised that this might eventually prove impossible, so that it was agreed that countries facing a 'fundamental disequilibrium' on their balance of payments would be allowed to adjust their exchange rates with the permission of the IMF. Hence the system came to be called the 'adjustable peg' system – that is, one in which exchange rates were *pegged* to gold through the dollar, but *adjustable* where necessary through governmental action. This arrangement was to last only until 1973, when a system of 'managed floating' was introduced for reasons to be examined in Chapter 5.

The third objective of the system was the creation of an effective means of international payment. This was achieved after 1945 through the use of the US dollar, which is still the main currency in which international transactions are settled, the form in which most countries keep their foreign exchange reserves, and the unit against which they value their own currencies. In 1945 the USA dominated world trade and production and held 70 per cent of its gold and foreign exchange reserves. The dollar was therefore the most sought after currency in the world and was universally acceptable outside the USA. It could thus be used both for the payment for goods bought from the USA and for payments for goods from other countries. The fact that the USA was willing to guarantee that its value would be stable and that it would be exchanged for gold ('dollar-gold convertibility') meant that countries which kept it in their reserves could be certain that its value would not have been reduced through devaluation when they eventually came to use the dollars they had saved. Thus the dollar rapidly replaced the pound sterling which had been used in the same way prior to the breakdown of the monetary system in the early 1930s. Sterling continued to be used in an international currency among the sterling area (i.e. Commonwealth) countries until convertibility, when it could be used more generally in the same way as the dollar. But the weakness of the British economy meant that its role was a marginal one, and it lost its special status altogether in the 1970s. In 1971, however, dollar-gold convertibility was terminated by the USA, although the dollar remained the leading centre currency in the system.

The fourth element of the Bretton Woods agreement related to the provision of credit for countries with serious balance of payments deficits. An agreement was reached to give the IMF the power to do this, and the major focus of the discussion was on the scale on which it would be enabled to do so. While the British recommendation put forward by Keynes was that this should be relatively large, and thus serve as an effective and automatic means of transferring resources from strong to weak countries, that of the Americans was very much less generous and, since it was to be American money that provided the agency with almost all of its resources in the first instance, it was the American view that carried the day. The Americans allowed their quota to be set at $2.75 billion in the first instance. This, together with the quotas of all the other countries in the system, has been progressively revised upwards since then. By 1978 total quotas were $39 billion, with the USA contributing 21 per cent (as opposed to 36 per cent in 1945), and the other nine advanced industrial countries 35 per cent.

The actual funds at the IMF's disposal are therefore provided by these 'quotas' contributed by each member. Each has to provide 25 per cent of this in convertible currency (originally in gold), and the remainder in its own currency. (This, of course, means that the IMF can only use the proportion of the quotas it receives in convertible currencies for lending to deficit countries, since they would not wish to receive the currencies of countries that were not large-scale exporters on the international market). The IMF is then in a position to use these resources to give balance of payments assistance to countries in difficulty, usually providing them with the money on a short-term basis (for less than three years) and doing so *only on the understanding that they adopt policies to deal with the problem which the IMF considered appropriate*. It is this imposition of *conditions* before loans are granted that gives the IMF the power to intervene in the domestic policy-making of individual countries which has been so important politically in recent years. In response to criticisms of the way in which it has exercised its role, the IMF has recently increased the amount of money that countries can borrow from it, has extended the period over which they can do so, and has begun to modify some of the conditions it imposes on them.

The issue of conditionality brings us to the fifth aspect of the system, namely the enforcement of adjustment policies appropriate to the maintenance of its stability and openness both on the domestic and the international levels. At Bretton Woods it was the

Americans who wanted to ensure that this principle was accepted, but no clear set of policies was actually set out. Instead the IMF's approach has emerged over time in response to the actual problems it has had to resolve in the countries in which it has been asked to intervene. Here we must distinguish between the policies it would recommend for countries with persistent deficits and those for countries with persistent surpluses, both of which are equally problematic for the survival of the system as a whole, as we saw in the previous chapter.

So far as the deficit countries are concerned, the IMF characteristically imposes policies that are highly 'orthodox', in that they seek to restore a balance of payments surplus by a reduction in consumption combined with an increase in investment. They have usually rejected the Keynesian, protectionist and structuralist arguments set out above and instead have insisted on policies which imply very heavy reliance on the market mechanism, the encouragement of private capitalist investment, and a reduction in state intervention. Thus a standard IMF 'package' of policies will usually involve the following: a reduction in state spending, and particularly in the provision of subsidies for the consumption goods of low income groups; some mechanism for reducing wages; a devaluation of the currency and even a possible reduction in foreign trade or monetary controls (though it does *not* impose free trade policies of a highly liberal kind); and the dismantling of controls on the activities of private capitalists, either local or foreign. The effect of all of these measures would be a reduction in the level of consumption and therefore of the consumption of imports, and an increase in the rate of profit because of the reduction in wages and taxes. It is therefore assumed that imports will decline very rapidly, and, as the increased profits are invested in more productive capacity, that exports will eventually begin to increase. Thus this approach seems to allow an 'adjustment' to the deficit which keeps the system open (by excluding any *increase* in protection), and which promises a quick return to a balance of payments surplus and a return a little later to economic expansion when consumption can again be increased on a more secure basis.

The IMF's ability to enforce these policies arises out of the fact that countries that wish to borrow from it have no option but to accept them in exchange for the loans. But no equivalent pressures can be imposed on the surplus countries whose policies, many would argue, are even more significant to a progressive solution to the problem of uneven development and unbalanced trade. At Bretton Woods the deficit countries did attempt to impose some pressure on the surplus countries through the inclusion of a 'scarce currency clause' (Article 7 of the Agreement), which indicated that deficit countries could impose controls on their imports from countries which remained in persistent surplus. But because the surplus countries (in fact at that stage only the USA) were opposed to this, the clause was formulated in a way which made it virtually impossible to enforce, and it has remained a dead letter. Thus the IMF's policy interventions not only favour very orthodox and conservative policies with respect to the deficit countries, but also take no steps at all to push the surplus countries into the adjustments that would be needed for an equitable solution to the problem of unbalanced trade as a whole.

The IMF therefore has quite extensive powers and has a political structure through which to exercise it that places most power in the hands of the strong countries. Final authority is vested in a Board of Governors and an Executive Board, together with a Managing Director who is formally subordinate to the Boards, but who in fact exercises a very powerful influence on both day-to-day decisions and on policy. The Managing Director has always been a European, and the composition of the Boards and voting rights on them are directly related to quotas and therefore guarantee the representatives of the advanced industrial countries an effective veto over all decisions. Indeed, the USA alone has had sufficient votes to veto any significant change of policy that it opposes. The Board of Governors is composed of senior Ministers of Finance or Governors of central banks, who meet annually and exercise final authority; the Executive Board is directly responsible for decisions and is in permanent session. Of its twenty members, five are elected directly by the largest member countries, and the remainder from groups of countries whose composition is such that at present only eight are drawn from the Third World. Thus the political power structure of the IMF closely correlates with the economic power of the countries of which it is composed and thus ensures that the orthodox policies preferred by the leading industrial countries will dominate the Board.

Thus we can see that the IMF has indeed developed into the sort of agency that the leading elements in the American capitalist class had in mind in 1944. Yet the weak countries did attempt to modify this bias at Bretton Woods, although it can be seen that their influence was very small. In 1944 their demands for interventionism took two forms: on the one hand they insisted on the right to maintain non-convertible currencies for as long as they needed to control deficits, while on the other they wanted the IMF itself to be given far larger resources to distribute than it was actually given in order to provide assistance to deficit countries. The main political demand put by the deficit countries was thus in effect the Keynesian suggestion that the organisation should become what amounted to a powerful international bank that would not limit itself to the provision of short-term balance of payments assistance, but which would actually provide deficit countries with the resources required to overcome their deficits through expanded investment and increased exports, rather than through deflationary policies and a reduction in imports (see pp. 50–1 above).

At Bretton Woods this amounted to a demand that the USA put a substantial percentage of its own resources at the disposal of the agency to be used as it, rather than its own government, determined, since it was only the USA that had the necessary resources. It was not willing to do this, and instead provided the IMF with only sufficient money to enable it to provide limited short-term financing. This, in turn, meant that the economic policies required to bring a country into surplus had to be that much more restrictive, placing more emphasis on the reduction in consumption than the increase in investment. This is a very important fact in determining the nature of the policies which the IMF imposes upon such countries, policies which are now generating so much political opposition. Thus the Keynesian intervention at Bretton Woods was an almost complete failure, the agency was strongly supported in the USA, and it has been widely seen as an important bulwark of the capitalist system as a whole since then.

On the other hand, however, these limitations in the IMF's powers have limited the nature of the role that it can play in deficit countries and has produced extensive opposition to its policies from the Left in both Third World and advanced industrial countries. These weaknesses first became visible in the 1960s when they generated a reform movement that led to the creation of a new form of international credit money (the Special Drawing Right) similar in conception but on a much smaller scale than that proposed by

Keynes in 1944. But they became critical at the start of the 1970s when the Americans unilaterally repudiated their obligation to maintain dollar-gold convertibility and fixed exchange rates and thus changed the nature of the whole system. Thus by the middle of the 1970s the system was very different from twenty years earlier, having suffered a significant reduction in stability but made a limited but important concession to the principle of unconditional international credit creation. The problems involved, however, became even worse when crisis ushered in a period of recession and mounting balance of payments deficits. This has led to the revival of interventionist theories, and to a growing political campaign in the Third World and on the Left in industrial countries calling for a more adequate provision of balance of payments assistance, and for a modification of the kinds of policies that the IMF imposes on those governments that are forced to call for its assistance.[3] The implications of all these changes will be considered in more detail in Chapters 5 and 8.

The World Bank

The Bretton Woods conference not only produced the IMF but also the International Bank for Reconstruction and Development (IBRD) as the World Bank is more properly known. The Bank was a response to the Keynesian call for some means of providing developmental assistance to the weaker countries in the system, and, in particular in 1944, to those whose economic base had been damaged by the war. Yet although it emerged out of this potentially radical concern, and although it was later to develop a more radical philosophy, it began as a very conservative institution.

Keynes's original proposal for an international bank assumed that it would be provided with very substantial official resources derived from the balance of payments surpluses of the advanced countries, and would be able to offer its help to the poorest countries on terms which they would be able to afford. The Articles of Agreement of the Bank did directly commit it to 'the development of productive facilities and resources in less developed countries', and to the promotion of the 'balanced growth of international trade' by encouraging investment in development. It was therefore directly concerned with the key problem of even development which lies at the heart of the international crisis. If the Bank had been given adequate resources and appropriate political direction, it might have been able to make a real contribution to the development of the productive capacity of the less developed countries. As an official, and not a private, bank, it does not have to operate on purely commercial principles, lending money purely on the basis of the profit motive.

Yet the Bank was a very conservative institution in its original form. The leading capitalist interests in the 1940s were opposed to the creation of an institution that would provide credit on genuinely non-commercial terms, and the Americans were certainly unwilling to provide it with the resources to do this on a large scale. When the Bank was set up it was therefore provided with very little money from the subscriptions of governments, and had to raise most of the funds it needed by borrowing from private financial institutions. This means that it had to charge commercial rates of interest to its own borrowers, and adopt the conservative financial policies approved of by the private banking authorities on which it depended for its resources. Thus, although it often lent to countries which at that stage would not have been able to borrow effectively from private bankers, it did so on terms which were just as restrictive as those imposed by them. It refused to lend at all to any country that had defaulted on earlier debts, lent only to countries and for projects which provided it with the best possible security, and therefore only operated on a very limited scale during the early years being considered here.

Like the IMF, the World Bank's governing bodies were composed on the basis of the economic strength of its members, and not on a direct democratic principle, so that it, too, is effectively under the control of the developed countries. Its President has always been an American. It was in fact only after 1960 that it established a 'soft loan' affiliate, the International Development Association (IDA) to provide loans for poor countries on non-commercial terms. Its development and orientation will be considered in Chapter 8.

The General Agreement on Tariffs and Trade

While the IMF and World Bank are concerned with the monetary and financial aspects of the international economy, the GATT is concerned with the other major area of concern, the regulation of tariffs and trade. Here again, fundamental issues of economic theory separated the approach of the surplus and deficit countries after the war, and in this case the possibility of arriving at an agreement was even more difficult. Indeed, the contemporary structure of the GATT is itself largely a historical accident, the by-product of a far more ambitious attempt, begun in 1945 and terminated in failure in 1950, to establish an International Trade Organisation (ITO) with the role of supervising the trading system in the same sort of way as the IMF was to supervise the monetary system. This failure was not an accident, however, but the outcome of the struggle between the dominant interests in the USA and those in the deficit countries. The structure of the GATT, and more especially its limited powers and liberal bias, was a direct reflection of this. We can therefore only understand the implications of this outcome by looking at the events that allowed it to come into existence while precluding the establishment of the ITO.[4]

Although they were ultimately to be responsible for destroying the ITO, the discussions held to establish it were in fact held on the basis of an American initiative taken in 1945. The Americans produced a draft charter for an organisation which was then discussed and extensively amended at conferences held in London, Washington and Havana between October 1946 and March 1948. At these the American insistence on economic liberalism in respect of Western governments came up against a far stronger resistance than had been encountered at Bretton Woods. Strong opposition to the liberal position was voiced in favour of the use of direct quantitative restrictions on imports (quotas), notably by India, while the Australians in particular led a general campaign in favour of the use of protectionism as a means of guaranteeing industrialisation and full employment. These governments, more articulate and better prepared than they had been at Bretton Woods, were not prepared to allow the commitment to full employment to take second place to that of free trade and market competition, and the Americans were forced to take their position into account.

The Havana Charter which emerged from these discussions was therefore a compromise, retaining the US commitment to a general expansion and liberalisation of trade, but incorporating a number of clauses which justified the use of intervention both to deal with balance of payments and developmental problems without having to adopt orthodox deflationary measures. It placed very heavy emphasis on the maintenance of full employment, and gave members the *right* to request the organisation 'to furnish them with appropriate advice concerning plans for economic development or reconstruction and the financing and carrying out of their programs, and to assist them in procuring such advice or study' (Article 10, 2(b)). The American administration which had been involved in the negotiations was prepared to accept the compromise, but the dominant elements in the American capitalist class were not. Thus the US Council of the International Chamber of Commerce attacked the Charter:

> because it accepts practically all of the policies of economic nationalism; because it jeopardises the free enterprise system by giving priority to centralised national government planning of foreign trade; because it leaves a wide scope to discrimination, accepts the principle of economic insulation and in effect commits all members of the ITO to state planning for full employment.[5]

Thus, despite strong administration support, the Charter failed to be ratified by the US Congress and this alone meant that it failed to produce an organisation which would have been in a position to approach trade problems from a very different point of view than the GATT and the IMF.

Although the ITO was never created, the GATT was brought into existence as a by-product of the negotiations intended to set it up. During 1947 the Americans wanted to organise trade negotiations, and the Geneva conference, then drafting a preliminary charter for the Havana meeting, was asked to produce a Draft Agreement on Tariffs and Trade to serve as a basis for these negotiations. This was signed on 30 October by twenty-three countries, and formally entered into force in January 1948. Although created as a temporary expedient, this was then to serve as the basis for the regulation of trade relations because of the collapse of the ITO. From an American point of view, however, this result could have hardly have been bettered, because the organisation in this form could never be anything more than a mechanism for regulating a system based on a generalised commitment to the reduction of protectionism on a multilateral basis.

Thus the GATT in this form is not so much an organisation as a *forum* and a *code of rules*, a place where countries meet to negotiate their tariff and other trade regulations on the basis of an agreed set of principles and procedures. It has no power or resources of its own (apart from those required to provide a secretariat to service these activities) and its effectiveness therefore depends entirely on the willingness of the countries involved (the 'contracting parties') to take part and to make binding commitments to each other on a reciprocal basis. Its liberalism is clearly inscribed in the preamble to the General Agreement itself, which quite specifically identifies 'the substantial reductions of tariffs and other barriers to trade and ... the elimination of discriminatory treatment in international commerce' as its primary objective. Since its initiation in 1947 it has organised seven 'rounds' of negotiations designed to do this, culminating in the most comprehensive of all, the 'Tokyo Round', which took place between 1973 and 1979. The most important reductions in tariffs have in fact been secured through the Tokyo Round and its predecessor, the 'Kennedy Round' (1964–67), each of which led to a reduction of more than 30 per cent in the tariffs prevailing between the leading industrial countries, and more limited ones among developing countries. In 1981, eighty-seven countries were fully committed to the GATT, and a further thirty had agreed to allow the GATT to be applied to the negotiation of their commercial policy, while ninety-nine countries were involved in the Tokyo Round. Thus GATT negotiations now determine the overwhelming majority of the capitalist world's trade, while its membership also includes the non-capitalist countries, Cuba, Czechoslovakia, Hungary, Romania and Yugoslavia.

The GATT rules are primarily designed to encourage non-discrimination between countries and the progressive reduction of tariffs. Thus all tariffs that are imposed must not favour one country any more than they do the others (the 'most favoured nation' clause); protection is to be given as far as possible through tariffs and not other methods; tariffs are to be stable once agreed and are not to be raised without further negotiations; all disputes are to be settled through consultation and conciliation; and quantitative restrictions on imports are to be eliminated as far as possible. Against these liberalising tendencies the code does allow for temporary action to limit the import of goods into a country where they are threatening injury to domestic producers, or where it is in serious balance of payments difficulties. It also allows for the establishment of regional trading arrangements between groups of countries seeking to reduce mutual trade barriers (like the EEC), and allows industrial countries to give preferential treatment to imports from LDCs. Much greater protection is allowed for trade in agricultural produce, and a special agreement (the 'Multi-Fibre Arrangement' or MFA) has been established to regulate the trade in textiles between developed and less developed countries, with the intention of limiting the growth of LDC exports in order to safeguard employment in the textile industries of the developed world. This agreement, which is now being renegotiated, is generally regarded as discriminatory in the LDCs that are attempting to industrialise through export promotion.

Since the GATT is mainly a forum, it does not have an elaborate structure of political representation. The enforcement of the decisions reached depends mainly upon *reciprocity*. Any country which unilaterally breaks its commitments will probably face retaliation from its main trading partners, thus threatening the stability of its leading export industries. Since all agreements can only be entered into where all the parties to them accept them, there will be no need for votes to be taken to determine the outcomes of any negotiations. All this, of course, is possible because of its dependence on the operation of the free market. Countries are merely deciding on the regulations that are to govern trade; the actual flows of trade themselves are the result of the competitive process, with state intervention becoming less and less significant as tariff and other trade barriers are progressively reduced.

It is obvious that any agency of this kind would be incapable of organising any significant degree of intervention into the actual flows of trade themselves, since this would require a large bureaucratic apparatus and the capacity to take decisions which would have to be politically binding on all the countries involved. Operating as it does on the basis of the 'most favoured nation' clause, it is also evident that it could not intervene over the long term to allow a particular country which needed protection to use it to build up its industries when they had been weakened by destructive import penetration.

The major exception to this orientation is the agreement to allow developing countries a separate status under the main agreement. After considerable pressure was exerted by the developing countries at the early conferences which set it up, a clause in the Agreement gave them the right to 'take protective or other measures affecting imports ... to implement programmes and policies of economic development' (Article XVIII), while three additional articles (Part IV, Trade and Development) were added in 1965 to strengthen this committment. But it has nevertheless been very difficult for the LDCs to get meaningful concessions out of the developed countries during the tariff rounds. The Multi-Fibre Arrangement is a constant source of resentment, since it means that textile exports from LDCs receive *worse* treatment in developed country markets than those from other developed countries. LDCs were also far from satisfied with the results of both the Kennedy and Tokyo Rounds, and their general feeling remains that any substantial increase in their exports of low-cost manufactures will be resisted by both working-class and capitalist interests in developed countries concerned to defend employment and wages in labour-intensive industries there.

4
Multinational Corporations, Nation States, World Economy

We thus see that the growth of the world economic process, having as its basis the growth of productive forces, not only calls forth an intensification of production relations among various countries, not only widens and deepens general capitalist interrelations, but also calls to life new economic formations, new economic forms unknown to past epochs in the history of capitalist development.

Nikolai Bukharin, *Imperialism and World Economy*, 1918

What is at issue is whether – in an era of international transfer pricing – government control of the private economy based on national price systems is any longer adequate.

Robin Murray, *Multinationals Beyond the Market*, 1981

A few hundred giant corporations now straddle the world, exerting a pervasive influence over its destiny. They control between a quarter and a third of all production, and a larger percentage of its trade. They sustain their predominant and expanding economic position through privileged access to technology, finance and marketing facilities, and also exert a powerful influence over the activities of smaller local firms which rely on them as suppliers, buyers, creditors and providers of high technology. Because they create employment and can usually afford to pay above-average wages, they can also often secure the support of trade unions and working-class political movements for their activities.

This economic power can also be translated into an equivalent amount of direct and indirect political and social influence. Since the prime responsibility of national governments must always be to maintain economic growth and stability, they can rarely afford to adopt policies that are likely to make MNCs unwilling to invest in their country, while MNCs' ability to move their resources about the world enables them to escape the effects of many attempts to impose nationalistic constraints on what they do. As though this were not enough, their access to financial resources, often in excess of those of the government of the country in which they are operating, makes it possible for them to exert a much more direct influence on key individuals in official positions and in public life.

This power is backed up by a less visible but no less pervasive influence over the way in which we see and experience the world. The control that MNCs have over the production process and advertising industry determines what we can choose and, indeed, what we choose to become. As Marx says, 'Production ... creates the consumer' (*Grundrisse*, p. 92). Their financial resources allow them to become major sponsors of academic research and teaching, of cultural events and sporting occasions. Their capital dominates the production of culture through their control over films, television, newspapers and publishing, enabling them to guarantee that few messages will be conveyed which question their role and the way in which they perform it. This influence is not exerted to defend the aspirations of any particular national capitalist class, but on behalf of capital itself – on behalf of an international class whose activities and aspirations extend beyond the boundaries of any particular nation state and extend to the creation of a global environment which will enable them to maximise their profits by excluding the constraints previously imposed upon their activities by particular political entities.

Orthodox economic and political science is largely silent about the implications of this concentration of supranational power, despite its immense significance for all of us. For the economists the world is one of perfect competition between firms which all 'have equal access to all productive factors'[1] and which are therefore regulated on a non-political basis through the market. In so far as a policy element does enter into the discussion, this is seen to be the prerogative of sovereign national governments with the ability and right to regulate the activities of all firms and individuals operating within their area of jurisdiction. Political scientists tend to use the same assumptions, treating MNCs as one among many 'pressure groups' in a pluralistic political universe, subject to national control by a system which provides all 'interests' with equal access to the state through the democratic process. In the dominant social democratic view which prevailed from the 1950s, it was widely assumed that the working class had now joined the capitalist class as potentially equal partners in the exercise of state power, thus guaranteeing that economic power could no longer be used by a minority to subordinate society as a whole.[2]

Yet the material presented in this study so far must surely suggest that this view is not so much inadequate as dangerously misleading. Not only is the competition between firms grossly unequal at the economic level, but this inequality can replicate itself at the political level through the mechanisms outlined above. More important from our point of view, the multinational character of these firms turns them into citizens of the world and thus allows them to operate in a political dimension which is largely inaccessible to the working class. And because they operate at this level they can also escape many of the controls supposedly exercised over national capital by nation states, and can also secure decisive competitive advantages over small-scale and purely national capitals. It is therefore clear that the political and economic realities of a world economy dominated by modern multinational capital can only be understood through a political economy of the *international* system which recognises as central the role that these corporations play within it.

Looked at as a totality, therefore, we have to see the world as a complex unity comprising a layered and discontinuous structure of political and economic power. Earlier chapters have already demonstrated that traditional assumptions as to the political autonomy of nation states no longer hold, given the authority already appropriated by regional and international agencies. Here we shall be concerned to demonstrate that an often assumed autonomy of the 'national bourgeoisie' has also ceased to exist as a dominant factor, given the internationalisation of capital through the MNC and the corresponding emergence of a class for which global profit maximisation must take precedence over a commitment to the development of any particular national location. This chapter will therefore attempt to give some indication of the reasons why this has happened, of the scale on which it has happened and, most especially, of its impact on the structure and distribution of power at the global level. In earlier chapters we have also been concerned with the relationships between official economic policy and institutions and the tendency towards even as opposed to uneven development. Here we shall look at the way in which these issues can be illuminated by examining how private economic power at the international level is related to them.

Orthodox theory, based as we have seen upon the assumptions of perfect competition, is incapable of providing us with any explanation for the continuous growth of international monopoly power represented by the emergence of the MNC as the dominant factor in the world economy. Using their assumptions of free access to all markets and diminishing returns to scale, large units will always eventually be displaced by smaller ones, and no *structural* tendency will emerge towards the centralisation and concentration of capital.[3] Many economists have therefore responded to this deficiency by accepting that their growth can be attributed to the existence of 'imperfect markets' (that is to say of situations where strong firms can use existing levels of economic and political power to secure additional advantages over smaller rivals) without seeing this as an inherent tendency in the evolution of the capitalist mode of production itself. Here we shall be concerned to look at the extent to which the process can be better explained through the Marxist assumption of its inherent tendency towards combined and uneven development, along the lines pioneered by Steven Hymer.[4]

In the real world competition is by no means 'perfect', but based upon the old adage 'to them that hath shall be given, from them that hath not shall be taken away, even that which they hath'. Modern production depends crucially upon the employment of larger and larger amounts of capital equipment to produce goods of ever increasing quality and decreasing cost. Far from causing efficient small new producers constantly to appear and challenge the position of existing ones, it constantly allows the most successful of the existing producers to reinvest their larger profits in new equipment and methods and thus to increase their dominance of the whole market. This process is not absolutely continuous, of course (if it was global production would now be controlled by a single firm), but it is still the predominant tendency in the evolution of the international capitalist economy. Thus productive capacity does not gravitate into the hands of individual entrepreneurs with a burning desire to become captains of industry and a willingness to abstain from personal consumption in order to do so, but remains in the hands of the giant corporations with access to their own and other people's savings, control over large research and development facilities, long experience in organising the production and marketing of commodities, and access to a large enough market to absorb the scale of output needed to sustain these heavy costs. Occasionally some new entrepreneur may be able to build a small company into a giant of this kind, but the great majority of MNCs are the direct descendants of small companies set up generations ago when most companies were still relatively small. They have grown to their present size by expanding their own productive capacity and by absorbing or destroying their less successful rivals along the way. Having now reached this size, they are able effectively to control the operations of smaller newcomers through the exercise of monopoly power.

Crucial to the ability to operate on a scale large enough to survive in the modern monopoly capitalist world is the ability to go multinational. With the possible exception of the United States, no national market is large enough to sustain the scale of output required to maintain production in all of the most important sectors of modern industry. Many small companies can survive by exporting internationally from a single national base, but the ability to produce directly in local markets gives their rivals some decisive advantages. A subsidiary in a specific region will avoid the transport and other communication costs and the tariff barriers that confront external producers; it will employ local personnel with intimate knowledge of local conditions; it may well maintain close and indeed privileged relationships with influential politicians and officials; its labour might be cheaper and more effectively disciplined than that in its home country; and many governments are prepared to provide MNCs with large subsidies and with monopolies over domestic markets. When these are added to the other advantages it can be seen that a company with 'global reach' is always likely to outperform any purely national company and thus threaten to displace it when times are hard. Their continuous growth relative to that of the firms operating only in one country is a clear demonstration of the importance of these considerations.

When we come to look at the scale and nature of this growth in private power we can establish not only its great importance, but also the way in which it is organically related to the processes of political internationalisation discussed in earlier chapters. During the period of international recovery financed by the USA from the end of the Second World War to the early 1960s, the major source of private overseas investment was, of course, American capital, with the British playing a subordinate but active role. Economically this was a reflection of the strength of American capital and, until the late 1950s at least, of the need to bypass protective barriers erected by host countries at the time. Politically it was a response to active encouragement by the US government, which not only used the Marshall Plan as a mechanism for ensuring open access for American capital, but also established 'incentives for US corporations to invest abroad' and looked for ways to invite American banks 'to lend abroad'.[5] The total outflow of private and official capital during this period reached a peak at the end of the 1950s and then declined into the 1960s because of a sharp decline in the growth rate of American private capital outflows in the second half of the 1960s. McEuan has shown that this fell in real terms from 7.8 per cent between 1955 and 1960, to 7.5 per cent between 1960 and 1965 but to only 4.4 per cent between 1965 and 1970.[6] The significance of the institutional arrangements described in the last chapter cannot be overestimated here. As Hood and Young put it:

> United States corporations were aided in their access to foreign countries by the Marshall Plan operations and subsequently by the gradual liberalisation of trade and payments; and they were in the unique position of having the capacity to export, and resources to expand, abroad. The convertibility of the dollar, the IMF, the formation of the GATT and so on were all part of a new situation.[7]

From the end of the 1950s, and more especially from the mid-1960s, European and Japanese firms began to internationalise very rapidly, quickly reducing the relative dominance of the USA and UK. While they controlled 70.4 per cent of all overseas investment in 1967, this had been reduced to 58.8 per cent in 1976.[8]

These changes correspond directly to the change in relative international economic power identified in the last chapter and which will be further explored in Chapter 5. The relative decline in the American ability to form new overseas affiliates was both a consequence of 'the rise of Japanese and European-based firms to the point where they could effectively compete with US multinationals throughout the world',[9] and one of the causes of the subsequent US inability to sustain its hegemonic position within the system as a whole.[10] US direct investment abroad actually *declined* by 2 per cent in 1982, the first such decline since 1945, while foreign direct investment into the USA increased by 13 per cent.

During the 1950s and 1960s the major expansion in MNC activity took place in industry and primary production (notably mining). From the end of the 1960s a new and crucially important element was added, with a very large expansion in the international activities of the leading Western banks. During the colonial period the main British banks had internationalised on a large scale, mainly throughout the Empire and Commonwealth, establishing an extensive network of branches in many countries. At the end of the 1960s the leading US banks began a dramatic process of international expansion, involving not only the establishment of a world-wide branch network, but also, and perhaps more significantly, a process of international foreign currency lending which created the so-called 'Euro-currency market', the critical importance of which will be assessed in Chapter 9. Here again, the early phase of expansion was dominated by American capital and subsequently emulated by competitors in Europe and Japan, to create an integrated though intensely competitive system which is now in deep crisis. Because the role of this banking function has such general significance for the operation of the economic system as a whole, and because the origins of the crisis require special examination, this issue will be left aside until it can be dealt with in full.

By the mid-1970s the dominant capitalist firms in the world economy had taken on a distinctly international structure. In 1976 nearly 11,000 companies operated some 82,600 foreign affiliates, and of these '371 operated in twenty or more countries; these were thought to account for more than three-fifths of all sales of MNEs'.[11] By the end of the 1970s Dunning estimates that the 'liquid assets of all kinds of multinational institutions were ... probably nearer three times ... the size of the world's gold and foreign exchange reserves'. By 1980 US multinationals, still by far the largest component of the system, earned $38.3 billion in profits, royalties and fees from their overseas investments, or 23.8 per cent of their total profits. This represents a growth from comparable figures of $3.5 billion and 13 per cent in 1961.[12] Associated with this growth has been an even more significant growth in the MNC contribution to trade. Thus Helleiner shows that 'in 1977 48% of all US imports originated with a party related by ownership ... to the buyer', and that to this figure 'should be added at least some of the US imports which are obtained on a subcontracting basis'.[13] So far as exports were concerned, an Economist Intelligence Unit study estimated that intra-firm trade accounted for '$43.7 billion, or 36.1% of total US exports in 1977 or $121.2 billion'.[14] These figures, it should be noted, relate to actual exchanges between the branch plants of the *same* firm, and were therefore not based on market considerations as these are normally understood (where transactions are supposed to be conducted on an 'arm's length' basis). When we look at total trade we find that some *97 per cent of US exports* can be accounted for by the operations of MNCs.[15] Comparable figures do not appear to be available for other countries, but it is very likely that those for the UK would be very similar to those of the USA, given the relative importance of MNCs there, while those for the other industrial countries would be less significant but expanding rapidly.

Finally, it is important to note that the international distribution of MNC investment is highly uneven. In 1975 74 per cent of all MNC investment was in developed countries, and only 26 per cent in LDCs, a percentage which had fallen from 31 per cent in 1974.[16] Within the LDCs the distribution is even more uneven, with the top ten countries and the OPEC countries between them accounting for 63.5 per cent and six small tax havens for a further 13 per cent of the total. Not surprisingly, this investment 'has focused heavily on those states with the highest level of incomes',[17] indicating that the pattern of MNC investment as a whole has closely followed, and by so doing strongly intensified, the structure of uneven development that has characterised the growth of the world economy since the war. More will be said about the implications of this process for LDCs in Chapter 7. The rest of this chapter will be concerned with a general examination of the implications of their growth for the associated problems of international political control and uneven development.

The international system, as we have seen, is governed by an uneasy collaboration between sovereign, and relatively highly organised, national state systems, and much weaker but nevertheless important international economic agencies. Economically, and notwithstanding the relative decline in US hegemony in the post-war period, it is characterised by an extreme degree of uneven development, with five-sixths of all industrial capacity concentrated within the bounds of the dozen leading countries. We have also seen that there is a close and problematic relationship between the functioning of these political institutions and the structure of uneven economic development on to which it is superimposed. On the one hand the growth of internationalisation of political control has been associated with a tendency towards the *liberalisation* of trade, financial and capital flows; on the other, inequality has encouraged the weaker links in the system to maintain protective barriers and practices which have inhibited the further integration of the system and the span of control of the international agencies. We have now to consider the implications of the growth of international private capital for these tendencies, before going on to consider its wider implications for the way in which we understand the operation of the system as a whole. Given that national governments are still seen to have the prime responsibility for regulating the development of the economic space under their jurisdiction, we can start by considering the nature of the relationship which this must involve with foreign private capital. A further important distinction must be kept in mind here between the needs and interests of capital-short as opposed to capital-surplus countries – between those which are net recipients of MNC investment and those which are net exporters.

In the pure neoclassical analysis, the fact of private overseas investment does not constitute a *political* problem because it can be seen as a purely economic response to market forces operating at the international level. Capital will choose those locations which enable it to maximise its rate of return and, in so doing, maximise both its own welfare and that of the world. In so far as host countries need foreign capital, this must be because they have no equivalent domestic resources capable of producing the same results. According to Meier:

> Direct foreign investment brings to the recipient country not only capital and foreign exchange but also managerial ability, technical personnel, technological knowledge, administrative organisation, and innovations in products and production techniques – all of which are in short supply. ... One of the greatest benefits to the

recipient country is the access to foreign knowledge that private foreign investment may provide – knowledge that helps overcome the managerial gap and the technological gap. . . . New techniques accompany the inflow of private capital, and by the example they set, foreign firms promote the diffusion of technological advance in the economy. In addition, foreign investment may lead to the training of labour in new skills, and the knowledge gained by these workers can be transmitted to other members of the labour force, or these workers might be employed later by local firms.[18]

Applying the neoclassical principles developed in Chapter 2 in relation to trade, we can see that this process will also tend to lead towards even development, since once any location has become a major recipient of foreign capital, wages and employment there will have a tendency to rise and this will lead investors to move on to more favoured locations where this has not yet occurred.

This view of the positive role of MNCs carries with it a corresponding orientation towards policy – essentially a willingness to treat them in the same way as national firms, while also taking account of their international position by allowing them to remit all of their earnings abroad even where national firms might be subjected to foreign exchange controls. Needless to say, this view is also the one that accords most closely with that of the MNCs themselves, who fully accept this positive view of their role and are therefore concerned to create an international environment in which they will be able to make decisions that will maximise their returns without having to take account of national locations from which they are drawn. They require governments that will provide them with a favourable environment within which to operate,[19] but which will not then attempt to force them into high cost locations or uneconomic activities in pursuit of their own nationalistic objectives. Indeed, it is easy to see that it is this view that underpins the liberal ideology of the dominant industrial countries and hence of the leading international economic agencies which was outlined in the preceding chapter. In these countries, where the great majority of MNC investment takes place, these liberal conditions do now apply, and there can be little doubt that they have played an important role in the continuous expansion in the phenomenon during the post-war period.

But the problem looks very different from the perspective of the weaker countries in the system, whose attitude to MNC investment has always been profoundly ambiguous. For reasons set out in Chapters 1 and 2, they cannot accept *laissez faire*, but are committed to the use of state intervention to increase growth and protect domestic producers from overseas competition. For as long as they feel the need to do this, neither a fully integrated liberal system of international political regulation can be created, nor an open environment for the maximisation of the freedom of manoeuvre of multinational capital. Thus we can see that the evolution of a coherent structure for the organisation of the political economy of the world economy must come to terms with the implications of the uneasy relationship between MNCs and the governments of host countries in the weaker centres. To understand this in what follows, the main concern will not be with the purely economic consequences of MNC activities, but with their political implications in the broadest sense – that is to say, with their capacity to exert effective leverage over policy-making, whether this is derived from their control over productive resources or their capacity to exert influence through political parties, pressure groups and bureaucracies.

When we come to look at this relationship it is important to recognise that the ambiguities it involves do not stem merely from a clear and easily recognised tendency for these companies to exploit host countries. For some varieties of (vulgar) Marxist theory, the interests of foreign capital are tied directly to those of a 'comprador' national bourgeoisie which controls the local state and uses it as an instrument to assist their foreign mentors in a continuous drain of surplus to the metropolitan centres, thus leading to the net impoverishment of the local society. Against this view the supporters of foreign capital can argue that it is the LDCs that have most successfully attracted foreign capital which have grown fastest and where wages are highest. They can also show that the industrialised communist states have increasingly turned to Western MNCs to provide them with new technology and capital, that the Chinese have now accepted this need, and that even the radical Marxist regime in Moçambique is doing so. It is because national governments of almost every political persuasion are willing to offer MNCs substantial inducements to invest in their territories that the latter exert such a powerful influence over domestic and international economic policy. Why should this be so?

Many of the reasons for this influence are set out very succinctly in the arguments summarised by Meier (cited on p. 89) since the resources listed there enable MNCs to bring substantial advantages to any country or region in which it chooses to locate a major subsidiary. While many governments would often prefer it if such enterprises were owned by nationals or by state or collective institutions, they will often have found that their indigenous capitalists lack the capital and expertise to produce the most modern goods successfully and that state-controlled production is inefficient and costly. MNCs, on the other hand, can almost guarantee the successful operation of a new subsidiary, since they will already be using the technology, will have access to the necessary financial resources, and will already have an established international marketing network through which to sell their output both locally and abroad. Their products will conform to international standards of quality and price, and, since the company raises its own capital, scarce public resources will not have to be diverted to allow it to be established except where direct subsidies are involved. Furthermore, since they usually employ the most advanced technology, they can usually offer their workers better wages and working conditions than their domestic counterparts. Thus any government which needs to cut unemployment and improve the balance of payments (and which does not?) is likely to find an offer to establish a local subsidiary from a multinational virtually impossible to refuse.

It is their ability to offer these advantages which enables the MNCs to exert a very powerful influence over the overall economic policies of particular countries, even where their executives play a very limited role in their day-to-day political life. Since there are always more countries looking for foreign capital than potential investors, all of them are forced to bid against each other in the attempt to offer the most favourable inducements. These are likely to include a favourable tax status, the right to repatriate unlimited amounts of profit, free access to foreign exchange for importing capital equipment and raw materials, direct subsidies from government and, in many Third World countries, direct prohibition of trade union organisation and strikes. These concessions have reached their most developed form in the 'free trade zones' set up in many Third World and some developed countries where foreign capital is allowed a completely free hand in relation to imports, exports and labour policies. The direct influence of the MNC connection is brought to bear on a country-by-country basis, but because all of them are involved in competitive bidding for investment, the effect is to produce an international environment uniquely favourable to the interests of this dominant section of the capitalist system.

The foregoing considerations relate to the attempt to encourage new investments, but the pressures on countries which already have substantial amounts of foreign investment are also considerable. Once a substantial foreign sector exists, the country will depend upon it for output and employment. Individual companies will then be able to threaten to move to a more favourable environment if policies are adopted of which it disapproves, or if an unacceptable degree of industrial militancy is allowed to develop. In these countries, too, their presence and resources enable them to develop close relationships with key individuals in the indigenous ruling class. Directorships and managerial posts can be offered to leading politicians and their relatives, distributorships and supply contracts to leading local firms. In many cases we know that the links are even more direct, with substantial 'commissions' passing hands in pursuit of important contracts. But even without the use of these dubious methods, the MNCs as a group exert a pervasive influence on the *general* orientation towards economic policy of many countries through their ability to promise them an apparently effortless solution to their economic problems if they toe the line, or to a serious economic crisis if they do not do what is expected of them.

Finally, we have to consider the sources of economic and political leverage open to MNCs when their interests are threatened by potentially hostile regimes. In such cases, of course, the threat of the withdrawal of new or existing investment and support can always be made, but it is always technically possible for a radical government to expropriate their assets and operate them independently. But here the international spread and organisational structure of these firms can have a very powerful influence on their ability to retaliate. Many new production processes are now carried out internationally, so that no final product is actually made from start to finish in any single plant or country. Components are made all over the world and only assembled in a single plant, like those for the Fiesta car, for example, which is produced in Britain, Spain and France. Almost all of the research and development for new processes is concentrated in the plants in the advanced countries, and is not available to the operatives in the less developed countries. As a result, it is likely that a hostile government will find it very difficult to continue effective production after expropriating a local plant since they will be unable to get access to key components or to a continuing flow of necessary technical information. Again, where the government is not willing to nationalise but attempts to use foreign exchange controls or taxation as a means of imposing its own priorities on companies, the latter can often evade these by exploiting their overseas linkages through 'transfer pricing', i.e. setting their own (non-market) prices for goods exchanged between international branches, and thus transferring profits or foreign exchange abroad.[20]

These arguments implicitly add up to an assertion that weaker counries are more or less obliged to accept foreign private investment because of the essentially positive contribution that it makes to their development. Extrapolating from this, we can then be persuaded to accept arguments which claim that the development of interventionist policies in weaker countries designed to harness the positive contribution of MNCs to growth must be the best means of ensuring even development in the system as a whole, and thus the possibility of eventually integrating the whole world into it on a liberal basis. This case, rigorously argued by Dunning,[21] is then backed by the selective use of evidence drawn from the post-war period, when the successful development of Western Europe, the former British Dominions and, more recently, the newly industrialising countries (the NICs) with substantial overseas foreign investment, is used to show that their contribution can be a positive one. If this were indeed the case, then the problems identified earlier in this work and in a mass of recent Marxist literature would only be temporary ones and liable to disappear, if only no counterproductive steps were taken to discourage MNC investment on either nationalist or socialist grounds. What can be said in response to what is clearly a very powerful body of argument and evidence?

Again, we can only do this by looking more closely at those arguments which do associate the expansion of foreign private investment with uneven development. This will establish the extent to which they may well promote it at the global level while making some real economic contribution to limited locations and regions in particular countries. Here we must consider two sets of arguments:

those which suggest that the contribution of MNCs to the countries within which they *do* operate is by no means as positive as their proponents suggest, and those which relate to their impact upon the process of uneven development at the international level.

Firstly, where an MNC is given special incentives to initiate a new activity in a particular country, and in particular where it is guaranteed a monopoly position (a common inducement in many Third World countries) it will be able to exploit this by keeping its prices high and extracting monopoly super profits. Where it moves into a sector in which small-scale domestic producers are already active, on the other hand, it will usually be in a position to undercut them through the exploitation of its superior technology or its superior access to financial resources. This might well drive the small producers out of business, thus destroying as many or even more jobs than the new investment has actually created. Thus its contribution to employment creation can often be much more apparent than real.

Secondly, where there are few opportunities for large-scale new investment in host countries, the MNC will probably have a much higher propensity to move its profits out of the country than domestic firms with stronger local commitments and limited external interests. Furthermore, many of the advanced types of manufacturing process favoured by MNCs rely heavily on the importation of a large proportion of their specialised components and raw materials. Thus the foreign exchange saving resulting from the new plant will be offset in large measure by these external payments, and this effect will be even more damaging where the prices charged for the domestically produced commodity are much higher than their imported equivalent, as they often are.

Thirdly, an MNC's control over the technology it uses tends to keep LDCs within which it invests in a state of permanent dependence. New processes and organisational methods are imported from the parent company, and no effort is made to build up any local capacity to carry out these critical functions. Thus the subsidiary cannot survive without its lifeline to head office, and local nationals do not acquire the skills which might enable them to move out and start a new business on their own. Where local nationals are employed at senior levels, as they often are, they are quite likely to put their loyalty to the company ahead of that to their country (or, perhaps more accurately, to lose the capacity to recognise that there could ever be any significant conflict between the two) and thus to identify with all the decisions the MNC makes. Since their own and other companies are very likely to be able to offer them prestigious jobs in other countries, their very identity as a 'national' of a particular country is quite likely to become blurred in the long run as they enter the expensive world of expatriate living and global mobility.

Fourthly, the MNCs have the capacity to move large quantities of money in and out of countries more or less when they choose by controlling the times at which payments are made and received between subsidiaries. This will directly affect the balance of payments and the money supply and even the overall level of economic activity itself. They are not directly and immediately constrained by market competition as smaller firms are, since their economic power can make it possible for them to set prices and provide services which would not be possible for smaller firms without the same resources. This does not mean that their activities are not controlled through competition (and especially through *international* competition) in the long run, since they do have to compete with other MNCs in most sectors, and some of them are now suffering real difficulties as a result. But their capacity to exert a much higher degree of control than small firms over both domestic and foreign activities means that they can exert a direct influence on the way the economy operates and undermine the ability of the government to use its controls – and especially those traditionally used by Keynesians – to achieve its objectives. Many of their critics feel that it is this power which has undermined social democratic governments' ability to maintain full employment and growth through the mechanisms developed in the post-war period, and has led to a reversion to pre-war strategies based on the uncontrolled use of the market mechanism combined with large-scale unemployment and public spending cuts.

Fifthly, the technology used by MNCs is designed to maximise profits in the conditions prevailing in the advanced countries, where 75 per cent of their investments are still located. Here labour is relatively scarce and expensive, but capital and the ability to service and produce complex equipment is plentiful. These conditions therefore lead them strongly to favour capital-intensive investment – that is to say, plants that use a very small amount of highly paid labour to produce very large amounts of production using very sophisticated machinery and work organisation. In the Third World, however, where the majority of the world's population lives, conditions are exactly the opposite of this. Here there are very large numbers of underemployed workers, limited supplies of capital (especially in the form of the foreign exchange needed to buy foreign machinery) and an even more limited indigenous capacity to service and maintain complex equipment. But MNCs find it almost impossible to produce using more 'appropriate' technology, since it is their control over these advanced techniques which gives them their competitive advantage over local firms in the first place. Thus their investments in these countries have a dramatic and damaging effect on the overall distribution of resources, generating very small amounts of employment (one economist estimated that all the MNCs in the Third World employed only about 4½ million workers[22]), monopolising scarce supplies of technically trained personnel, requiring large outflows of foreign exchange to cover the costs of the capital intensive equipment, and producing relatively sophisticated and sometimes expensive commodities conforming to the standards and requirements of Western markets, and not those of the periphery.

The effect of the growth of a large MNC sector (in the small number of countries actually able to attract any substantial amount of foreign investment) in these circumstances must therefore be greatly to intensify existing levels of inequality *within* countries and regions. A few powerful modern plants come to be concentrated at a few points surrounded by a growth of sophisticated services and facilities for the favoured few employed by them. The same cities will then attract a much larger number of marginal people hoping for better employment or living off semi-legal or totally illegal activities designed to capture a few of the crumbs falling from the MNCs' table. Outside these centres, however, there will be almost no effective growth in genuine manufacturing capacity and, in many cases, an actual decline as the result of the penetration of local markets by the new products of the MNCs. The result, of course, will be a serious problem of uneven development internally and a very weak growth of the domestic market. Since few will be able to earn effectively, few will have much to spend. The internal market will be small, thus discouraging further investment in local production to meet local needs, leading to a perpetuation of the situation in which small islands of prosperity coexist with huge areas of misery and stagnation. The result must also be intense regional and class conflicts, political instability and a tendency to political dictatorship, the prevailing condition in the great majority of Third World countries at present.

Finally, in countries where governments are very weak, the presence of large foreign companies with easy access to large resources can intensify the corruption of the indigenous ruling class, which is especially possible where access to valuable mineral resources is at stake.

Taking all of this together, therefore, we can understand the strength of the criticisms made by Third World theorists of the 'new international division of labour ... with its new agent: the international manufacturing oligopoly', generating an increasing internal polarisation 'between modern dominant and advanced economic activities social groups and regions on the one hand, and backward, marginal and dependent activities, groups and regions on the other'.[23] Within this context we have to emphasise the growing weakening of the control exerted by national governments over economic policy as a result of the leverage exerted by MNCs, both in terms of the concessions required to keep them there and their capacity to control the flows of profits and money through transfer pricing. This marginalisation of political control *within* countries through the leverage exerted by monopoly capital is one aspect of the problem of international political organisation, because it has a crucial impact on the extent to which the nation state itself can still serve as a valid mechanism through which the working class of particular countries can attempt to overcome the crisis through the capture of the state and an attempt to build some form of 'socialism in one country'. But before it can be put in the context of the problem of political power at the level of the world economy, we must look at the implications of the present pattern of MNC investment at that level and not merely at the national level, as is so often the case.[24]

At the international level we can first identify a tendency towards the creation of a hierarchical division of labour based on a division within the firm between day-to-day enterprise operations, regional office management, and overall goal determination and planning.[25] The locational effects of this division make themselves felt internationally with a concentration of overall planning in the world's major cities, which therefore become 'the major centres of high-level strategic planning';[26] regional management will be concentrated in the larger cities, often the capital cities where access to political influence is easiest; the lowest level production processes will then be located in these cities or other already developed urban locations where specific advantages can be identified with respect to access to markets, skilled labour, social amenities, and so on. The corresponding social and political effect of this tendency will be a concentration of wealth and amenities in these areas, a weakening of control in the peripheral areas, and an intensification of the tendency towards uneven development.

These effects can then be further intensified by the nature of the technology normally used by MNCs. Their competitiveness usually derives from their ability to produce very large numbers of products from highly efficient plants using expensive machinery and small labour forces, together with their control over advertising, marketing, research and financial assets. Almost no countries in the Third World (and not very many in the advanced countries) have markets large enough to absorb the minimum output of even the smallest of these modern plants, so that they are only likely to consider setting up in a country where the level of economic activity is already very high (so that the domestic market is relatively large) and there are real prospects for exports, preferably to the industrial countries themselves, but also to the smaller markets of other Third World countries. Once a particular site has been chosen by a few MNCs, more are likely to follow in order to gain access to the markets and other services which they create, thus leading to a greater and greater concentration of activity at that point. In Eastern Africa, for example, the MNCs centred on Nairobi in Kenya, and now dominate the markets for many sophisticated consumer goods in a region comprising Tanzania, Uganda, Rwanda, Burundi and even Zambia and the Southern Sudan when transport conditions permit. This means that MNCs can point to a process of dynamic manufacturing development in the region when looked at from a Kenyan perspective, but in doing so ignore the dramatic problems of intensified stagnation in the rest of the region, where virtually no foreign investment takes place and local producers of simple commodities like soap and shoes are actually forced out of business.[27]

This tendency towards uneven development is compounded by the indirect effects that it has on the effectiveness and stability of the governments in the favoured, as opposed to the disfavoured, countries. In the favoured countries the growth in revenues stemming from the relatively successful development of MNC enterprise can be devoted to improving the services required to attract more of them. Better roads, telecommunications and social services can be provided in the major urban centres, and a wide range of amenities, public and private, can be provided to make life in the Third World palatable to hard pressed foreign executives and their families. A few of these benefits may trickle down to the mass of the indigenous population, but their effect is constantly to increase the relative attractiveness of favoured locations to foreign enterprise.[28] In these countries the growth in governmental resources may also enable it to provide some benefits to enough of the population to sustain a higher degree of political stability than elsewhere, and it will certainly enable them to increase the size of the army and police force and use it for the same purpose when other methods fail. But in the neglected areas exactly the opposite process goes on. Revenues fail to keep pace with expenditure, services fall into decay, it becomes more and more difficult to do business, and existing firms drift away to better locations. Political discontent cannot be effectively contained, governments are continually in crisis, and conditions for effective investment worsen even further.

What can be seen as a process of national disintegration – clearly visible across the Third World countries like El Salvador, Uganda and Bangladesh – then also becomes one of *international* disintegration, since their failure compounds the global recession by leading to a reduction in markets for the established producers in the already favoured areas. Eventually they, too, find it increasingly difficult to sell enough of their output, and the process of degeneration moves from the poor areas to the favoured areas. The effects of this process are now clearly visible in the capitalist world, as unemployment escalates in even the most successful countries and the viciousness of the competitive struggle for international markets intensifies. Yet the private and individualistic nature of the MNC, and the weak and atomised nature of the nation-state system, makes it impossible for effective, planned, *social* solutions to be found for what is essentially an international problem.

Finally, it is important to note that the growth of monopoly capitalism embodied in MNCs also has the effect of creating large inequalities between different groups of *workers*, which can have significant implications for the struggle for socialism. Many years ago Lenin pointed out that some more favoured workers in the advanced countries could be given part of the surpluses extracted from the Third World and thereby turned into allies of the system.[29] The development of advanced production techniques by MNCs has now greatly exaggerated this tendency. Using highly advanced technology and small workforces, MNCs can afford to pay relatively high wages. Their workers are, of course, still being heavily exploited by capitalism, which can make even higher profits out of them than their smaller competitors, who pay lower wages, because of their greater productivity. But for the workers themselves what is important is the absolute level of the real wages, rather than the amount of surplus that is being extracted from them. Many of these workers are industrially very militant, often the most militant sectors of the whole working class. But they, and more especially their trade union leadership, are also quite capable of recognising the advantages which they themselves obtain from their privileged access to highly paid jobs, and thus support policies which favour further MNC investment, even those which attempt to do this by attracting investment that would otherwise go to neighbouring countries. In this way they can associate themselves with the ruling class in their own country in nationalistic policies which intensify the tendencies to international dislocation because they fail to recognise the need for an international solution to what is an essentially international problem. The political implications of this argument for the workers' movement are immensely complex and contradictory, and will be taken up again in the concluding chapter.

We can now conclude by reviewing the major points that have been made:

1. It is clear that a major expansion of the activities of MNCs has taken place since the war which has transformed the international division of labour, transferring an immense quantity of surplus to the advanced countries in the process,[30] but also generating significant new concentrations of industrial power at certain favoured points in the world economy, mainly in already developed countries, but a few of them in LDCs. This process has occurred not merely at the level of circulation (the exchange of goods, services and money) but of production itself, thereby making the possibility of a reversion to autarchic nationalistic solutions to the current crisis increasingly problematic.

2. This global expansion has been greatly accelerated by, but has itself also greatly assisted, the liberalisation of the world economy mediated by the international agencies – a process which has reached its most developed stage in the EEC, where something very close to a supranational federal authority is now in existence. But this process of capitalist expansion has also been directly assisted by the attempt by weaker countries to use state power, including protectionist methods, to induce MNCs to locate within their territorial space. In so doing their activities have partially contradicted the *laissez-faire* principle at the global level, but the effect has been to intensify the internationalisation of production and exchange and thereby to weaken the long-term capacity of nation states to control their economic destinies on an autonomous basis.

3. While liberal and reformist theorists assume that the expansion of international private capital must eventually lead to an evening up of levels of development on the global scale, a closer examination shows that it is in fact intensifying and altering a situation which is dominated by a tendency to further inequality and dislocation. In the early post-war phase, the expansion of US capital, in association with large net official transfers abroad, did allow a process of very rapid growth to occur in Europe and Japan, but this has now had the effect of weakening the control of US capital both at home and abroad. Subsequently a number of smaller but still significant new centres have emerged in Latin America and Asia and these have become important foci of capitalist expansion. But these remain isolated concentrations, and the effect of their emergence is to impose added difficulties on neighbouring countries whose position will be undermined by the competitiveness of the foreign industry in the favoured areas.

4. All of these considerations suggest that the creation of a viable structure of international political authority capable of managing the tensions and dislocations that must arise out of these processes will be fraught with extreme difficulties. In so far as any process of market competition tends to generate a process of uneven as opposed to even development, it can only be sustained in the long run where an effective political authority exists that is capable of redistributing surpluses from strong to weak areas and from dominant to subordinated classes. In the nineteenth century British dominance was overcome through the emergence of strong nation states on the Continent, in the USA and Japan, capable of using

protectionism and imperialism as an effective means of building up their own industrial base to the point where they could eventually out-compete Britain. In the early post-war period, the combination of US disbursements and protectionism in a few centres allowed domestic capital to expand to the point where it could pose an effective challenge to America. But now this process itself has undermined the structures which allowed it to operate, without replacing it with an equivalent mechanism capable of allowing it to be taken further in a positive direction. Instead, weak centres are being encouraged to reduce protectionist controls, while the international agencies have not been given the resources required for an effective redistribution to the weaker areas. The result is a political vacuum and an intensification of the tendency to disintegration at both national and global levels.

Capital, having internationalised itself and taken advantage of its ability to operate at the global level, where it has escaped the direct controls previously established by interventionist social democratic states to control it, now finds itself without the capacity to organise an effective *political* defence of the structure it has created. The implications of this failure are of the utmost significance for the future of humanity. In the chapters that follow it will only be possible to look at some of its most obvious consequences.

PART II

The Industrial Countries in the International System

5
American Deficits, Global Boom and Crisis

Financing the post-war boom, 1947–1961

The establishment of the IMF, World Bank and the GATT in the 1940s, involved, as we have seen, a series of compromises between the objectives of the USA as a strong surplus country committed to trade liberalisation, and those of the weak deficit countries in most of the rest of the world committed to protectionism and planned trade. The USA had extracted from the rest a long-term commitment to liberalisation in exchange for the right to retain controls in the short term and to receive some degree of US assistance with their expected balance of payments problems. Believing as they did that trade would induce a tendency towards equilibrium between weak and strong, the Americans originally assumed that these controls would soon be dismantled and that their direct assistance could be relatively small – a view clearly demonstrated in their dealings with Britain, which will be reviewed in Chapter 6. From the Marxist perspective set out in Chapter 2, however, we would expect the opposite to be the case – indeed, contemporary Marxist observers were convinced of the inevitability of 'economic crises in the post-war Western world'.[1] Liberal theorists now associate the post-war recovery with the free trade policies which in fact were only to be consistently implemented in the 1960s. A close look at the recovery period itself, however, suggests an entirely opposite conclusion, and one which is far more compatible with an analysis based upon the necessity for planned redistribution – an analysis which can best be developed by looking at the way in which the economic policies of the time were forced to come to terms with the facts of uneven development if crisis was to be averted.

In 1945 the problem of uneven development manifested itself in the dominant position of US producers in the international manufacturing system, and of the dollar as an international currency. The productive capacity of the rest of the world could only be rebuilt quickly through a rapid inflow of US capital equipment, which, in turn, could only be financed with dollars acquired out of loans, gifts or export surpluses. If the orthodox theory set out in Chapter 2 were to hold, the unemployment and low wages in the deficit countries should have given them a clear competitive advantage in US markets and induced an automatic tendency towards equilibrium. Instead the opposite occurred: between 1945 and 1947 American exports continued to dominate world markets, and its balance of payments surplus remained, totalling $19.5 billion in 1946 and 1947. This exhausted Western foreign exchange reserves, so that imports would have to be cut unless some *political* means could be found of financing them. The problem thus presented itself to the international community as a 'dollar shortage' arising out of the inability of the weaker countries to trade on equal terms with the USA and of the failure of the USA to accept the Keynesian proposals for automatic recycling through the international agencies. This failure thus threatened a serious economic crisis comparable to the one that had occurred after the First World War, and one which would also threaten American exports and the viability of its own industries.[2]

This crisis coincided with an intensification of the cold war and of American concern for the political stability of the capitalist systems of Western Europe. It marked a critical turning point in post-war history, and forced the USA to accept not only a strongly interventionist orientation on the part of these governments and that of Japan, but also the necessity for a far more generous use of its own military and financial resources to stabilise the situation. This American view was clearly set out in a memorandum writtten by Will Clayton, Assistant Secretary of State for Economic Affairs, on his return from a visit to Europe early in 1947:

> Communist movements are threatening established governments in every part of the globe. These movements, directed by Moscow, feed on economic and political weakness. The countries under Communist pressure require economic assistance on a large scale if they are to maintain their territorial integrity and political independence.

At one time it had been expected that the International Bank could satisfy the needs for such assistance. But it is now clear that the bank cannot do this job.

The United States is faced with a world-wide challenge to human freedom. The only way to meet this challenge is by a vast new programme of assistance given directly by the United States itself.[3]

The outcome of the USA's response to the communist threat was twofold. On the one hand there was the Marshall Plan, which committed substantial resources to the rebuilding of the European economies on very generous terms; on the other there was an expansion in overseas defence spending which turned the American surplus on their balance of *trade* into a deficit on their balance of *payments*. Thus, as Balogh noted, the emergence of the US deficit owed nothing to the 'natural' tendency for weak countries to catch up with strong ones propounded by orthodox theory, and everything to central government policy and direct governmental expenditure. He wrote:

It took $84,000 million of grants and loans ... or 15 times the original dollar component of the IMF and 6½ times the total maximum lending power of the [World] Bank; and military expenditure and supply grants abroad of an average of well over $5,000 million per annum since 1952 to restore balance. American domestic demand was buttressed by military expenditure which between 1951 and 1961 amounted to $451 millions.[4]

Thus, as Spero clearly shows, the crisis was resolved through mechanisms which owed little to the market mechanism and almost everything to conscious political intervention:

From 1947 until 1958 the US deliberately encouraged an outflow of dollars, and from 1950 on the United States ran a balance-of-payments deficit which provided liquidity for the international economy ... In addition ..., the United States assumed the international management of imbalances in the system ... It dealt with its own huge balance-of-trade surplus and the European and Japanese deficits by foreign aid and military expenditures. [It] abandoned the Bretton Woods goal of convertibility and encouraged European and Japanese trade protectionism and discrimination against the dollar. For example, the United States absorbed large volumes of Japanese exports while accepting Japanese restrictions against American exports. It supported the European Payments Union, an intra-European clearing system which discriminated against the dollar. And it promoted European and Japanese exports to the United States. Finally, the United States used the leverage of Marshall Plan aid to encourage devaluation of many European currencies in 1949 and to promote national programmes of monetary stabilization.[5]

In Germany and Japan the combination of an undervalued exchange rate, generous American aid, the close economic management of industrial investment, the increase in demand created by the Korean war boom, and the availability of a large labour surplus and correspondingly low wages, generated economic 'miracles' which would not have been possible but for these uniquely favourable external circumstances. Both rapidly moved into balance of payments surpluses based upon rapid and continuous capital investment which sustained high levels of employment and rising wage rates, while simultaneously keeping down wage costs and thus guaranteeing international competitiveness. Germany moved into surplus in 1952 'during the Korean boom' and, 'against all textbook wisdom', remained so in every year barring two until 1980.[6] The Japanese economy benefited particularly strongly from the Korean war boom and American spending,[7] and it also successfully followed policies designed to increase its foreign market penetration of an extremely interventionist kind.[8] By the end of the 1950s it had restructured its industrial base so effectively that it was to begin a process of unprecedented export expansion which was to make it, too, a structural surplus country with significant and problematic implications for the period that was to follow.

Against this triumphant experience, that of the US economy was much less spectacular, since the long-term effects of the deficit were to induce a relative deterioration in its competitive position. The large external flows of official and private capital, together with the manpower and money tied up in unproductive military activities, meant that the USA (and, as we shall see, the UK) could not sustain the same levels of investment and productivity growth as those achieved in its former adversaries. The resulting change in the relative levels of output in the leading countries in the system is

Figure 5.1 Per capita GNP of selected countries as percentage of US per capita GNP, 1913–79

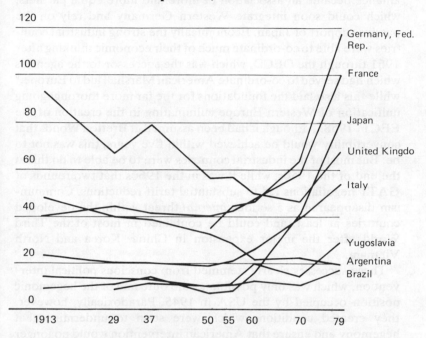

SOURCE: World Bank, *World Development Report*, 1982, p. 21

clearly demonstrated in Figure 5.1. The transition from crisis to boom between 1947 and the end of the 1950s had clearly been based on the initiation of a process of even development in the world economy involving a substantial relative decline in the position of the erstwhile leading economies, the USA and the UK, and a corresponding improvement in those of the industrial countries which had suffered occupation during the war. But although this transition conforms closely to the macro requirements for stable global development identified in orthodox theory, it was achieved by methods which were the exact opposite of those to be found in the orthodox textbooks, methods involving extreme forms of state intervention and international economic management, which, as we have seen, were the essential prerequisites for the results that followed.

Associated with this process of even development was an equally important process of political integration. Militarily the NATO alliance became an association of more and more equal partners, which could soon integrate Western Germany and rely on the passive support of Japan. Economically the strong industrial countries were able to co-ordinate much of their economic thinking after 1961 through the OECD, which was the successor to the agencies which had served to co-ordinate American Marshall aid to Europe,[9] while this also laid the foundations for the far more thoroughgoing unification of Western Europe culminating in the creation of the EEC in 1958. Although it had been assumed at Bretton Woods that convertibility would be achieved within five years, this was not to be. But most of the industrial countries were to be able to do this at the end of the 1950s, while it was in the 1960s that two rounds of GATT negotiations led to substantial tariff reductions. Communism disappeared as a serious *internal* threat within the developed countries at least, and could be contained in most of the Third World after the major expansion in China, Korea and North Vietnam.

These successes clearly stemmed from conscious political intervention, which was only possible as the outcome of the hegemonic position occupied by the USA in 1945. Paradoxically, however, they created conditions which were soon to undermine that hegemony and ensure that American intervention would no longer have the positive effects which were so gratefully received at the time. Yet this no longer seemed to matter, since, with the weaker countries restored to competitiveness, it now seemed that the political element in the system could be eliminated through the creation of the liberal market conditions recommended by orthodox theory. The USA could simply become one among a self-regulating community of relatively equal traders and allow the equilibrating forces of the market to guarantee a dynamic yet orderly development of the world market. What was not yet clear to liberal observers, however, was that the process which had eliminated the old structure of inequality had merely replaced it with another. Although the strength of the American balance of payments and the 'dollar shortage' had been the key feature of the crisis of the 1940s, its new weakness and the corresponding 'dollar overhang' was to become the crucial element in the political economy of the 1960s and 1970s.

Reform and crisis, 1961–1973

During the 1960s the boom continued, with the benefits widely dispersed throughout the system: there were annual growth rates of 5.2 per cent in the industrial countries, 5.9 per cent in the middle income LDCs, and 4.4 per cent in the low income countries.[10] This should have provided the basis for stable trading and monetary arrangements, but the fact that it did not was made brutally clear on 15 August 1971, when Nixon unilaterally announced that the USA was abrogating the Bretton Woods agreement by ending dollar-gold convertibility, devaluing the dollar and imposing a 10 per cent tax on imports.[11] In December a new system of parities was negotiated, involving a further devaluation of the dollar; at the start of 1973 a period of sustained speculation against it finally convinced the authorities that fixed exchange rates could no longer be defended and a period of 'managed floating' ensued, in which stability could no longer be guaranteed. The weakness of the dollar, which produced these problems, had been recognised during the 1960s, and serious attempts were made to deal with it. By looking at these efforts and the reasons for their failure we can further demonstrate the weaknesses of orthodox theory in practice and identify some of the factors which undermined it.

The reason why the start of the 1960s can be chosen as marking an important break in the evolution of the post-war world economy is because this was the point when the effects of the American deficit and the reduction in international monetary management first became visible and began to demand attention. In 1961 the dollars held by overseas countries as foreign exchange reserves came to exceed the value of US gold and foreign exchange reserves for the first time. At about the same time the leading countries also ended currency convertibility and began negotiations through the GATT which were to lead to a substantial reduction in the overall levels of protection. Trade liberalisation had now begun in earnest, and this meant that the first line of defence against balance of payments difficulties had been removed. A new system had emerged which would be less easy to manage than the old.

The viability of an international economic system based on free exchange, it will be remembered, depends upon the ability to establish currency convertibility, stable exchange rates, a secure centre currency, and national economic policies which guarantee free trade and balance of payments equilibrium. In the 1950s the dollar deficit was fundamental to the solution of all these problems, since it guaranteed the availability of the centre currency for the financing of trade and development, and enabled weaker countries to maintain balance of payments surpluses and thus keep their exchange rates stable and adopt convertibility. It also gave the Americans immense moral authority in international negotiations because of the benefits it allowed them to confer on their allies, and thus enabled them to persuade reluctant governments to adopt liberal policies before they would probably have done so of their own volition. At the start of the 1960s, however, the emergence of the so-called 'dollar overhang' (the excess of American overseas liabilities over domestic foreign exchange reserves) made it clear that these conditions could not last forever. Once American reserves fell to unacceptably low levels in relation to overseas liabilities in the form of dollars which foreign owners could convert into gold at $35 to the ounce, the USA would either have to turn its deficit into a surplus, or devalue, or end the guarantee of dollar-gold convertibility. This, in turn, would mean a restructuring of the whole Bretton Woods system, which, as we have seen, depended in all its aspects upon the dominance of the dollar.

The need to find an acceptable alternative to the dollar in the international economic system can therefore be seen as the key to its restructuring from the early 1960s onwards. Although it tended to be treated as a purely technical and economic problem, it is clear that it was actually a reflection of the uneven development of productive capacity which had occurred up to then in the post-war period, and more especially of the slow growth of the US economy relative to the strong performers. The problem at the time was stated most coherently by Robert Triffin, who showed in 1959 that the existing system incorporated a fundamental contradiction.[12] While the dollar deficit had been essential to the growth of the rest of the system, its effect had been to undermine the relative economic strength of the US economy itself. Yet, because the dollar was not only the international currency, but also the *national* currency of a particular state, its value relative to other currencies must depend directly on the viability of the productive capacity of that state, and of the policies adopted by its government. If the American economy became so weakened that it could no longer be relied on to compete effectively overseas, or if its government adopted inflationary policies which increased the balance of payments deficit, its reserves would soon disappear and it would be forced to devalue and/or adopt protectionist measures (as Nixon did in 1971) to deal with the problem. This would then have dramatic international consequences, because it would effectively reduce the value of all overseas holdings of dollars (thereby making a substantial transfer of real resources to the USA) and constitute a direct attack upon the liberal principles on which the system was based. Thus the *supply* of dollars to the rest of the world depended on the US deficit, while the *stability* of dollar (once the American gold stock had been significantly depleted) depended on the ability to return to surplus. By the early 1960s it had therefore become clear that the international redistribution mechanism established in 1947 could no longer function without intensifying this inherent contradiction (the 'Triffin paradox'). Fundamental change was essential if the system was not to collapse.

Although the Triffin paradox appeared to pose purely technical and economic problems, the attempt to deal with it exposed a conflict-ridden and intensely political situation. What was at issue was the relative power positions of the various countries in the OECD alliance, the nature of the responsibilities and the extent of the costs to be sustained by each in the restructuring of the system, and the possibility of establishing the basis for another period of even development by restoring the balance in growth rates between the USA and UK (the weak performers) and the strong OECD countries on the one hand, and by overcoming the much greater inequalities that still existed between the whole of the industrialised world and the Third World on the other. The specific problems posed by the weakness of the UK and Third World will be considered in the next two chapters; here we will purely be concerned with that which stemmed from the relationship between the USA and the strong industrialised countries.

To resolve the Triffin paradox the nature of this relationship had now to be fundamentally restructured. The US deficit had to be reduced, even turned into a surplus before it threatened the American ability to guarantee the long-term stability of the dollar. But since this would end the long-term flow of dollars to the rest of the world and threaten to reduce the general expansion of trade and economic development, it was essential that an alternative source of internationally acceptable money (of 'international liquidity', to use the technical term) be found which could serve the same purpose. And just as it was only the USA as the leading surplus country which could provide this facility in 1945, it was only the newly established surplus countries in the OECD which could do so on a stable basis in the 1960s. They, too, would only be able to do this if they were to accept the conditions which applied to the USA in the 1940s: they would either have to allow their economies to run into deficit and thus allow their foreign exchange resources to be transferred to what had previously been deficit countries, or they would have to take steps to lend or donate the necessary resources to those countries directly. Again, it is clear that the underlying problem was one of overcoming the perrenial problem of uneven development which was emerging again in a new guise. How, then, was this problem approached?[13]

Two major campaigns can be identified in the politics of international economic management in the 1960s: the attempt to set up alternative sources of international credit to those provided by the flow of dollars from the USA to the rest of the system, and that to persuade the USA to bring its deficit under control. The first had some very limited successes, the second was a resounding failure. Let us now consider how the interaction between these various pressures and tendencies shaped the system as a whole during these years.

The provision of new forms of official international credit by the surplus countries meant that they had to accept a political obligation to allow their own savings to be used by deficit countries so that the latter could pursue their economic programmes more successfully. At the end of the 1960s, and more especially in the 1970s, the major part of this task was to be taken over by the international private banks and performed on an unofficial basis with results which will be explored in Chapter 9. This did not require direct political agreements to be reached, but official credit creation required government-to-government negotiations as well as the active intervention of the IMF. Given the technical complexity of the issues involved and, more expecially, the conflicts of interest that they generated, the negotiations were confined to a small circle of experts and spread over a number of years. Who, then, were the main protagonists involved?

In the 1960s the surplus countries were now those whose prospects in 1945 had seemed so doubtful – Germany, France, the Benelux and Scandinavian countries in Europe,and Japan in Asia. The deficit countries still included the Third World, but now as independent states rather than as colonies. But they had also been joined by the former victors, the USA and UK, whose position as one-time dominant industrial countries with a long experience of international financial management and internationally used currencies separated their problems decisively from the rest. Given that it was the surplus countries whose resources would have to be made available if any form of the monetary system was to succeed, it was inevitable that they would play a critical role in the negotiations. Since the dollar was still the key currency in the system, it was equally true that no effective change could occur without the consent of the American goverment. The British position was now highly marginal, however, since the pound sterling's role in the system was relatively limited, while its own economy was consistently weak and in balance of payments deficit. This reduced its political influence to almost zero, since it came to the international agencies mainly as a supplicant looking for the assistance required to resolve its own problems. By the early 1960s the great majority of the Third World was independent and involved in the IMF. They were therefore entitled to participate in those aspects of the problem which were negotiated through the IMF, but their influence was to be very limited. A great many crucial decisions and most of the negotiations leading up to them were conducted in forums from which they were specifically excluded, their voting rights at the IMF were limited by the small size of their quotas, which ensured that the rich countries would exercise a veto over all decisions, and, most important of all, they too were essentially demanding an increase in the supply of credit provided to them by the surplus countries. Since the latter could not be forced to part with their funds, the final say in any decision inevitably rested with them, whatever the prevailing constitutional arrangement. What demands were each of these groups putting forward?

The situation in which the strong countries found themselves was a contradictory one. Their balance of payments surpluses ensured that their foreign exchange reserves were constantly expanding, most of them in the form of dollars. If the dollar were ever to be devalued they would immediately lose an equivalent part of the value of their savings, so they were anxious to ensure that the

Americans brought their deficit under control before possibly being forced to take this step. If, on the other hand, they simply allowed the American deficit to continue and stockpiled more and more dollars in their reserves, this would have uncontrollable inflationary effects on their own economies. This is because the dollars earned by, say, German exporters, which were accumulating in the Central Bank, would have been converted into the local currency and available for spending in the domestic economy. This would increase the money supply without an equivalent increase in the supply of goods, thus leading to an increase in prices unless the government stepped in to modify the situation. Thus all of these countries saw a clear willingness on the part of the USA to adopt the policies needed to move back towards surplus before its reserves of gold were exhausted as a necessary element in any solution of the problem. Indeed, as the decade went on and the deficit increased rather than diminished, their demands became stronger. They began to look for American policies that would generate a sufficient surplus to enable them to reduce their existing holdings of dollars and convert them into some other internationally acceptable form of money.

Yet this was easier said than done. As the governments of highly successful capitalist countries, their political standing depended on their ability to maximise the economic success of their own producers of goods and services on both the home *and* the world markets, since this determined their ability to guarantee their voters full employment, rising wages and improved social services. They could only do this by *increasing* their exports not only to the rest of the world but also to the USA (their biggest single market) and thus making it *more* difficult for the latter to eliminate its balance of payments deficit. Thus their domestic and international economic policies stood in direct contradiction to each other: while they spent huge sums on the economic infrastructure required to increase the international competitiveness of their basic industries (the success of the Japanese Ministry of Industry has become a byword in this regard) and thus generated a continuous expansion in exports, they spent their time in international economic negotiations lecturing the Americans and the British on the need to export more and import less. We have already seen how, faced with the same contradiction in the 1940s, the Americans had only resolved the problem through an expansion in aid and more especially in defence expenditure. What was now at issue was whether the new surplus countries could find some new mechanism which would have similar effects.

The position of the Third World, on the other hand, was much like that of the weaker industrialised countries in 1945. They saw themselves as suffering from what could be called a 'development deficit' – the fact that a gap necessarily existed between what they needed to import and what they were capable of exporting stemmed from the costs they would have to incur in building up their infant industrial base to the point where it could be internationally competitive. The arguments they presented, summarised in Chapter 2, were a logical extension of those put forward by Keynes at Bretton Woods, which stressed that they would only be able to build up their economies without excessive sacrifices if they were given access to concessional assistance by the strong countries either in the form of aid or through the creation of new forms of international credit designed to achieve the same purpose. The implications and outcome of these demands will be considered in more detail in Chapter 7; here we shall be concerned with the relatively limited implications of their interventions for the development of the system as a whole.

The position of the USA in all this was perhaps the most complex of all, both technically and politically. In the 1960s the Americans were essentially having to respond to demands (the reduction of their deficit and the creation of new forms of credit) which at bottom reflected the need for a substantial reduction in their own dominant role at the centre of the international economic system. The willingness and ability to do this, of course, would depend upon the extent to which the maintenance of existing arrangements contributed to their own well-being, and more especially to that of the most influential groups in their political system. When we look at the costs and benefits involved, we find an array of contradictory tendencies at work which made it virtually impossible for the US government to take a consistent position in negotiations and more especially, to do anything effective to overcome the growing difficulties involved in maintaining the integrity of the system that it had been so influential in creating at Bretton Woods.

The existence of the American deficit made many Americans very rich and powerful. Its huge defence component had generated the most sophisticated and extensive military machine of all time and a correspondingly powerful political lobby to go with it. The Pentagon, the generals and admirals, the private firms (the most powerful in the land) which supplied them with their equipment, all maintained a constant and highly successful pressure in favour of increasing spending, and this was further backed up by similar demands from America's overseas allies. These pressures were given a sharp and irresistible urgency with the escalation of the Vietnam war in the mid-1960s which was soon costing the country billions of dollars. Furthermore, a good many of the dollars which were being stockpiled overseas could be used as credit by American MNCs to expand their foreign activities, thus increasing American capitalist control over the world's economic assets. And finally, a large percentage of American aid expenditure was tied to orders from American companies, often at prices higher than those prevailing on the open market. Thus the US 'military-industrial complex', the dominant force in American society, had a strong vested interest in the maintenance of the system inherited from the 1960s, and their demands made it very difficult for any administration to adopt policies that would reduce the benefits they received from its operation.

The benefits did not stop there. The American balance of payments deficit was an outflow of paper money in exchange for which the USA obtained some very concrete returns – an international military presence which enabled it to exert a powerful influence over the political and economic choices made by virtually all of the countries in the Western system, the ability to buy potentially profitable overseas assets, and the ability to import foreign goods without having to export an equivalent amount of American goods to pay for them. For as long as foreign countries were obliged to go on receiving these paper tokens in payment for these goods and services, neither the government nor the population at large would have to reduce its consumption or increase its output or reduce its costs in order to establish the usual balance of payments equilibrium expected of countries which did not enjoy the advantage of providing the world with its international currency. This, of course, was of fundamental political importance.

Any other country which ran a persistent deficit (like Britain, for example, at the same time) would very quickly have to make adjustments of this kind which are invariably very difficult and politically very damaging because they mean lower wages, worse services and the need to increase productivity. Thus the key position of the dollar in the system protected a very wide range of people in American society from having to come to terms with these demands, and at the same time enabled their government to carry the costs of the country's international imperialist role without having to ask its voters to bear its real costs.[14] These advantages became more and more evident as the war escalated. Between 1967 and 1971 the deficit totalled $33.4 billion, expanding from $2.9 billion in 1967 to *$19.8 billion* in 1971, when the system collapsed. And US foreign liabilities (their foreign debt) increased from $33.2 billion to $67.8 billion over the same period.[15] In effect the USA was using its key role in the system to pay for the costs of its international military and economic presence and of the war by exporting paper tokens abroad and obtaining very real assets in exchange. Given the nature of the system, the only thing that foreign countries could legally do about this was to ask the Americans to meet the obligation they had accepted at Bretton Woods and convert these dollars into gold at the official price of $35 an ounce.

Yet this right was far more apparent than real. By 1961 we have already seen that all foreign liabilities already exceeded the value of gold and other foreign exchange reserves. By 1965 reserves were $15.45 billion and liabilities $25.18 billion; by 1971 these figures were $13.19 billion as against $67.81 billion.[16] In 1965 de Gaulle demanded that the USA convert a substantial proportion of France's dollar holdings into gold, thus threatening to reduce American holdings to unacceptable levels and threaten the value of the dollar itself. This was treated as a hostile political act by the USA, and intense political and diplomatic pressure was applied both by the USA and its more sympathetic allies to stop the rot.[17] It is now clear that the right to convert dollars into gold existed on paper only, and that there was no effective way in which the surplus countries could stop the USA from continuing to solve its own economic and political problems at their expense. An American deficit which had once seemed a lifeline to their own prosperity had now become a millstone around their necks.

Yet these very real benefits to many sectors of American society were being bought at considerable cost to the underlying strength of the US economy as a whole. During the 1950s and 1960s American defence expenditure was always significantly higher than that of its leading industrial competitors, and a large percentage of this was

spent overseas, as we have seen. Although this contributed significantly to the health of its arms industry, its overall effects on the
relative strength of the domestic economy was certainly negative,
tying up very large numbers of workers and huge amounts of raw
materials and sophisticated capital equipment in unproductive activities which contributed nothing to the modernisation of the social
and economic infrastructure, or to the strengthening of the productivity and competitiveness of the productive sector itself. Thus the
growth in the productivity of labour in the USA was far slower than
that of its immediate competitors, being 2.7 per cent between 1960
and 1975, compared with 5.6 per cent in France, 5.7 per cent in
Germany and 9.7 per cent in Japan. This, of course, was a reflection
of the catching-up process that was going on in the world economy,
as the US lead was continuously reduced, but it was now creating an
internal problem of a serious kind for the US government, and an
even more serious one for the system as a whole.

   In the 1950s it was assumed that the Americans would be able to
move back into surplus with little difficulty when the system needed
them to do so, because of their basic economic strength. But in the
1960s this became increasingly difficult, both because of the long-
term effects of their declining competitiveness, and the escalation of
international conflict during the Vietnam war. In the 1950s and
1960s the USA ran a continuous surplus on its *trade* with the rest of
the world, an indication that its former industrial supremacy had not
entirely disappeared, but this was on a sharply declining trend. The
surplus totalled $6.6 billion in 1964, but only a little more than $600
million in 1968 and 1969, and then moved into a deficit of $2.7
billion in 1971 after a limited improvement in 1970. This decline
coincided with the rapid escalation of American aggression in
Vietnam, which led to a large increase in the deficit on military
spending (up from $2,122 billion in 1965 to $3,335 billion in 1969)
and thus to a sudden growth in the overall deficit just as the stability
of the system demanded a substantial reduction. In 1971 it seemed
that American gold reserves would fall below $10 billion for the
first time, and they took the step which many had feared for some
time. In August President Nixon announced that they would no
longer convert dollars into gold on request, that they would not
guarantee the value of the dollar at its existing parity, and that they
would introduce temporary controls over imports until the deficit
was brought under control.

This decision signalled the end of the era of American economic hegemony and ushered in one of increasing instability in which no single country could establish any firm authority. It also demonstrated that the attempts at monetary reform of the previous decade had been a failure, the result of irreconcilable conflicts of interest which had made any far-reaching changes impossible. We can therefore complete this section by looking briefly at the fate of these attempts which, it will be remembered, related to the creation of new forms of international credit as a means of replacing the dollar as the key currency, and providing an effective means of financing the developmental efforts of Third World countries.

At the start of the decade, responding to the emergence of the 'dollar overhang', the leading industrial countries got together and formed the Group of 10 (G-10), which agreed to provide reciprocal credit facilities for each other through the IMF known as the General Arrangement to Borrow (GAB). This still exists and provides the IMF with $6 billion for use in this way, though it is important to note that all but the industrial giants are excluded from this arrangement. (The members of the Group are Belgium, Canada, France, Germany, Italy, Japan, Netherlands, Sweden, the UK and the USA. Switzerland, a non-member of the IMF, has been associated with the group since 1964, so that it should in fact be one of 11.) Once in existence, the G-10 began discussions for the creation of a new credit mechanism of a much more ambitious kind – the development of a new form of international credit money intended to supplement the dollar as the American deficit was brought under control. This initiative eventually gave rise to the creation of Special Drawing Rights (SDRs) through the IMF, in effect a form of international money created by political agreement between all of the countries involved in the IMF who now have the right to use it. The technicalities and the political background to this event are very complex, and cannot be developed in detail here. It will only be possible to give a brief indication of how SDRs work, of how they were created, and of their limitations in relation to the problem they were designed to solve.[18]

SDRs are in fact 'drawing rights' allocated in specific amounts, proportional to IMF quotas, to the countries which belong to the IMF. Countries that are in deficit on their balance of payments can then transfer their SDRs to countries that are in surplus, and the latter must provide them with convertible currencies in exchange.

Deficit countries can use all of their SDRs in this way and no conditions are attached to the transaction; they will eventually be expected to repay the currencies and to re-acquire (technically to 'reconstitute') the SDRs which they disposed of, but this obligation is no longer as stringently enforced as it was. Countries pay interest on the SDRs they have disposed of and receive interest on those they hold in excess of their original quota. This rate was originally very small, but is now set at about 80 per cent of the average rate prevailing in the leading countries. No country can be expected to accept more than a certain number of SDRs in excess of its allocation, but is *obliged* to accept up to that amount from any country which brings them to it and to provide it with convertible currency in exchange. The value of the SDR was originally directly tied to that of the dollar, but at present each SDR is worth about $1.3 dollars, and its value is determined on the basis of the relative values of the five leading currencies in the system.

What we have, therefore, is a system which provides all of the countries involved with a specified amount of *unconditional* international credit which they can use to cover any balance of payments deficit and enables them to maintain a level of economic activity which would otherwise be impossible. It depends upon the continued willingness of the surplus countries to provide credit in this way, and on the ability of the deficit countries to pay their interest and repay their debts in due course. The resemblance to Keynes's suggestions for the IMF at Bretton Woods is very close, and there can be no doubt that it does represent a potentially progressive initiative of great importance. However, only a relatively limited number of SDRs have ever been issued (nine billion between 1970 and 1972, and twelve billion between 1978 and 1980), and its role in international monetary relations has been correspondingly limited. We have now to consider why this should have been so.

Between 1962 and 1966 the discussions on this issue were confined to the industrialised countries, incorporating the representatives of the G-10 and the management of the IMF. Here the surplus countries were mainly concerned to use any concessions they might make as a means of forcing the USA to reduce its deficit, while the latter wanted to transfer part of the responsibility for financing international economic activities to the new surplus countries, without losing any of the special advantages that it obtained from the structure of the existing system. It constantly made verbal commitments to the need for policies which would reduce its deficit, but just as constantly failed to put them into practical effect, as we have seen. In the early stages the industrial countries wished to exclude the developing countries from the scheme altogether, since they had a long-term tendency to remain in balance of payments deficit and might therefore not be abe to be trusted 'to assume the obligations as well as the rights entailed in the convention and its workings.[19] After 1966, however, the discussion was broadened to include not only the G-10, but also the Directors of the IMF, and this drew the nine who represented the LDCs into it. It was now agreed that the scheme should cover all countries in the IMF, but while the developed countries wanted the LDCs to obtain SDRs only in proportion to their level of economic activity, the LDCs themselves wanted to have a more than proportional allocation, thus turning the SDR into a form of aid. This demand for a 'link' between SDRs and aid has remained a continuous feature of all LDC interventions in the international monetary debate since then.[20]

In 1969 a final compromise was established. SDRs were to be made available to all the countries in the IMF who wished to make use of them, but the allocation was to be directly proportional to quotas, which meant that less than a third would go to LDCs. This would increase their access to credit, but only on a very limited scale: the 'link' had not been conceded. The USA, despite the strong pressures imposed on it by the surplus countries to do so, accepted no binding obligations to reduce its own deficit at the price of their willingness to use their own reserves to back the new asset. Having failed to get this concession, the surplus countries were willing to make only a very limited amount of credit available: of the SDR 9 billion issued in the early 1970s, less than half actually went to deficit countries which could ever be expected to use them, and their actual use was limited by a number of regulations, some of which have since been eased. Thus a new form of collectively created unconditioned credit had been created, revolutionary in the principles on which it was based, but very limited in its application. The proportions involved can be gathered from a look at some related figures: American external liabilities (overseas dollar holdings) to central banks increased by almost $27 billion between 1970 and 1971 alone, while the major private banks lent $47 billion from the start of 1970 to the end of 1972. The carefully controlled credit creation provided by the SDRs pales into insignificance by comparison, and they have, indeed, only played a very marginal part in the international monetary system since then.

The creation of the SDR was the major monetary reform of the 1960s, but it did nothing to shore up the tottering Bretton Woods edifice, which, it will be remembered, was based upon a commitment to the maintenance of stable exchange rates and to the convertibility of the dollar into gold at a fixed rate. In 1967 the British were forced to devalue after a long and costly struggle with a balance of payments deficit; in 1968 the French were forced to do the same as the outcome of the economic crisis created by the events of May. Meanwhile the inexorable escalation of the costs of Vietnam continued, making it clear that there was no way in which the Americans could bring their deficit under control or stem the growth in their external debts. By 1968 they had made it clear that devaluation was being strongly considered to increase the competitiveness of American industry, but this was strongly resisted by the strong surplus countries, who saw that it would reduce the value of their reserves and make it more difficult for their exporters to penetrate the US market. Because a change in the value of the main currencies seemed imminent, speculation on a huge scale began. The price of gold on the unofficial market increased sharply, since a devaluation of the dollar would mean an increase in the price of gold, and money also flowed out of dollars into other currencies – notably Deutschmarks – in very large amounts. Under these intense pressures it became more and more difficult for central banks and governments to manage their foreign exchange holdings in such a way as to secure the stable exchange rates to which they were committed. Nixon's 1971 announcement signalled the end of an era in which this had been possible, and opened one in which the relative value of currencies was to fluctuate dramatically, thus substantially increasing the risks and costs of conducting international trade and payments, and one in which the guarantee provided by the USA to maintain the value of the world's most important international reserve asset had been unilaterally removed.

At the end of 1971 the major Western countries gathered at the Smithsonian conference in the USA and arranged a realignment of the relative values of the main currencies, which involved a dollar devaluation of about 9.7 per cent against the strongest, and of 7.5 per cent overall. This change was insufficient to solve the problem, and a further run on the dollar started at the end of 1972, which was only stemmed by the middle of 1973 when the devaluation of the dollar against the stronger currencies had reached about 17.5 per cent. At this point it was accepted that it would no longer be possible for central bankers to guarantee stable exchange rates, and it was agreed that the relative values of currencies could be changed more or less at will in order to adjust to both balance of payments changes and the impact of currency speculation. The 'adjustable peg' system had given way to 'managed floating', which made it far easier for the authorities to deal with international pressures, but at the cost of a real increase in the instability in the system as a whole. Two of the foundation stones of the Bretton Woods system – dollar–gold convertibility and stable exchange rates – had been removed, the outcome of the fundamental shift in the international balance of economic power that had occurred since the war and which the political arrangements for international economic organisation had proved incapable of handling.

From crisis to crisis, 1974–1984

These significant breaks in the mechanisms for the control of the international economic system occurred in a context of continuing prosperity which caused many people to overlook their real importance. But the basis of this growth was deeply insecure, as it was significantly fuelled by the American deficit which was continuously worsening the underlying crisis. Expanding demand for imports in America stimulated output and employment everywhere. Payment for these imports was then made through an increased outflow of dollars which were translated into increased spending power in the exporting countries. This, of course, had inflationary effects (indeed, in 1973 a leading German banker accused the USA of 'forcing monetary debauchery on surplus countries',[21] but it did ensure that a very high level of economic activity would be sustained both in the industrial and raw material exporting countries. At the end of 1973, however, the bubble burst, and a new downswing began which is still continuing. The effects of this regression have not been evenly distributed, either in time or space. Particular events have provoked difficulties for some and benefits for others. An overall decline in 1974/5 was followed by a limited recovery which has again given way to what is now almost certainly a far more serious decline. But the overall tendency is now undoubtedly downwards, and there are few who seriously believe that any effective recipe for a general recovery has been found. What we can attempt to do here is look at the international dimensions of this failure and more especially at the way in which it relates to the new inequalities in the world economy as a whole, and to the accumulating weaknesses in the international economic agencies designed to deal with them.

During the 1970s the inequalities which had produced the 1971–3 crisis continued to manifest themselves, but were now intensified by two new factors. On the one hand the very specific position of the main oil-exporting countries (and notably those organised through OPEC) made it possible for them to push up the price of oil very dramatically at the end of 1973 and again at the end of 1979. This enabled them to join the ranks of the surplus countries overnight, provided them with huge accumulations of foreign exchange to dispose of both internationally and domestically, and seriously impoverished their customers, and in particular those in the Third World. This change, and a gradual deterioration in their overall balance of payments position, seriously worsened the economic prospects of the Third World as a whole, thus threatening their capacity to import and imposing deflationary pressures on the economies of the industrialised countries which have always been their main suppliers. The wealthier LDCs like Brazil, Mexico and South Korea managed to maintain their level of economic activity by increased borrowing, but the poorer ones could not, and many of them, notably those in tropical Africa, have suffered catastrophic declines in production and welfare as a result – an issue to be taken up later.

Within the industrial countries, on the other hand, the stresses which had generated the earlier crisis continued to operate, but now in conjunction with additional adverse effects produced by the increases in the price of oil. The latter put the whole of the industrial world into deficit in 1974, and again in 1980, but the stronger countries, notably German and Japan, were quickly back into surplus in 1975, and show every evidence of doing so again now. The USA remained in heavy deficit, totalling $55 billion in 1977 and 1978. The dollar fell very sharply against the main currencies as a result. In 1978 the Swiss franc had appreciated by 85 per cent over its value set at the Smithsonian conference, the Deutschmark by 41 per cent and the Japanese yen by 40 per cent.[22] The dollar meanwhile had fallen by 12 per cent, so the losses in the value of these countries' dollar reserves were very large. In effect the Americans had written off a very substantial proportion of the value of their foreign debt at the expense of all the countries in the system which were using dollars as their main form of foreign exchange. One of the most fundamental prerequisites for the maintenance of a stable token money system – a belief that the monetary authority will act in such a way as to guarantee the value of the currency – had been eliminated. The resulting insecurity produced a revival in the fortunes of gold. While it had remained stable at £35 an ounce until the late 1960s, its price constantly increased throughout the 1970s, reaching a peak of $850 dollars an ounce early in 1980, and falling very sharply thereafter, a clear indication of the growing insecurity afflicting the system as a whole.

The authorities responded to these escalating problems in two ways: they had now to repair the damage inflicted on the Bretton Woods system between 1971 and 1973 by establishing a new basis for dealing with exchange rates and foreign currency reserves, and they had to attempt to find some way of overcoming the growing inequalities in productive structure which were the primary cause of the breakdown in the monetary mechanisms. We can conclude this chapter by considering the very limited achievements recorded in each of these areas.

The American repudiation of the Bretton Woods agreement in 1971 meant that the Articles of the IMF had to be amended to provide a retrospective legitimation for what had been done, and to establish a new basis for its work. In 1972 it set up the Committee of 20 (C-20) to produce these reforms and, in particular, to deal with the problem of the dollar and of unstable exchange rates. This reported in 1974 without securing any effective agreements,[23] and was then replaced by the Interim Committee, a standing committee of the IMF which has had to deal with these problems since then.

The theoretical analysis in earlier parts of this book suggests that the problems manifesting themselves in the monetary system were the outcome of the failure to achieve an even development of the productive resources throughout the world economy. The 'dollar overhang', now expanding on an exponential scale (American external liabilities increased from £67.8 billion in 1971 to $278.5

billion in 1980, while their foreign exchange reserves only increased from $13.2 billion to $23 billion during the same period) could only be reduced through a move back from deficit into surplus. The fluctuations in exchange rates again took the form of a continuous relative decline in the weak currencies (the dollar and the pound sterling) against the increase in the value of the strong ones like the Deutschmark and the yen, and this could only be reversed if the latter countries moved from surplus into deficit, as all the textbooks said they should.

The political debate inside the international forums during these years essentially concerned the terms on which such a transition might be made, and all of them foundered on the fact that it was impossible to bring it about without serious and politically unacceptable costs being incurred on both sides. During the 1970s the growth in productivity was again very unevenly distributed, with growth in the USA down to only 0.2 per cent as opposed to 3.2 per cent in Germany and 3.4 per cent in Japan, so that the inequalities in competitiveness continued to widen. This was then reflected in a continuing deterioration of the American balance of *trade*, which was positive briefly in 1973, but worsened in each succeeding year to reach $27 billion in 1978. The strong countries were in deficit in 1974 as a result of the oil price increase, but moved rapidly back into surplus and remained there until the end of the decade and the next oil price rise.

In these circumstances it was virtually impossible to create viable monetary arrangements. The surplus countries were being forced to consider the possibility of creating an alternative to the dollar which would necessarily rest upon the strength of their economies (mainly through the creation of an expanded role for the SDR) but were only willing to do this if the USA could be made to give up its right to export dollars at will and to accept a firm and binding commitment to reduce its overseas liabilities as the role of the new currency expanded. This would have meant the adoption of domestic policies of a very deflationary kind, which would have meant declining consumption, falling services and cuts in military spending. All of these would have been strongly opposed by a wide range of highly influential interests and been politically damaging in the extreme. The Americans, for their part, wanted the surplus countries to adopt expansionary domestic policies designed to draw in a large increase in imports, as well as much larger contribution to the unproductive military costs involved in maintaining the Atlantic Alliance. These, in turn, were rejected as inflationary by the surplus countries, which felt that their competitiveness would decline if they were forced to accept them at a time when 'stagflation' was becoming a reality and unemployment a growing problem. In these circumstances the teachings of neoclassical theory carried little resonance, and a solution which could be seen to bring clear benefits to both sides was not to be found. To use the words of a distinguished liberal economist directly involved in the negotiations, the result was not a solution, but 'a decision to learn to live with the non-system that had evolved out of a mixture of custom and crisis over the preceding years'.[24]

In 1976 the Articles of Agreement of the IMF were amended effectively to eliminate the role of gold from the system, and to allow countries to change the value of their currencies in response to significant changes in their balance of payments position. The former meant that no mechanism existed to stop the Americans from continuing to debase the most important international currency in the system if it suited their domestic or foreign needs to do so. The latter provision was supposedly to be supervised by the IMF itself, which was given the right to exercise 'firm surveillance' over changes in par values in order to ensure that they were not being manipulated for competitive balance of payments purposes. But this control has never been used, so we are now back with an international currency system susceptible to political manipulation in which very large fluctuations can take place. These are particularly noticeable in Third World countries, but have been very important in the advanced countries as well. This has also given rise to the creation of the European Monetary System, which has attempted to maintain a high degree of stability between the leading European countries. This, of course, does involve a break with the commitment to universality in monetary arrangements envisaged at Bretton Woods, but has been relatively successful up to the present. However, the intensification of problems inside the European economy, and in particular the negative response from capital to President Mitterrand's experiment in France, is making it increasingly difficult for this stability to be sustained.

Although it is very difficult to talk with confidence about the immediate past and future, it seems very likely that the end of the 1970s witnessed another important break which signals the end of the long period of prosperity and the onset of a serious depression. The oil price increase in 1973/4 brought about the first real decline in industrial output since the war. But the surpluses accumulated by the OPEC countries were rapidly recycled by the bankers, leading to another upturn. The large American deficits of 1977/8 continued this inflationary process, since they, too, allowed lending to continue unabated and with it the level of effective international demand. But the competitive struggle generated by the growing over-capacity in the world economy made it essential that every government impose rigid attempts to cut costs on its own producers, leading to the emergence of monetarism as the new panacea. Thus the inflationary tendencies generated by the increase in international credit were now being offset by increasingly restrictive domestic policies in all the leading states, and , most importantly of all, in the USA itself.

Towards the end of 1978 the Federal Reserve Bank introduced the era of tight monetary policy, using high interest rates to reduce domestic economic activity, intensify competition and cut costs. At last they were doing what the surplus countries had been demanding, and the balance of payments moved back towards surplus and the long fall of the dollar was halted. This change was immediately followed by a renewed increase in the price of oil, and another escalation in the deficits of the non-oil-producing countries. High American interest rates have led to rising interest rates everywhere, and thus to increasing costs and declining production. The reduction in the American deficit also meant a cut in international markets and thus imposed a deflationary pressure on the system everywhere. After having demanded American efforts to reduce the deficit for many years, their leading partners were soon condemning the restrictiveness of their policies and demanding a reduction in interest rates.

The Reagan administration, however, allowed the Federal Reserve to maintain its relatively tight monetary policies, but soon initiated a rapid growth in deficit spending on military hardware, which by 1983 had reached the point where it was providing the economy with a strong reflationary impetus. After rising sharply as it has done in the rest of the industrial world, unemployment began to fall and output to rise, particularly in the first half of 1984. Although elected on a monetarist commitment to public spending cuts, the administration's obsession with defence has transformed it into a leading exponent of Keynesian deficit spending, to the apparent benefit of both the domestic and the international economies. Yet this experiment has produced some serious and almost certainly terminal side-effects. The combination of tight money and a large deficit has meant a very large increase in real interest rates, which has had the effect of drawing large amounts of foreign savings into the USA and thus pushing up interest rates and cutting profits elsewhere. Simultaneously, high US interest rates have led to a strong appreciation of the dollar which, while defending the value of overseas dollar assets, has reduced the competitiveness of US industry and produced a trade deficit which is large even by American standards.[25] These high interest rates and the strong dollar have also imposed unsustainable burdens on the leading borrowers from the Euro-currency banks, thus threatening a breakdown in the international financial system.[26] A limited reflation has been induced in Europe and Japan, in part as a function of their ability to expand exports to the USA, but its viability is now threatened by the continuation of high interest rates and the likelihood that the deficit will soon have to be reduced.

Merely to list this welter of contradictory tendencies is to highlight the collapse of authority and order in a system which can no longer be effectively managed by its once dominant power, and is as yet unable to develop a more collective alternative. Once a hegemonic force, able to impose its own vision on the system, the USA is neither able to provide a rational solution to its own problems or those of the world economy as a whole. If this analysis is correct and the present reliance on market solutions to the problem continues, then the next period must be one of deepening depression and intensified instability.

6

Britain's International Decline

The British case will be explored here at some length, partly because its links with the international system have been relatively little explored, but mainly because of its direct relevance to the general concerns of this book – the problems of global economic management, the negative effects of uneven development on deficit countries, and the political implications of the constraints imposed upon national sovereignty and autonomy by the requirements of economic management within a liberalised international system. This chapter will therefore provide an opportunity to explore the contribution to global economic management made by the country which stood second only to the USA in power and responsibility in 1945; to consider the negative effects of the balance of payments deficit, mainly created by those responsibilities, on its economic development; and to demonstrate the contradictory implications of the attempt by a deficit country to sustain welfare-oriented social democratic policies in the context of an open and unplanned international economic system. While all of these problems are central to the international concerns of this book, the material presented here should also be of interest to those purely interested in British political and economic history, since it involves an interpretation of the role of the state and of the management of economic policy which is sharply at odds with a number of very influential accounts.

Post-war British economic policy can be interpreted as an attempt to reconcile the consequences of three central and widely accepted commitments: to Keynesian social democracy as the basis for a stable compromise between capital and labour; to the full liberalisation of trade and payments; and to an international political and economic role as junior partner of the USA in the stabilisation of the world economy and the strengthening of the anti-communist military alliance. All of these involved important breaks with pre-war experience and the need to overcome internal opposition, but were effectively established as something close to a national consensus by the end of the first Labour government in 1951. Yet it is now clearly evident that they were neither mutually compatible nor in line with the country's diminished economic resources. The attempt to serve all of them, critically important, too, to the evolution of the liberal international order, was to disintegrate in the 1960s and 1970s and give rise to a fundamental crisis at the level of economic structures and political theory. The political battles of the last decade can all be traced to the consequences of this failure, a failure which has led the Conservative Party to attempt to rescue liberalism and the Atlantic Alliance at the expense of social democracy; the Labour Party to rescue social democracy at the expense of liberalisation and military pre-eminence; and the Liberal/Social Democratic Alliance to attempt an uneasy compromise between Keynesianism, free trade and the weakening of trade union power. Each of these options involves a very different pattern of both domestic and international orientations than that which prevailed in the past, and has important consequences both for national development and for the structure of the international system. By looking at the way in which the original consensus emerged, was destroyed, and is now being restructured, we can provide an effective means of linking external and internal, political and economic factors in the evolution of the post-war capitalist system in a key industrial country.

We will attempt to do this through close examination of the relationship between domestic policies and the external constraint from 1945 to the present, trying to explain the crucial and usually negative impact of this relationship upon economic performance. This historical account will use a periodisation derived from an identification of the major breaks which occurred in the building and then demolition of the consensus outlined in the previous paragraph. Four such periods have been identified:

1. The post-war reconstruction from 1945 to the outbreak of the Korean war in 1950, which created the social democratic

framework but still forced the UK to operate with stringent internal and external controls;

2. The period of liberalisation and centre currency status, but with diminishing success from 1951 to 1967;

3. The loss of centre currency status and intensified destabilisation between 1967 and 1976;

4. The subsequent attempt, under 'monetarist' influences, to jettison the fundamentals of social democracy and find an orthodox solution to the crisis by accepting rising unemployment as the necessary precondition for the continued integration of the international capitalist economic order.

The social democratic foundations, 1945–1950[1]

The reconstruction period is often regarded as an important but somehow isolated episode in Britain's post-war economic development. In this view it is an abnormal period when old industries were rebuilt using emergency measures inherited from the war, measures which, having achieved their purpose, had inevitably to be discarded once 'normality' had been re-established. There is obviously some truth in this view, since the transition from war to peace necessarily demanded an altogether unusual degree of restructuring and gave those who managed it access to controls over economic allocation and personal freedom which was quickly done away with in the 1950s. But it also ignores much more important continuities between the 1930s and the 1940s and the whole post-war period which must be clarified if the period itself is to be adequately interpreted and, more importantly, its consequences for subsequent development properly understood.

In 1945 social democracy meant the central planning of domestic resources to ensure full employment, and a dramatic extension in the provision of health, education and social services. This meant a major break with the 1930s (though a continuation of important developments of the war itself) when direct controls had been of very limited importance in domestic economic management. But these objectives could only be achieved if they could be reconciled with a number of external obligations which could not be avoided and were likely to impose heavy additional burdens on the country's war-damaged productive capacity.

Firstly, Britain was still central to the sterling area made up of the dominions and colonies and now a substantial debtor to it. Here it obtained the bulk of its raw materials, found the main markets for its manufacturers, and sent the largest proportion of its foreign overseas investment. Secondly, and generating an important tension with the links with the sterling area, the war had produced a fundamental increase in dependence on the USA which had begun with lend-lease supplies of war materials, and had now to continue because of dependence on American finance and capital equipment for industrial reconstruction. Thirdly, as a leading element in the victorious alliance, Britain would be a major protagonist in the plans to rebuild Western Europe and more especially in the administration and re-equipment of Germany, whose cities had been destroyed and whose population was on the verge of starvation. Finally, there was the the threat of communist expansion created by Russian victories in Eastern Europe which were quickly consolidated at the political level, and subsequent expansion in Asia, and notably in Korea at the end of the decade. It was to be the interaction between these external requirements (and most especially the need to come to terms with the Americans) and the internal commitment to the social democratic consensus that was to dominate policy-making during the period and will therefore provide us with our major focus.

While the interventionist domestic policy of the Labour government involved a sharp break with pre-war experience, its external orientation was far more consistent with both British and foreign practice. After a long and unsuccessful attempt to defend the liberal principles of its nineteenth-century heyday, Britain had capitulated to the protectionism of its major competitors in the early 1930s. In September 1931 the gold standard was abandoned and the pound depreciated by a total of 30 per cent before the end of the year. For the rest of the decade the exchange rate was deliberately managed by the Bank of England to maintain the external price competitiveness of British goods and to create the external conditions required to allow for an internal regime of low interest rates – of 'cheap money'. Then, six months later, in a second spectacular change in British policy' there followed 'the final abandonment of free trade in favour of a general tariff and imperial preference'.[2] Now this solution to the external problem imposed a very particular stamp upon British policy: direct controls were used to control trade with the non-sterling world (and especially the USA), but free trade remained within the sterling area, where it was assumed that the reciprocal needs of colonial and dominion raw material producers and British manufacturers would guarantee a mutually advantageous interaction combining the advantages of a global division of labour and a unified trading, monetary and financial structure.[3] During the war these arrangements were consolidated, which turned the sterling area into 'a closely integrated monetary association, almost a union', and subsequently made possible 'the post-war development of a dollar discriminatory club and a banker-customer relationship between Britain (with depleted reserves behind her) and her sterling associates'.[4] At the end of the war this involved a banker with reserves of convertible currency and gold of £610 million, as against external liabilities (the 'sterling balances') of £3,567 million, about two-thirds of which were held in the sterling area countries.[5] These represented 'in varying degrees a potential call on the reserves of the United Kingdom',[6] and therefore served as a potentially serious constraint upon domestic policymaking.

Against this sphere of free trade, dealings between the whole sterling area and the USA were closely controlled and the supply of dollars to any user strictly rationed – in these circumstances the full convertibility of the pound into the dollar would involve not merely the loss of control over Britain's economic relations with the USA, but that of the rest of the sterling area as well. During the 1930s other leading industrial countries, and Nazi Germany in particular, had themselves established tightly controlled trading systems which were also sustained into the post-war period. In these circumstances foreign economic relations necessarily had to be based upon centrally negotiated bilateral arrangements, whatever the theoretical and ideological inclinations of the individual countries.

Earlier chapters have already considered both the theoretical and the practical implications of this structure of nationally regulated trading blocs, and more especially the American commitment to liberalise it. It is therefore easy to understand the broad orientation of their approach to the British problem; in addition to their general dislike of protectionism, their major exporters had always demonstrated a powerful dislike of the operation of the sterling area as a mechanism for the exclusion of their goods.[7] In order to gain access to American financial assistance, the British would have to come to terms with these views, as well as with the American desire to build a military wall around the Soviet Union and, later, China. The question which now has to be asked is whether these changes were to be compatible with the obligations to the sterling area and more especially to the maintenance of full employment and welfare spending.

What exactly were the problems? Critically, full employment required protection, because British industry could not compete on equal terms with American, so that many existing jobs would have been lost and new investment jeopardised without it. Furthermore, the resulting balance of payments deficit would have required deflationary policies designed to reduce domestic consumption, and this would have meant cuts in welfare spending. At the same time, however, rapid industrial development depended on access to the most modern capital equipment, only available from America and to be paid for in dollars. Thus access to these dollars was to be a key factor in economic policy-making, and the 'dollar shortage' arising out of the relative strength of American industry and that country's correspondingly large balance of trade surplus was the major constraint on the Labour government's freedom of action both at home and abroad. The solution to this problem was to have fundamental long-term political and economic consequences.

Two basic alternatives were canvassed at the time, one assuming that American credit could be secured to cover the whole deficit; the other that it should be overcome through an intensification of protectionism and the further extension of bilateral trading agreements to guarantee essential imports and external markets. The former position would inevitably involve coming to terms with the American commitment to trade liberalisation; the latter could be seen as a continuation of the attempt at imperial self-sufficiency in the 1930s, but now associated with a socialist commitment to use it as a mechanism to escape the constraints which would otherwise inevitably be imposed upon the capacity to plan for domestic full employment. In the event, the liberal solution was to gain over-whelming support in Britain, as in the rest of the world, as we have seen. Let us now consider why this should have been so.[8]

This argument was presented with greatest coherence in a key memorandum prepared for the Cabinet by Keynes as adviser to the Treasury in April 1945.[9] He opened by noting that 'a prime objective of Treasury policy' during the war had been to maintain a financial position which did not leave us hopelessly at the mercy of the United States', not in order to establish 'our own self-sufficiency, assisted by a chain of bilateral bargains with those countries which cannot afford to lose our markets' and the full severity 'of the present Sterling Area arrangements', but in order 'that in negotiation we should feel and appear sufficiently independent only to accept arrangements we deem acceptable' (p. 1). Keynes then set out at length the extent of actual external sterling liabilities and the continuing military and other official spending overseas, which he saw as 'wholly responsible for our financial difficulties' (p. 4). He argued that these would impose unacceptable levels of austerity on the population and 'our withdrawal, for the time being, from the position of a first-class Power in the outside world' (p. 9) if they had to be entirely covered from the country's own depleted financial and industrial resources. Most important, this would involve several years of 'rigid domestic controls and strict rationing of consumption, and with an organisation of foreign trade after the Russian model', an alternative 'certainly not compatible with the restoration of free enterprise', and which would be bound to lose the support of all but the very few countries 'prepared to denounce their commercial treaties with the United States and forgo all prospect of borrowing easy money from that country' (p. 1). Against this Keynes felt that an offer of credit from the USA, 'not so much generous as just' (p. 8), of $5 to $8 billion at 1 per cent repayable at 1 per cent a year for ten years after a ten year grace period and 2 per cent thereafter, would enable them to meet all their internal needs and external commitments and, in the process, enable them to create the liberal financial conditions which would 'recover for London its ancient prestige and its hegemony' (p. 9). Thus an effective act of international redistribution designed to recreate the conditions for an integrated and open trading situation was here posed as the necessary alternative to the disintegration of the system into autarchic units.

The paper was prepared for the coalition government, but Keynes remained in office when Labour took over and fully accepted the strategy he had outlined. In the autumn of 1945 he was sent to Washington to negotiate the American loan on which so much depended, having argued in his paper the necessity of keeping alive the possibility of recourse to 'the disagreeable, indeed the disastrous [bilateralist] alternative' as the means of avoiding the necessity to accept excessively unfavourable terms (p. 8). Yet when Keynes reached Washington and began the negotiations he found the 'hostile forces' far stronger, and those 'of light and friendship' far weaker than he had expected. But having made so much of the negative consequences of self-sufficiency, he was unable to resist a series of dreary capitulations, well summarised by Dalton, then Chancellor of the Exchequer:

> So, as the talks went on, we retreated slowly and with bad grace and with increasing irritation, from a free gift to an interest free loan, and from this again to a loan bearing interest; from a larger to a smaller total of aid; and from the prospect of loose strings, some of which would be only general declarations of intention to the most unwilling acceptance of strings so tight they might strangle our trade and, indeed, our whole economic life.[10]

The loan only provided $3.75 billion at 2 per cent repayable over 50 years, starting in 1951, and involved a major concession on financial and trading policy by requiring full currency convertibility to come into force only a year after final ratification – in the event in June 1947. This seemingly technical requirement was of the utmost significance and was widely accepted, because it would make it impossible to protect the reserves through central controls since all foreign holders of sterling assets would immediately be free to convert them into dollars if they felt that they could meet their needs more effectively by buying in American than in British markets, as they almost inevitably would. To offset this the British would have to follow classic deflationary policies which would be bound to conflict with both full employment and welfare objectives.

Both Bevan and Shinwell opposed the loan in Cabinet, the latter correctly describing it as 'incompatible with the successful operation of a planned economy'.[11] But Keynes felt it was the only way of financing the government's domestic policy, and Dalton agreed that the otherwise inevitable increase in austerity and especially 'practically no smokes' would lead to 'sure defeat at the next election'.[12] Access to the dollar loan also made it possible for Britain to maintain its commitments to the sterling area, despite American opposition, and with complex consequences which will be considered later.

In this regard, by providing the loan, and earlier help during the war itself, and by supplementing it with Marshall Aid after 1948, the USA had become, in Strange's words, 'the ultimate guarantor of the sterling area',[13] and of an area, moreover, committed to becoming an integral part of an emerging multilateral trading system, rather than a basis for imperial self-sufficiency as it had been before the war. Capitulation to American hegemony had been rapid and complete. In exchange for this support and for subsequent 'acts of financial and economic favouritism' the British gave American policy support which was even 'sometimes slavish and faintly ludicrous', and gave up the possibility of attempting to follow a more autonomous and self-sufficient line, with fundamental long-term consequences.

There was a good deal of opposition to this settlement both from the Left, which believed that a bilateralist solution would have been possible, and from the old imperialist Right of the Conservative Party, which had been responsible for the creation of imperial preference in the 1930s.[14] But it was passed in the Commons by 347 to 100, and signalled an important long-term commitment to liberalisation and American dependence which has never been reversed or even threatened since then.

In the short-term this decision greatly eased the government's situation without appearing to require any fundamental shifts in its strategy. The additional resources enabled consumption, investment, contributions to European reconstruction and overseas defence to be reconciled without the need to make significant and politically difficult cuts. The Americans, despite widespread opposition to the 'socialist' experiment, did not apparently attempt to interfere too directly with internal policies, while external economic policy would only have to be modified in July 1947 when convertibility was to be enforced. The fact that the first two years of Labour rule are still widely seen as the most successful period of social democratic reformism in our recent history is a direct outcome of this situation.[15]

Yet the longer-term consequences, heavily disguised by a series of short-term problems which limited the impact of the original agreement, were to be far more serious. Two key elements need to be distinguished here: the extent to which American support served to underwrite Britain's overseas obligations and thus allowed them to be sustained at a level which could not be realistically maintained without undermining industrial and social investment, and the way in which it came to require an increasingly impossible reconcilation between domestic spending and production and an open foreign trading policy. The tensions involved in reconciling these conflicting objectives were to be clearly visible during the 1940s, though strongly moderated by the maintenance of war-time controls over both internal and external resource allocations. These controls were opposed by powerful elements in America, and were eventually allowed to survive with bad grace and because a major crisis was precipitated by the attempt to relax them. But even though they were directly responsible for the very considerable social and economic successes of the reconstruction period, they were increasingly seen by the Labour Right and, more especially, by the Tories who were to succeed them, as a temporary and 'unnatural' expedient required to overcome the immediate effects of the war and to be replaced by a full acceptance of the American strategy as soon as possible.

If this argument is accepted, it then becomes possible to understand the events of the next thirty years as a process of gradual transition from centralised controls to liberalisation backed by access to the American resources required to meet inevitable shortfalls which Britain's weakened position inevitably produced. This support turned Britain into a willing American client, while the resulting symbiosis allowed many short-term problems to be resolved with less sacrifice and stress than would otherwise have been necessary, but at the cost of creating conditions that were to guarantee a gradual decline into economic and political mediocrity, and the collapse of the system itself. Let us now look at a few of the key events in this depressing saga.

Firstly, the loan allowed Britain to take its place alongside the USA as a major supplier of the resources required to fund international economic recovery and defence against communism. Thus, while Keynes and Dalton were capitulating to the Americans to gain $3.75 billion and thus stave off an unacceptable austerity, the government was to spend almost $8 billion between 1946 and 1951 on overseas military and other programmes.[16] Secondly, with full employment and a desperate need for exports in a seller's market, domestic military spending also imposed a direct burden on both industrial reconstruction and the balance of payments. Yet in 1946 there were still more than 1,200,000 in the armed services and about 500,000 in the supply industries, while expenditure 'still stood at ... £1,736 million, or one-fifth of the gross national product'.[17] After the 1947 crisis a half-hearted attempt was made to reduce spending and manpower, but the spending was still about £720,000 in 1950, and Britain was still spending 'a higher proportion of her national income on defence (some 7%) than any other member of NATO'.[18] a proportion which was to increase dramatically a year later in response to the Korean war, as we shall see in the next section. As Bartlett points out, given the national commitment to an international role, 'only imminent national bankruptcy' would have led to a drastic reappraisal of these commitments, but the American loan and subsequent economic expedients 'made it possible for Britain to bear the heavy military burdens of a global power for many years to come'.[19] With Germany and Japan virtually debarred from any expenditure of this kind at all, it is hardly surprising that their levels of industrial and social expenditure soon greatly exceeded Britain's.

Thirdly, while the American loan eased the balance of payments constraint in 1946 and the first half of 1947, the enforced attempt to introduce convertibility in July, after a particularly severe winter, led to a major crisis. The drain on reserves which had been an average of $75 million per month in 1946, was $498 million in July 1947 and $650 million in the first twenty days of July, as sterling holders rushed to switch their money into dollars. Convertibility was suspended on 20 August and the full range of controls reintroduced. Because of these, and only because of them, the government did not have to fall back on the full range of deflationary measures which subsequent sterling crises were to impose on their successors, but the crisis did nevertheless require a fundamental reorientation in policy. The decision to nationalise steel was postponed in July in order to increase exports, in Bevan's view 'a negation of the principles of the party'.[20] Cripps then took over at the Treasury and introduced what he called a 'disinflationary' policy involving a cut in social services, a rise in interest rates and curbs in capital investment in sectors which were thought to be less important than others in the reduction of the dollar gap.[21] Wage and dividend restraint was also introduced with TUC backing, which led to a decline in the real wage by 1950,[22] and the Chiefs of Staff were forced to accept that defence spending would be cut to less than £700 million in 1948.[23]

Yet despite the strong similarities with subsequent deflations, the return to managed trade made its effects very different. The maintenance of the full array of external and internal controls made it possible for the reduction in consumption to be associated with full employment and a substantial expansion in investment and output. Disinflation, as opposed to deflation, made it possible to plan 'a comprehensive export programme' involving 'allocations, supplies, shipping, fuel and power, and labour being guided to the industries and firms of greatest need in the attainment of their targets'.[24] Full employment was sustained, domestic capital formation increased from £2.1 billion in 1948 to £2.5 billion in 1950, while the balance of payments assisted by the 1949 devaluation from $4 to $2.80, was in comfortable surplus and industrial production grew by 7–8 per cent each year, a level which has never been sustained since. Despite the excessive burden of defence, an economic performance was achieved which closely matched the best in Europe for the only time in the post-war period.

> Figures compiled for the Economic Survey of Europe show that during 1947–50 the United Kingdom increase of 29% in industrial production much exceeded that of Sweden and Belgium, and was slightly more than that of Italy and Denmark, but rather less than that of France and Norway, which reached 31%. During 1950–56, however, the British percentage increase slipped back to 21, while Sweden rose 10 points to 27, France 18 points to 49, Belgium 23 points to 36, and Italy more than doubled its increase to 63; Germany, a unique case, actually doubled total production, in these years of European recovery from which Britain opted out.[25]

Without the crisis created by convertibility, the huge reserve losses of July/August (almost a third of the original loan) would have been avoided. And although subsequent American Marshall Aid disbursements, starting in 1948, served to ease the situation, the need for them was in large part accounted for by these losses. Indeed, the favourable balance of payments stemming from the Cripps programme 'led Britain to announce that it would be able to dispense, ahead of schedule, with Marshall Aid'.[26] Had orthodox deflationary policies been tried without the re-imposition of direct controls, however, the recovery would almost certainly have collapsed, as it did soon after the First World War with devasting consequences for both the British and the world economy.

Fourthly, American assistance allowed the sterling area to continue, initially as an exclusive club of the old kind, but only on the understanding that the relationships involved would give way to full multilateralism as soon as possible. The effects of this intervention were to be complex and ambiguous, but undoubtedly a significant element in the long-term tendency to British decline. In 1945, far from being a source of strength, the sterling area involved major liabilities for Britain in the form of its indebtedness to its members accumulated during the war and totalling £3,567 million in 1945,[27] four times the size of the eventual American loan. Most of the money was owed to very poor Third World countries, particularly India, Egypt and the colonies. One solution to the balance of payments problem might therefore have been a full or partial repudiation of these debts, although this would inevitably have involved strong political opposition in the countries concerned and made it almost impossible for the old relationship of trust between Britain as central banker and the rest as willing depositors to have been maintained. Keynes himself recommended that some £880 million of these debts be cancelled (£500 million belonging to India), and that a further £1,500 million be funded on terms which would be little short of outright cancellation.[28] In the loan negotiations the Americans, too, wanted 'a drastic scaling down' of the balances,[29] recognising that if this occurred the possibility of an effective transition to convertibility would be greatly eased. In their view 'total releases to sterling area countries in 1946–50 would be limited to £200–250 million ... [and] would be offset by equivalent contribution from the overseas sterling area and thus would involve no net drain on the reserves'.[30] At the time they assumed that the British had accepted this general principle at least, and that by repudiating these debts would no longer require external monetary controls in order to sustain its international position. Thus their assumption that convertibility could be established without serious problems in 1947depended on their belief that Britain had been persuaded to repudiate a large proportion of its debts to some of the poorest countries in the world. The poorest were, yet again, to be asked to pay the price required to create the preconditions for the establishment of capitalist freedom.

The British certainly gave the impression that they had accepted this general principle,[31] but in the event, and to their credit, ultimately failed to do so. According to Gardner, the desire to maintain their banking reputation, to ensure that sterling balances be used to finance British exports, and to ease the transition to independence in India, outweighed the immediate advantages of renegotiation.[32] This failure was entirely inconsistent with the commitment to convertibility, as we have seen, since sterling holders rapidly used their new freedom to switch their resources out of sterling into dollars so rapidly that the former controls had to be re-introduced and tightened up. The sterling balances had indeed proved 'a major obstacle to multilateral trade',[33] as the Americans had anticipated, and a crucial element in forcing the British Government to continue with its regime of close central controls.

The result of the 1947 crisis was 'closer cooperation among members of the sterling area'[34] and its survival as an organisation based upon direct discrimination against American exports, the principle that the Americans were most concerned to destroy. Yet, paradoxically, it was only the access to American credit in 1945, and again after 1948 with Marshall Aid, that enabled Britain to treat the sterling balances as favourably as it did. The original obligations were run down gradually on the basis of arrangements which certainly favoured Britain and depended in large measure on the enforcement of very conservative economic policies in the colonies, which turned them into the major suppliers of dollars to the central pool.[35] Meanwhile, it was Marshall Aid and subsequent support to Britain under the NATO Mutual Aid Agreement that continued to underpin a system which the British economy itself was no longer powerful enough to guarantee. Yet before we make too much of this American generosity, it is important to recognise its source. We have already seen that a major part of Britain's weakness stemmed from its excessive spending on defence, both domestic and overseas. The only way in which Britain could have met its sterling obligations and sustained full employment would have been through a reduction in these to the level of its European rivals, and this would have been seen as a direct threat to the anti-communist alliance. Thus Strange is quite right in arguing that this support 'was a reflection of the American political interest in building a world-wide alliance system, first in Europe and then, after Korea, in Asia'.[36] It was because Britain was prepared to make so many debilitating sacrifices in this area, and because they had conceded that the controls over sterling would eventually be removed, that the Americans were prepared to provide it with this temporary support.

While the maintenance of the controls around the sterling area were crucial to the success of reconstruction, as we have seen, the willingness to allow it to operate in the particular form in which it did was nevertheless to have very damaging longer-term consequences. Firstly, it greatly encouraged a very large outflow of capital, and more especially of private capital, since no limits were imposed on these flows within the area, although they were only permitted for designated projects outside it. Thus £910 million of private investment went into the sterling area between 1946 and 1951, and a further £380 million into the rest of the world.[37] Combined with overseas public investment of £345 million (£86 million to the sterling area) we thus discover a further leakage of £1,635 million to support 'first-class power' status and the 'ancient prestige and hegemony' of London after financial and political independence had been sold to the Americans for far less. There can be little doubt that this leakage was an important element in the lower levels of investment in Britain than in European and Japanese industry which began in the 1940s and became much worse later on. While British private capital now followed closely behind American in building up the multinational system, its future rivals in the rest of the industrial world were financing the productivity gains which were soon to alter the balance of economic power decisively in their favour. There can be little doubt that Shonfield was quite correct in identifying this as a major source of British weakness[38] which has yet to be overcome.

Secondly, the successful operation of the sterling area itself depended on the extent to which all the countries involved maintained a viable balance of payments relationship with the external world, and especially with the dollar area. Although their policies could be strongly influenced, they could not be controlled, so that the possibility always existed that a poor performance by Britain or by a combination of countries within the system could threaten a fall in reserves and, especially after payments had been liberalised in the 1950s, a run on sterling. Since the exchange rate was fixed (and was subsequently to become increasingly overhauled) the only defence against these pressures was an attempt to keep Britain in continuous surplus and the readiness to push up interest rates at the first sign of any difficulties. Both implied very cautious economic policies with a powerful tendency to discourage investment and hence inhibit growth. This problem only really manifested itself in an extreme form during the 1947 crisis during reconstruction, but was to become the root cause of the 'stop-go' cycle which was to become the dominant feature of the 1950s and 1960s.

Thirdly, and with far less persuasiveness, it has been argued that the lack of innovativeness in British industry can be attributed in large part to its access to protected markets in the Empire, of which the post-war sterling area was a continuation.[39] Now although it is very likely that a good many incompetent producers survived who would otherwise have failed as a result of their protected access, this argument leaves aside a number of crucial facts. Before the war protectionism was widespread and closely correlated with economic success, not just in Britain, but also outside, while major gains over Britain in Europe and Japan were made as Britain reduced its external controls and these other countries maintained them. Furthermore, it ignores the losses that would have been incurred with the collapse of weaker firms in a situation where high interest rates, a tight labour market and a shortage of capital equipment stemming from the commitments to defence spending and capital outflows made it almost impossible for British firms to match their foreign competitors. Without the modification of these far more significant policies, the removal of the few advantages gained in protective markets would have destroyed the least efficient without creating the resources to put anything better in its place – the direct outcome, as we shall see, of subsequent attempts to force British industry to modernise by exposing it directly to the bracing winds of foreign competition.

Having looked at reconstruction in some detail because of its significance in establishing a general pattern for the future, it should be possible to deal with subsequent developments rather more quickly. But before doing so it is important that we re-emphasise the essential ambiguity of that experience and more especially its very positive achievements. Whatever the long-term capitulation to liberal principles, the contingencies of the immediate situation forced the Labour government to plan both for domestic full employment and external balance, and provided them with mechanisms of central control which made it possible for them to sustain their momentum despite conditions which were far less favourable than those which have confronted their successors. An important shift in the balance of power between capital and labour did take place during these years, creating a legacy of full employment and welfare which was to be a major source of strength to the working class later and is only now being systematically dismantled. Although it is also essential to stress that a series of capitulations to capitalist orthodoxy mainly in the fields of foreign defence and economic policy also took place, which were themselves to become a crucial element in the processes which were eventually to destroy both that internal balance of power and the country's external strength, it is important that we should not lose sight of the fact that it was the use of methods entirely opposed to the teachings of neoclassical orthodoxy that allowed these achievements to be sustained. For it is now widely assumed that it has been the liberalisation of the trading system which created the basis for the long boom, but what the British experience makes clear, and was equally the case elsewhere, is that the stability and continuity of the first and most critical phase was entirely dependent on the use of interventionist methods that were entirely alien to the principles of economic orthodoxy.[40]

The contradictions of liberalisation, 1951–1968

The period from the Korean war to the Basle Agreement on sterling spans the golden years of the long boom funded by the American deficit and characterised by entirely unprecedented rates of growth in the world economy. It also spans the decisive move from protectionism to liberalisation through convertibility at the end of the 1950s, the completion of the Kennedy Round of tariff reductions in the 1960s, and the establishment of the European Economic Community (EEC) and the European Free Trade Association (EFTA). It ends with the emergence of clear evidence that the underlying basis of the Bretton Woods system was seriously threatened by the British devaluation of 1967, the intensification of the Vietnam war and the establishment of the two-tier gold market in 1968.

The chief concern in this chapter, however, is not with the successes in the most successful industrial countries, but with the relative failure of the British economy to keep pace – failure which was to turn it into a chronic deficit country by the early 1960s and thus a significant threat to the integrity of the structures which sustained the liberal international economic system. We shall attempt now to demonstrate that it was primarily the incompatibility between domestic and external commitments which produced both the inadequacies in economic performance and its inevitable and disastrous external consequence. Only the most central features of the period will be dealt with here; further substantiation of the argument can be found in the powerful accounts provided in the works of Strange and Pollard.[41]

During these years the dominant feature is a sharp alternation between periods when growth almost reached that of European levels, and those when it fell far short. Thus in the nine fat years between 1950 and 1951, 1953 and 1955, 1959 and 1960, and 1963 and 1964, growth was more than 4 per cent. During the remaining years it was not much above 1 per cent, producing the overall average which left Britain bottom of the European league. We have to understand, therefore, what it was about the British experience that made it impossible to sustain these bursts of expansion without the need for equal periods of drastic and damaging retrenchment. The general arguments will be reviewed in the final section of the chapter; here we will attempt to look briefly at the conditions that precipitated each phase of deflationary policy. In each case there can be no doubt that external commitments and pressures were the major factor, with the problem of economic management continually intensifying as external controls came to be progressively loosened.

Between 1947 and 1950 cuts in defence expenditure, devaluation and external controls had sustained rapid growth and balance of payments equilibrium; the Korean war produced an immediate regression. Responding to American demands,[42] a huge rearmament programme was immediately announced involving an expenditure programme of £4,700 million over three years, after it had fallen to £750 million in 1949, the diversion of a large percentage of scarce heavy manufacturing and research capacity into the defence industries, and cuts in social services.[43] The corresponding expansion in imports and contraction in exports, together with rising raw material prices and deficits in many sterling area countries, produced an inevitable balance of payments crisis. Deflation was inevitable, and as a result manufacturing production fell by almost 3 per cent and GNP by more than 1 per cent in 1952. Thus the first major break in post-war growth had been consciously engineered to enable the country to meet external demands far in excess of those imposed on any of its major competitors. In the early 1950s British arms production 'exceeded that of all her European NATO partners combined', and was 'contributing more than 40% to the total defence spending of the European members of NATO'.[44]

In 1953, however, the balance of payments pressures eased and expansion again became possible. Raw material prices had fallen and the world economy was expanding so that it became possible to sustain increased defence expenditure and investment while simultaneously beginning a drastic reduction in both external and internal controls. The balance of payments on current account remained in surplus in 1953 and 1954, but without creating a margin sufficient to build up the reserves. In 1955 it was again in deficit and, when the overall figures which include both current account and long-term capital movement are considered, it becomes clear that there had been small deficits in 1953 and 1954 as well.[45] Hence the end of 1955 saw the beginning of a new deflation, but now with the need for a much stronger use of deflationary monetary policy because of the lifting of controls, as Worswick makes clear.[46] The Suez war in 1956, while having a limited effect on the real economy, nevertheless produced sharp movements out of sterling as speculators attempted to defend against a possible devaluation, and this, too, intensified the need for high interest rates. Despite the resulting losses, with growth rates forced down to pre-war levels, in 1958 'the pressure from the City ensured that the final reckless step was taken of making sterling wholly convertible, so that the economy, which was already in imbalance of a long-term lending programme it could not sustain, had to carry the further strain of short-term lending also'.[47]

Even leaving aside the negative impact of the increases in defence expenditure on exports, the break in 1955 can be wholly attributed to the negative outflows of private and government capital and of overseas defence. The total deficit on current and capital account was £400 million between 1953 and 1955, while private foreign investment totalled £900 million and government defence and other spending £335 billion; between 1956 and 1958 there was an overall surplus of £300 million, compared with private outflows of

£1,663 million and official outflows of £538 million.[48] As if this were not sufficient, the country's position as chief of sterling led the Treasury to believe that they should not merely aim to maintain an overall equilibrium, but a substantial surplus designed to build up the reserves to a point where they would be sufficient to deal with external threats to the reserves. This surplus was put at £300–£350 million in the mid-1950s, and £450 million by 1959,[49] figures which necessarily required extreme caution in economic policy-making since the underlying strength of the economy was not such that they could be achieved without cutting back on domestic consumption and investment. As the Treasury itself put it, the 'facts of the external position necessarily limit our freedom in our general economic policies, including monetary policy', and any failure to meet external targets 'even by small amounts, can have disproportionate effects on the whole economy'. As a result, on no account should they 'take risks in the management of the domestic economy of a kind that affect the balance of payments'.[50]

Operating within this highly restrictive framework, it is not surprising that two years of expansion in 1959 and 1960 were followed by two more years of retrenchment in 1961 and 1962, when yet another external deficit led to the usual response of rising interest rates, spending cuts and a wage freeze. By this time it had become evident to at least some that the country was falling behind internationally at an alarming rate, and a token commitment to planning on French lines was introduced, presumably on the assumption that the problem could be solved through a more rational use of resources. But nothing was done to eliminate the major outflows of private and public resources, with private overseas investment totalling £719 million and military spending and other government spending £896 million in 1963 and 1964 alone.[51]

The constraints on investment of the previous dozen years now meant that insufficient capacity existed to meet the increased output sought by the expansionary programme designed by Maudling in 1962 and implemented in 1963 and 1964, so that imports of basic materials and of manufactured goods increased much faster than exports.[52] The result was a dramatic worsening in the balance of payments in 1964, and a legacy to the incoming Labour government which was to 'dominate almost every action of the Government for five years of the five years, eight months [it] was in office.'[53]

The Wilson government was directly committed to the solution of the long-term problem of relative economic decline, and of the underinvestment in public sector infrastructure which the periodic bouts of spending cuts had inevitably introduced. Yet it was entirely unprepared for the constraints which the problem of the weakness of sterling imposed on it, as is shown by Wilson's own account of his dealings with the Governor of the Bank of England in the context of the major sterling crisis which greeted his arrival as Prime Minister. By 24 November the Governor,

> Claiming that our failure to act in accordance with his advice had precipitated the [sterling] crisis, he was now demanding allround cuts in expenditure, regardless of social or even economic priorities, and fundamental changes in some of the Chancellor's economic announcements.
>
> Not for the first time I said that we had now reached the situation where a newly elected government with a mandate from the people was being told, not so much by the Bank of England but by international speculators, that the policies on which we had fought the election could not be implemented; that this government was to be forced into the adoption of Tory policies to which it was fundamentally opposed. The Governor confirmed that this was, in fact, the case.
>
> I asked him if this meant that it was impossible for any Government whatever its party label, whatever its manifesto or the policies on which it fought an election, to continue, unless it immediately reverted to full-scale Tory policies. He had to admit that was what his argument meant, because of the sheer compulsion of the economic dictation of those who exercised decisive economic power.[54]

At this point Wilson insisted that he would not accept this diagnosis, because to do so would be 'to bring down the curtain on parliamentary democracy', and put the control of policy into the hands of foreigners.[55] Threatened with the possibility of a major intensification of the crisis and a threat to the exchange rate, the Governor then had recourse to swap arrangements negotiated under the General Arrangements to Borrow (GAB) established in 1962, and borrowed $3,000 billions from the central bankers, thus defusing the speculative pressures.[56]

For Wilson this was a triumphant assertion of the autonomy of his national government and presumably of the sovereignty of Parliament, but his optimism was misplaced. This easy access to foreign credit enabled the government to finance a greater programme of public spending than would have been possible otherwise, but by the middle of 1965 the underlying deficit was still there, together with far more insistent pressures from the bankers whose direct control had been greatly increased because of the money they had lent. Thus we find the usual policies of high interest rates and credit controls over consumption and private construction, and the formulation of an incomes policy on the basis of 'considerable communication between London and Washington at various levels', and 'including intensive talks between the heads of the two central banks'.[57]

What the bankers had actually done by putting together this package was to make it possible for the exchange rate to be held at a level that was no longer viable, given the damage which the economy had suffered as a result of the lost years of the 1950s and early 1960s. Entirely failing to recognise the negative effects of overseas leakages and never stopping even to consider the re-imposition of direct controls, all the weight had to be placed on a classic deflation – the 'Tory' policies which the electorate had rejected in electing him to office. Thus Bacon and Eltis note that the National Plan put forward by the newly created Department of Economic Affairs at the end of 1965 might have created the basis for a sustained expansion, provided that there was a devaluation. But this was strongly resisted by Wilson, who appears to have assumed that the whole problem was created by the greed and malice of external speculators, and by the establishment of the Treasury, Bank of England and the City more concerned with the country's external obligations and earnings than with industrial development and full employment. As a result,

> There were severe expenditure cuts and no devaluation. Expansion therefore ceased, the National Plan was abandoned, and nothing was done to make it possible for the spare resources released to go to exports where they could lay the foundation for the future.[58]

The contrast with the experience under Cripps, when effective measures to control the external balance were immediately adopted and investment actually increased, could not have been clearer. From this point onwards policy was again to be entirely restrictive until a surplus had been restored in 1969. A major opportunity had been lost. One can hardly disagree with Bacon and Eltis, who claim that 'this was to prove the decisive turning point after which the structure of the United Kingdom economy deteriorated almost without interruption',[59] although one would want to argue that rather more than a simple devaluation would have been necessary to produce a fundamental change of the kind envisaged in the Plan.

Yet this victory of the establishment was also to prove the last gasp of the old order. The underlying weakness that their policies had created was now so extreme that the old commitments to sterling and international policing had to be drastically revised. In November 1967 the immense pressure of speculation finally forced a devaluation and recourse to the IMF. The resulting policy negotiated with the IMF entirely foreclosed all possibilities of expansion and social betterment. The democratic will of Parliament now clearly counted for much less than the requirements of the country's creditors[60] and Wilson and Jenkins, the new Chancellor, had to cut investment and public services, enforce wage policies and, in 1968, even attempt to introduce legal penalties for certain forms of industrial action, thus breaking the most powerful of the understandings which united the trade union and constituency elements in the Labour Party. This time, however, the damage was even worse than before, since the 'stop' phase of the old cycle had to be extended further than ever, and an ominous growth in unemployment also emerged for the first time. As a result of these policies Beckerman argues:

> the 'go' phase of what would normally have been a 'stop-go' cycle beginning with the 'stop' of 1966/7 never materialised; the economy stayed in the 'stop' position. By 1970 output was over 2% below the trend level, and the trend rate of growth itself had no doubt been depressed by the sluggish growth of output over the whole period and the gradual slackening of the pressure of demand. And the average unemployment rate over the years 1967 to 1969 inclusive (2.5% for the UK) was higher than any previous consecutive three-year period.[61]

Although not everyone could see it, this clearly demonstrated the impossibility of a stable association between Keynesian social democracy and liberal external policies in a country attempting to sustain Britain's overseas commitments. Externally again, the devaluation of the pound was the first step in the process which soon was to lead to the collapse of the dollar and of the Bretton Woods agreement. More directly, devaluation meant considerable losses to overseas holders of sterling balances, who rapidly made it clear that they would move into other currencies unless steps were taken to safeguard their position from a repetition. As a result, the 'Basle Agreement' was negotiated in 1968, under which Britain agreed to sustain the dollar value of the sterling deposits in the event of another devaluation, in exchange for a 'standby credit to Britain of $2 billion to be repaid within ten years'.[62] Although this still left Britain with the prime responsibility, it now made it clear that its old role as sole guardian of the monetary stability of the former British Empire had passed for ever. Finally, the spending cuts of this period also involved a serious review of defence spending, with a firm commitment to withdraw all troops east of Suez, and an acceptance that Britain's role would henceforth 'be concentrated mainly in Europe and the North Atlantic area'.[63] Spending continued at levels which were far higher than most of the leading countries, but Britain no longer foresaw a permanent defensive role in the Third World – a fundamental break with the imperial past.

These changes add up to a major shift in the country's international role and in the mechanisms which sustained it, but one which was made only after the damage to the underlying structures that had put Britain ahead of its major overseas rivals had been done. The cumulative effect of the inability to reconcile growth with external balance, and the damage it inflicted, comes out very clearly in Table 6.1.

Table 6.1

	Annual growth in UK industrial production (%)	UK balance of payments, current account (£m)	UK current account (excluding govt invisibles) (£m)
1953–55 expansion	5.6	+ 145 to − 155	+ 211 to − 17
1955–58 stagnation	0.4	− 155 to − 336	− 17 to + 555
1958–60 expansion	6.2	+ 336 to − 275	+ 555 to + 8
1960–62 stagnation	1.1	− 275 to + 101	+ 8 to + 462
1962–64 expansion	5.6	+ 101 to − 393	+ 462 to + 40
1964–66 stagnation	1.5	− 393 to − 61	+ 40 to + 411

SOURCE: *The British Economy, Key Statistics, 1900–66*, published by *The Times* for the London and Cambridge Economic Service.

Here we can see the direct connection between deficits, deflation and industrial decline, together with a long-term tendency for the deficit to worsen in each cycle.[64] By 1967 the strain had become too much, and the first steps were taken to change the way in which the system worked. But nothing could replace the investment lost during the wasted years, and the response was to be both too little and too late.

Disintegration, 1969–1976

The failures of the 1950s and mid-1960s had occurred in the context of the international boom fuelled by the dollar (and to a far smaller but still significant extent) pound deficit, and defended by the international military alliance to which Britain had made an entirely disproportionate contribution. The policy response to the 1967 crisis marked a decisive break in Britain's post-war development, involving as it did the effective surrender of the third of the policy commitments outlined at the beginning of this chapter – the maintenance of a central role alongside the USA in the management of the international economic and security system. It is perhaps not surprising, therefore, that this decline in international pretensions directly paralleled the country's uneasy relations with Europe. Rejecting membership of the EEC in the 1950s when it might have been a major element both politically and economically, Britain attempted to create a leadership role for itself in the European periphery through EFTA. Having failed, and beginning to recognise its increased international vulnerability, it attempted to negotiate entry during the 1960s, but was rejected twice on the probably valid grounds that its external commitments to the sterling area and the USA were too strong. By the early 1970s, however, these obstacles were no longer seen to be significant, and the country was finally drawn back into a union which was to ensure, for the first time for centuries, that its relationships with its nearest neighbours were to become far closer than those with its dependencies beyond the seas, a change involving not merely a geographical shift, but a fundamental switch in the terms on which these relations were to be conducted. The end of the Empire was finally at hand.

Equally important as this transformation in national status was the break in the dynamism and stability of the international economic order that was also to become visible at the end of the 1960s, of which, indeed, the sterling devaluation was itself an early sign. At the point when Britain was attempting to make a new and more self-sufficient strategy for growth, the external conditions required to make this possible were becoming dramatically less favourable as the long boom began to give way to the oncoming long recession. In the earlier period, the phases of deflation could always be followed by equally extensive phases of growth, because over-seas demand was still buoyant enough to absorb even the high-cost products of British industry. As a result, deflation did not require the sacrifice of the commitment to the welfare state, full employ-ment, complete legal freedom for the trade union movement and continuously rising wages. These commitments, together with the assumption that each period of deflation would be the last, were the fundamental basis of the compromise between capital and labour which sustained the liberal social democratic state system.

But as the international recession began to intensify, these pos-sibilities were to disappear progressively. Competition intensified in domestic and foreign markets (and, indeed, with monetary reforms and tariff reductions, the distinction between these markets itself became increasingly unimportant), British goods were in-creasingly pushed into a no-man's land between the high technol-ogy output of the advanced countries and the low-wage output of the NICs, the rate of profit fell precipitously,[65] and this in turn further inhibited the investment on which future progress de-pended.

Thus it is also evident that the end of the 1960s marked a significant shift in the way in which Britain's international problems related to the central issues of this book – to global economic management and uneven development. From 1945 to 1968, as we have seen, the key problems arose out of a misguided attempt to play a central managerial role, and the failure documented in the preceding sections must therefore be read as a further extension of the inherently contradictory implications of any purely national attempt at this role already explored in relation to the decline of the USA over the same period. But during these years, although British resources were poor by comparison with the USA, they were substantial by comparison with all of its other competitors, so that Britain was not having to overcome the inherent problems con-fronting a weak country attempting to establish its position in the face of the superior competitiveness of a strong one – the problems, in other words, of uneven development. By the end of the 1960s, however, it had been overtaken by its major competititors in Europe and Japan and had now to attempt to match their levels of performance in an international market-place from which almost all protective barriers and special privileges had been eliminated. Stripped bare of its former advantages and unwilling to concede that it would be unable to meet this challenge without external aids, British industry inevitably failed in this attempt, which generated not only a further phase of accelerated economic decline, but the destruction of the social democratic consensus and its Keynesian theoretical underpinning.

The nine years separating the devaluation of 1967 from the IMF intervention at the end of 1976 were marked by a series of vacillations in policy which culminated in the final demise of the liberal Keynesian thinking that had dominated the post-war period. Repudiation of these policies in response to external deficits gave way to attempts to restore them in order to regain the political support which they guarantee with the mass electorate, but these in turn proved to be incompatible with the economic viability of the national industrial base. The events of these years finally demonstrated that the basis for the old compromises between the social Toryism of Macmillan's *The Middle Way*, and the right-wing reformism of Crosland's *The Future of Socialism* no longer existed, with fundamental political and economic consequences both at home and abroad.

Thus the Wilson/Jenkins strategy in 1968 and 1969 involved a significant repudiation of many of the elements of the old position, notably a direct attack on the industrial working class and on welfare services. The latter suffered substantial cuts in the economic programme negotiated with the IMF in November 1967. The former suffered under the impact of record increases in unemployment (from 1.4 per cent in 1965 to 2.6 per cent in 1970), the imposition of a wages policy, which reduced real earnings and an attempt to introduce legal controls over the right to organise and strike. Thus while in the 1940s planning was based on the manipulation of the foreign balance in order to sustain full employment and welfare, in the late 1960s employment and welfare were being adjusted downwards to the point where the external balance could be sustained.

Needless to say, this change involved a massive loss of political support and caused deep strains within the Labour Party. Having established the surplus at the end of 1969, the government attempted to begin a new expansion designed to make good the losses, using this as the basis for the appeal to the electorate in the middle of 1970. But the political damage had been too great, and the Conservatives took over, a clear demonstration of the organic connections between political and economic variables and between foreign and domestic requirements.

In opposition the Tory party had responded to the evident inability of the old social democratic strategy to solve the economic problem or to sustain political support by calling for a return to traditional free market policies. Their programme committed them to the encouragement of competition, the elimination of subsidies to inefficient industries, the abolition of interventionist agencies set up by Labour, such as the Industrial Reorganisation Corporation, and the system of regional grants, and the restoration of free collective bargaining. To ensure that the latter was not to be exploited by the best organised workers, they introduced the Industrial Relations Act, which was designed to impose legal controls on union organisation and industrial action. Externally they had inherited a substantial surplus, and therefore did not anticipate immediate difficulties. In the longer term, however, they assumed that the problem could be taken care of on purely liberal principles – accession to the EEC (finalised in 1973) to give free access to a very large and expanding market, and, after 1972, the adoption of a freely floating exchange rate to take care of external price competitiveness. This decision, combined with the imposition of the same controls on private overseas capital investment in the sterling area as had previously operated in the rest of the world, finally terminated the attempt to sustain centre country status.[66]

But this strategy, too, was to be fraught with contradictions. The return to free collective bargaining was followed by a dramatic increase in wage settlements and industrial disputes, which the Industrial Relations Act proved unable to resolve. Thus wage increases averaged 4.9 per cent per annum and days lost through industrial disputes totalled 3.7 million between 1964 and 1969; these had increased to 12.6 per cent and 13.9 million between 1970 and 1973.[67] Productivity increases remained far behind wage increases, and manufacturing continued to fall, at 20 per cent in

1968, 16.7 per cent in 1970, 17.2 per cent in 1972, 14.9 per cent in 1973 and 6.3 per cent in 1974.[68] In the early years the pressure on profits could be offset to some extent by reflation and, more importantly, an inflationary increase in prices, since the balance of payments constraint had been loosened. But, with an increasingly open economy this merely increased import penetration, which involved an increase in the share of the domestic market for manufacturers from 13 per cent in 1970 to 19 per cent in 1974.[69] The pressure on marginal companies intensified, and the withdrawal of subsidies threatened some major bankruptcies and the actual collapse of Upper Clyde Shipbuilders and Rolls-Royce. Responding to the threat of industrial militancy and unacceptable increases in unemployment, a retreat was soon organised involving a restoration of direct assistance.

From 1972, the desire to push up the growth rate became overwhelming, and demand was allowed to expand rapidly. The corresponding increase in wage inflation and threat to profits and the external balance produced a reversal on wage policy, leading to compulsory controls over both wages and prices. Furthermore, while it was assumed in 1972 that devaluation would take care of the external balance, it failed to do so. By the first half of 1973, assisted by a dramatic increase in the export of private capital (£501 million in 1970, £1,272 million in 1972, £2,073 million in 1973[70]) it had begun to reach unsustainable levels; by the end of the year, greatly worsened by the escalation in oil and other raw material prices, it was out of control. The year 1973 saw what was probably the last attempt at an old-fashioned Keynesian reflation, with full employment and an open border. After the longest period of low growth in the post-war period, an expansion of 6.5 per cent was registered, but by the end of the year the combination of external deficit and domestic industrial disruption made it impossible for the process to continue. The Heath government had neither created an effective system of competition and controls over labour, nor a workable structure of centralised controls. In an external environment which now intensified internal difficulties rather than moderating them, the end result was an ideological and economic collapse. While governments up to 1970 could all claim to have 'achieved successes rather than failures', Bacon and Eltis could claim that 'what was unique about Mr Heath's 1970–4 administration was that failure was total'.[71] There can be no doubt that it was this experience that enabled the proponents of economic orthodoxy led by Mrs Thatcher to capture control of the party during the next few years, and to refuse resolutely to make further compromises with Keynesianism after they took power in 1979.

The Labour Party in opposition had also begun a retreat from the old social democratic consensus, but in this case towards policies involving a much more radical attack on liberal orthodoxy than that contemplated during the 1950s and 1960s. A new critique of the role of multinational capital in destroying the conditions under which Keynesian policies could operate had emerged, which claimed that their monopoly power and external linkages made it possible for them to evade the normal disciplines imposed by market competition and the controls over external flows at the disposal of the nation state.[72] To ensure that future reflations actually generated real increases in investment and output and to enforce price competition, it was decided that there would be significant state acquisitions in each major industrial sector, and the creation of new investment institutions, notably a National Enterprise Board. The Industrial Relations Act was to go and wages regulated through a voluntary 'social contract' negotiated between both sides of industry and the state, while spending on social services was to be restored. But although there were now important economic advisers in the party arguing for a return to import controls,[73] the lessons of the 1960s had not been generally learnt, and these were not seen to be an important element of the overall programme.

But these ambitions were to be brought to a very rapid end, and the circumstances of these early years conspired to turn this administration into the agency for the initiation of a fully fledged monetarist strategy after 1976. The leadership which took office in 1974 was almost the same as that which had presided over the deflation of 1967 to 1969, and it almost certainly had much less faith in radical measures than the rank and file of the party. Furthermore, there was no overall parliamentary majority in February 1974, and one of only three after the election held in October, so that it could be argued that insufficient support existed for radical measures. However, most important of all, they came to power in external circumstances worse than any experienced since 1945, and with none of the domestic and external controls that had enabled their predecessors to overcome those problems without recourse to draconian cuts in public spending and economic activity. As we have seen, the Governor of the Bank of England had explained to Wilson that such circumstances would require 'Tory measures' whatever the opinion of the electorate, and his views had eventually prevailed. Between 1974 and 1976 this experience was to be repeated, with even worse results for economic development and political support.

At the start of 1974 the immediate response to the escalating deficit was again to fund the promised spending programme and sustain an economic expansion through foreign borrowing. While total borrowing was £3 billion in 1973, it was £7.1 billion in 1974, £8.9 billion in 1975 and £14.2 billion in 1976.[74] In the first instance this allowed spending and wages to be increased (no doubt making a useful contribution to the electoral victory at the end of the year), but without reducing external weaknesses. Instead, access to foreign borrowing allowed the Bank of England to hold the exchange rate at a higher level than would have been possible otherwise, while unprecedented increases in oil and other raw material prices and the inflationary effects of the dollar deficit, discussed in Chapter 5, led to a surge of imported price increases. Responding to these, an increasingly militant labour force pushed wages up to equally unprecedented levels, and earnings rose nearly 28 per cent from July 1974 to July 1975. Inflation was now around 25 per cent, ahead of all industrial countries, and the balance of payments deficit was £3.6 billion in 1974.[75] Since there were no improvements in productivity between 1973 and 1975, not even this rate of inflation was sufficient to maintain profits, and those in manufacturing fell from 14.9 per cent in 1973 to 6.3 per cent in 1974 and to 3.8 per cent in 1976.[76]

In these conditions the possibility of a complete collapse into hyper-inflation and industrial bankruptcy could not be excluded. Without access to any direct controls, the government had now to take up where it had left off in 1969 by taking active steps to contain wage increases, cut spending and restrain demand. Joel Barnett therefore records a life as Chief Secretary to the Treasury spent in a continuous round of negotiations designed to wrest spending cuts out of a succession of reluctant Ministers.[77] An agreement was secured with the TUC to restrict wage claims to a flat rate of £6 in 1975/6, and the tax burden on company profits was significantly reduced. The only concessions to the radicalism of the manifesto were the establishment of the National Enterprise Board in 1975, though without the resources required to make a major impact on investment, the bringing of British Leyland into public ownership (though this was in response to bankruptcy, not to socialist principles), and the creation of the British National Oil Corporation in 1976 with important powers over the whole North Sea field.

But the retrenchment and wage restraints agreed in 1975 were to be insufficient to offset the effects of domestic cost-push pressures (wage increases were still at 16.5 per cent in 1975/6, despite the agreement) and the international recession which was now at its deepest. The exchange rate was still at just over $2 at the start of 1976, and was maintained there only through massive external borrowing, a lot of it in the form of short-term deposits, mainly from the OPEC countries whose holdings alone equalled the value of total reserves.[78] While the authorities accepted that this rate was too high, they did not want a very large fall, since this would have worsened inflationary pressures and led to an outflow of credit which would have exhausted the country's reserves and forced a drastic cut in imports. Whatever one may think of the nature of the concessions which came to be made to obtain the resources required to defend the pound in 1976, it is important to recognise that a failure to do so would have required even more fundamental adjustments to consumption patterns and economic organisation than those that were eventually imposed.

In 1976 OPEC depositors began to take their money out on a large scale. In March the Treasury attempted a limited and controlled devaluation, but, given the lack of overseas confidence, this soon got out of hand and the pound rapidly fell into the $1.70s, and eventually reached just over $1.50 in September.[79] Rather than allow an uncontrolled run on sterling to develop, and refusing to impose direct controls, the government was to spend the next nine months negotiating external credits with the Americans, the Germans and, ultimately, the IMF. The American objective in these negotiations was twofold: to offer enough money to induce the British to sign, but to do so on terms that would tie the government into the liberal policies required to sustain the existing international economic order. Thus Yeo at the US Treasury told Fay and Young: 'We feared that if a country like Britain blew up, defaulted on its loans, introduced foreign exchange controls and froze convertibility, we could have a real depression.' In his view the British now 'had a higher standard of living than the country was earning', and the only answer was a classic deflation by 'cutting public expenditure, and thus government borrowing; and imposing strict controls on the expanding supply of money, to control inflation. If taxes could also be reduced, so much the better'.[80]

In the Cabinet there was fierce resistance to the implications of these recommendations, especially from the spending Ministries which had already had to digest unacceptable cuts. But it was now evident that a fundamental choice had to be made between accepting the highly conservative policy prescriptions of the foreign creditors within the existing framework of trading and monetary management, or adopting import controls to defend the border as the means of overcoming the payments crisis. The latter was strongly pressed by a minority in the Cabinet as the basis for an 'alternative economic strategy', but it was defeated by the weight of evidence presented by the Treasury, mainly based on the probable consequences of the international retaliation that it would provoke. Thus in September discussions began with the IMF on a credit package which was finalised in discussions in London in November/December. Agreement was reached on the 14 December and the Letter of Intent was published the following day. [81] High interest rates, substantial public spending cuts, wage restraint and an agreement to sell off £500 million worth of BP shares were agreed in exchange for an IMF credit of about $3.5 billion dollars, and a pretty well guaranteed line of credit to the private banking system of rather more.

This capitulation to the demands of orthodox theory has been chosen to mark the start of a new phase of economic development, because it represented a clear-cut rejection of the Keynesian full employment/demand management principles which had continued to exert a strong, if increasingly untenable, influence over policy till then. But now demand was being savagely cut back, with unemployment at the unprecedented post-war level of 5.2 per cent and it was well understood that it would expand further before it could be brought down. The needs of the external balance had taken priority over the commitment to domestic expansion in a more thoroughgoing way than ever before, and in an international context so depressed that earlier returns to some degrees of prosperity were no longer possible. The fundamental capitalist principle that wage bargaining could only produce an adequate level of profit by the reality of large-scale unemployment had been re-established thirty years after the first majority Labour government had taken power, committed to eliminating it for ever. This commitment was to be taken over and applied far more consistently and ruthlessly by the Conservative government which took power in 1979, but it was clearly visible in the policies adopted by Labour in December 1976–1984.

Liberalism in crisis, 1976–1984

In September 1976 James Callaghan officially informed the Labour Party conference of the government's conversion to orthodox theory:

> We used to think that you could just spend your way out of a recession and increase employment by cutting taxes and boosting government spending. I tell you in all candour that that option no longer exists, and that insofar as it ever did exist, it worked by injecting inflation into the economy. And each time that happened the average level of unemployment has risen. Higher inflation followed by higher unemployment. That is the history of the last twenty years.[82]

Three months later a Letter of Intent to the IMF confirmed that the policies designed to put these convictions into effect had received the official seal of approval from the international financial community, and for the next two years the government valiantly implemented them. The traditional combination of high interest rates, public spending cuts and restrictive wage policies was followed now backed by a Treasury which had finally exchanged monetarism for Keynesian fiscal policy as its dominant *modus vivendi*.[83] Earlier deflations had been more or less exclusively concerned to reduce consumption by enough to eliminate an external deficit, but this objective now had to be combined with the elimination of inflation. To do this it was necessary to stop the total supply of money in the economy from expanding and thus allowing inflationary wage increases to be turned into price increases. The necessary consequence of this was a willingness to allow unemployment to rise to the point where it dissuaded workers from demanding too much, and eliminated all those employers unable to sustain sufficient labour discipline and to meet the higher levels of efficiency required by the intensification of overseas competition.

During these years, as a result, unemployment increased, though only marginally, the real wage fell, while actual government expenditure was reduced between 1975/6 and 1978/9 by '£3,100 million in current items and £4,900 million in fixed investment'.[84] These policies had a significant effect on both the deficit and inflation, since the former recovered from a deficit of about £1 billion in 1976 to a surplus of the same amount in 1978, while inflation fell from 16.5 per cent to 8.3 per cent at the same time. But growth was again suppressed, though the loss was disguised by the beginnings of oil and natural gas production. Industrial production excluding the latter only increased by a total of 3.3 per cent between 1975 and 1979, when it was still 4.1 per cent lower than it had been at its peak in 1973.[85] Yet despite these developments, the commitment to orthodoxy was not yet total. In particular, after confidence in sterling was restored in 1977, strong upward pressure on the exchange rate led to attempts at control through direct intervention and reductions in interest rates, while the major source of downward pressure on wages remained 'the direct though largely voluntary, restraint on prices and incomes'.[86] Furthermore, even though the use of orthodox methods was the dominant feature of policy during these years of crisis, there is little doubt that the preference of the government (though not of the Treasury and Bank of England) would have been to return to Keynesian expansionism as soon as inflation and the external balance permitted. Indeed, in 1979 an initial expansion was attempted, but with the problem of productivity and profitability still unresolved, the effect was mainly to initiate an import boom and to push the balance of payments back into deficit.

The major damage stemming from the deflation was incurred in the relations between capital and labour, which now, in a context where wage increases had become an aspect of government policy, necessarily involved a break in the relations between the trade unions and the Labour Party. In 1978 the TUC refused to renew its commitment to wage restraint, and in the winter of 1978/9 a number of strikes among low-paid workers, mainly in the public sector, produced a massive level of public discomfort and negated all of the advantages the government had expected to derive from the expansion then under way. As a result, the Thatcher government was elected, resolutely committed to the implementation of a fully fledged orthodox policy which was to combine stringent policies to restrain demand through public spending cuts (with the significant exception of spending on army, police and prisons) with a willingness to allow interest rates and the exchange rate to appreciate to the point where rising costs would push unemployment up to the level required to bring down the wage rate and eliminate industrial militancy. Thus not only was there to be no interventionist policy to assist unprofitable industry, but wages and the exchange rate were also to be taken out of the political sphere and determined by market forces alone.

These policies were dressed up in the guise of a sophisticated advance in economic theory, popularly known as monetarism, which sought to attribute a scientific basis to what was essentially an exercise in destroying the capacity of the working class to resist wage and social welfare cuts. Indeed, the Bank of England has itself conceded that the adoption of 'monetary targeting' was essential as a means of distracting attention from the real objective, 'for, *inter alia*, output and employment' which, if disclosed, 'would either have been unacceptable to public opinion or else inadequate to secure a substantial reduction in the rate of inflation or both'.[87] In a masterly critique of the strategy (and, indeed, of the failures of the whole post-war period) Pollard sees it as operating in six steps:

> Its sole objective is to bring down the rate of inflation (step 1). The key mechanism for doing that is to reduce the quantity of money (2). In turn the reduction in the quantity of money, or at least its rate of increase below the inflation rate, is to be achieved by the two parallel methods of high interest rates (3a) and a cut-back in government spending (3b); this will create more unemployment (4) and incidentally thereby weaken the unions. With less money and credit available firms will have to reduce their price and cost increases (5) and in particular will have to resist the unions' wage demands, on pain of bankruptcy. Once the inflation has been 'squeezed out' of the economy, healthy growth without inflation may then be expected.[88]

The results of these policies have been almost entirely negative. Although wage increases have slowed down, trade union resistance has maintained them at levels above productivity growth, so that profits have hardly improved. Thus unemployment has been the major means of cutting consumption down to match reduced output, and this is now apparently to be allowed to remain at levels only reached reached during the worst years of the 1930s. Output fell in 1980 and again in 1981 by about 2.4 per cent; by the end of 1981 industrial production excluding oil and gas was 19.2 per cent below the 1973 peak, and in 1982 a weak recovery of 1 per cent was recorded.

In 1983, however, with the election in mind, a strong expansion took place in consumer spending based on the relaxation of hire-purchase regulations and a reduction in savings. Interest rates were brought down and with them the rate of exchange, particularly against the dollar. Exporters have been able to take advantage of the favourable conditions prevailing in the USA outlined at the end of Chapter 5, and growth has therefore risen to around 3 per cent. Yet this has yet to be established as a long-term trend, since the lack of investment has yet to be made good and serious problems still exist. Import penetration has increased sharply and a deficit on the balance of payments in manufactures emerged in 1983 for the first time since the industrial revolution. High US interest rates and the falling pound forced 2.5 per cent increase in the British rate in July 1984; should the American deficit be closed, as most observers feel it must, the deflationary effects on Britain and the rest of the system are likely to be severe.

Since 1981 the contribution to the balance of payments of oil has been about $20 billion a year, but in that year the actual surplus was about half that, declined to $6 billion in 1982, and is expected to disappear altogether in 1983[89] Without this fortuitous contribution, the effects of monetarist policies would have been unimaginably destructive; the fact that these policies have now so weakened the productive base that a deficit is just around the corner in spite of it, merely emphasises the seriousness of the situation.

To emphasise the fact that the worst aspects of the old habits of the 1950s and 1960s have not yet disappeared, the government has excelled its predecessors in its propensity to encourage the export of private capital and engage in military adventures of an absurdly expensive and vainglorious kind. In 1979 all controls over capital outflows were finally removed, on the assumption that this would help to keep down the exchange rate, and that, after an initial increase, there would be no large-scale outflow. In the event, despite a decline in the domestic savings ratio, these have grown astronomically, with outward portfolio investment alone totalling £4.2 billion in 1981, £5.8 billion in 1982, and £5.7 billion in 1983,[90] to the point where the foreign earnings of North Sea oil which have not been used to sustain domestic consumption have gone to finance external investment – a decision for which the country must pay dearly before very long. This response on the part of capital is entirely rational from a private point of view, since monetarist policies have been unable to bring the domestic rate of profit into line with that prevailing abroad, but it will, of course, further reduce the competitiveness of the industrial base and worsen an already bad situation. Again, the government has also organised a conscious regression into the practices of the imperialist past, committing itself to increased spending on defence in real terms each year and, in 1982, allowing itself to be drawn into a full-scale war in the South Atlantic. At a time when the social and economic infrastructure was being drastically reduced, an armada was dispatched to fight a ruinously expensive war to retain a piece of land supporting a population insufficient to occupy fully a single city street. Yet again, long-term commitments involving significant diversions from the urgent tasks of domestic reconstruction have been entered to support an overseas role which is both dubious in its own terms and impossible to justify in relation to the resources available to the economy as a whole.

Thus, what we have experienced in the 1980s is a remarkable combination of all of the worst policy errors of the past thirty years. With the immediate balance of payments constraint temporarily lifted by North Sea oil, the government has organised a deflation more savage than any undertaken in the past to meet the most serious external crises. It has combined the inevitable loss of domestic investment stemming from these policies with the active encouragement of the foreign investment of a very large proportion of domestic surpluses overseas, thus ensuring that they should be used to strengthen further the position of those competitors whose products are driving domestic production out of our own markets. To complete this catalogue of imbecility, the further growth of these surpluses is being guaranteed by cutting social and economic infrastructure investments by the state, while non-productive investment in the weapons of destruction and in the assertion of an essentially nineteenth-century imperial role is being increased. It is little wonder that the problems of future adjustment are being created which must soon involve disruptions on a scale as yet entirely unimagined.

Evaluation

The material contained in the preceeding pages is intended to substantiate two broad propositions: that the British commitment to a centre country role between 1945 and 1972 was a major factor in its international economic decline, and that its attempts to deal with the problems of decline in an increasingly open and market-determined international environment from the mid-1950s onwards has become an increasingly counter-productive contributor to yet further decline. These arguments, if accepted, then serve to substantiate the central hypotheses of this book – that no national economy can bear the weight of international economic management without undermining its own viability and thus its ability to sustain the role over the long term, and that once forced into a position of relative weakness,the operation of an open, competitive international economic system will intensify problems of uneven development rather than moderate them. These conclusions, in turn, require that we accept that the price of international integration must be the creation of a multinational agency – *a form of world government* – capable of redistributing sufficient resources from strong centres to weak to offset the tendencies to inequality and destabilisation which will inevitably emerge in its absence. Where this does not exist, weak countries like Britain must either adopt protection or deflate in response to balance of payments deficit, and thus, by cutting consumption and investment, solve the short-term problem by intensifying their underlying structural weakness.

The current structure of the international economy is based upon the body of orthodox economic theory which assumes a natural tendency towards even development, and which therefore entirely underestimates the costs involved in both international management and in the deflationary policy responses which have always to be accepted by deficit countries where the government is allowed neither adequate external resources, nor the policies that enable it to organise a controlled domestic investment programme protected from the worst effects of international competition. The British case clearly demonstrates how mistaken these views are. While it is probable that Britain might have avoided the worst effects of its post-war failure by refusing to take on the international burden – by refusing to re-arm, repudiating much of its debt, prohibiting out-flows of capital and rebuilding its own economy within protective barriers as did Germany and Japan – this would also have greatly increased the load on the Americans, intensified isolationism there, and possibly induced a breakdown in the system much earlier than the one that eventually occurred in 1971. Thus it is important that we should not ignore the positive consequences of the British role, but it is equally important that we recognise that a system which requires self-destructive sacrificies on the part of the centre country can hardly hope to maintain itself over the long term. Furthermore, when we now survey a society in which there is 16 per cent unemployment, a continuous reduction in the level of social provision, the wholesale destruction of productive resources, and growing and increasingly violent social tensions, we can also see that the long-term costs of constant recourse to deflationary policies are so great that they must inevitably lead to a reversion to protectionism unless some positive international solution can be found.

In Britain such a solution has already been put forward as a central plank in Labour Party policy, and it is now being seen by many French socialists as the only alternative to the austerity into which their government was forced as a result of a balance of payments crisis in 1982. Defending the Brettons Woods agreement in the House of Lords in 1944, Keynes asserted that its provisions would forever remove the need for sacrifices of this kind and therefore open up the way for international interventions capable of sustaining the conditions for full employment in the world economy as a whole.[91] In the event, the machinery he helped to design has been proved too flimsy to bear the weight imposed upon it. Unless it can be improved, the pressures stemming from the weaker countries must induce a reversion to the protectionism of the 1930s.

Before taking up the most serious aspects of the problem of uneven development in the next chapter, it is perhaps worth saying a little about other arguments which some would claim are far more important than the problem of the external balance in explaining the underdevelopment of the British economy. Other accounts have emphasised the high cost and restrictive attitudes of the British labour force, the organisational and psychological inadequacies of the managerial and entrepreneurial elite, and the excessive growth of the state apparatus and of welfare provision. Space does not permit a full examination of all of these, nor is this entirely essential, given the brilliant exposition of the case argued in this book to be found in Pollard's now classic economic history and his recent monograph.[92]

Rather than go through all of these arguments, therefore, it seems more useful to emphasise not so much the superiority of an externally oriented approach, but the way in which it serves to explain the persistence of many of the phenomena identified in these other accounts. Looked at at any point in time, it is no doubt true that British labour has been paid more than its productivity warrants, that managers have not shown the entrepreneurial flair required to maintain their international role, and that state provision has been so expensive that it has crowded out the 'marketed goods' sector. Yet all of these problems, as Pollard effectively demonstrates, depend in turn upon the long-term failure to sustain the rate of investment required to ensure that innovations can be turned into new products, taxes increased to finance services without excessive pressure, and, most especially, wages increased without eliminating the rate of profit. Thus, as he says, 'the difference between British and foreign experience was not that money wages rose here; but that the increased costs were absorbed by rising productivity elsewhere, but not in the United Kingdom'.[93]

Once this inadequacy in managerial performance and imbalance between wages and productivity is consolidated, of course, it has the effect of creating a vicious circle which further worsens the problem and becomes an independent variable in its own right. But what the historic record shows is that the problem of the external balance pre-dated the emergence of this discrepancy, and that it was the policies adopted to deal with it which pushed down the rate of investment to the point where these further imbalances became inevitable. We have attempted to show in some detail that each phase of deflation, inevitably involving lost production and a massive disincentive to investors, was initiated by the need to defend sterling in the particular circumstances that had come into existence after the relaxation of external controls in the early 1950s. Pollard writes:

Thus, in the crisis of 1947–51 some future growth was sacrificed though the productive capacity was not wasted. It was merely diverted from investment to exports. Since then, however, this approach has become a permanent, and increasingly effective, feature of the British economy. Moreover, as it became increasingly difficult to market potential exports, the capacity abstracted from capital formation was no longer diverted to exports but was kept unemployed. Thus the main cause of the low investment, and hence the low growth rate, in Britain is easily stated: the whole of the considerable apparatus of Government economic power, especially as exercised by the Treasury, has been applied during the major part of the period under discussion to achieving it.[94]

The cumulative effects of the succession of deflations which external weakness imposed on policy from the mid-1950s onwards had thus reduced Britain to the status of a second rank industrial producer by 1976, and left the government with two choices: either to accept mass unemployment and further stagnation as the price to be paid for external balance with free trade, or to revert to the protectionism and interventionism which had made reconstruction and the post-war boom possible. The fact that both the Labour government in 1976 and the Tories in 1979 adopted the former has since immeasurably worsened the underlying problem and guaranteed that the final rejection must involve far heavier costs than would have been necessary if a more adequate policy had been arranged either on the basis of a more adequate system of international co-operation or, if that had failed, through a more thoroughgoing restructuring of the country's external policies and commitments. Much more needs to be said about the costs and difficulties implicit in both of these options, but this must wait until the final chapter.

PART III

Underdevelopment in the International System

Prologue

The gap in productivity that still exists between North and South is, without doubt, the most significant feature of the contemporary world economy. Access to an immense accumulation of skills and technology provides some peoples with great wealth, its absence elsewhere confines others to lives of drudgery and destitution. This inequality enables the rich nations to appropriate the lion's share of the earth's resources, and to exercise a dominating influence over the opportunities open to the rest. It is in large part because the Third World is too poor to consume what the First World can produce, and too ill-equipped to compete on equal terms in international markets, that the world system is now in crisis and must be restructured on more equitable lines if it is not to disintegrate altogether. Nor can we assume that the situation is getting any better. As the second Brandt Report points out:

> In the 1970s the developing countries' imports from the North, partly financed by their commercial borrowing, helped to prevent the recession in the industrial countries from getting worse, sustaining production and employment ... Today that effect is reversed; the downturn of growth in developing countries deprives Northern exporters of their markets: and the decline in developing countries' imports is accelerating as major countries in Africa and Latin America run short of foreign exchange. Even more dangerous ... the plight of these countries threatens the international financial system itself.[1]

Thus one concern of this section must be with the nature of the international policies and relationships that have impinged upon this structure of uneven development, and with their broader political implications.

Yet when we come to look at the South, we find that its own internal structure is also marked by cleavages almost as sharp as those which cut it off from the industrialised countries. Within a small number of countries, centres of industrial activity have emerged which have been characterised by rapid rates of growth in productivity and social organisation, growth rates which have in some cases been faster than those ever witnessed before. Against this we find vast regions, containing the bulk of the world's population, where growth has been slow, intermittent, or even negative. Thus the problem of uneven development involves not merely the implications of the unequal relationship between the Third World and the First, but also those of the increasingly unequal relationships that have developed between countries and regions within the Third World itself.

Now the implications of these inequalities, and more especially of the way in which they have evolved since the war, are very difficult to evaluate, and have been the subject of intense theoretical disagreement. Indeed, even apparently objective descriptions of the present conditions of the Third World present us with strongly contrasting pictures of it, depending upon the ideological and theoretical orientations of their authors, orientations closely related to the three intellectual positions set out in Chapter 2.

For many liberal observers the predominant feeling is one of optimism – a belief that a number of former colonies and dependencies have transformed themselves into 'newly industrialising countries' (NICs) by appropriating Western technology, finance and markets, and using them to sustain unparalleled rates of growth in industry, agriculture and in the skills and resources of their peoples. By adopting rational market-oriented strategies, and by fully exploiting both domestic and external opportunities, they have broken out of the vicious circle of underdevelopment and given the lie to those who have asserted that this can only be achieved by those willing to 'de-link' from the capitalist world economy. For these observers the many failures in the Third World are the result not of the necessary operation of the capitalist market mechanism, but of the 'irrational government interventions' introduced in response to incorrect theories designed to correct its supposed imperfections.[2] Thus although they recognise that only a small proportion of the countries in the Third World have taken off into sustained growth, they see their achievement as clear evidence that any other countries will be able to do so if only they, too, are willing to adopt the policies that are essential to make it possible.

For many Marxist theorists, however, the dominant feature of the Third World is the fact that a billion of its people now live in conditions of absolute and deteriorating poverty. Because they cannot buy, the rich in the First World cannot sell, so that food mountains grow and factories and workers stand idle. Because their poverty and exploitation breeds crime and revolt, their governments are run by soldiers who use their resources to buy weapons to repress their own peoples rather than the machinery with which to liberate them. Because their repression breeds apathy and corruption, opportunities for progress cannot be taken and the resources that are available are squandered. And because exploitation in the Third World enriches many in the First, the governments of both are joined in a conspiracy of violence designed to hold together an edifice which would otherwise disintegrate under the pressure of its inner contradictions.

None of these views can be entirely rejected, since each chooses to emphasise particular pieces of experience which are manifestly real and which legitimately support the inferences that each draws about the nature of the operation of the system as a whole. The dynamism of the NICs is as real as the squalor and degradation of the masses of the poor, and the need for rational structures of economic management and of competitive market-oriented solutions to a wide range of micro-problems cannot be denied. Yet we cannot simply juxtapose these two views and leave it at that, since, in their pure form they imply contradictory understandings of reality and contrasting solutions to the problems that confront us. If the optimists are right we must all work to 'ensure that the post-war *liberal* international economic order is maintained',[3] in the confident expectation that the elimination of irrational interferences with it will sooner rather than later allow the poor to catch up with the rich and provide an effective basis for the organisation of a productive and equitable global division of labour. If they are not, as this book has argued, then new forms of global and national intervention will have to be found that are capable of offsetting both the negative effects of unfettered competition as well as much of the irrationality, corruption and waste associated with a very large proportion of the interventionist policies that have been tried in the past.

Between these two extreme views can be found a third, strongly influenced by Keynesian and protectionist theory, which recognises a 'structural' tendency to inequality and underdevelopment in the South arising out of existing international arrangements, but which assumes that this can be effectively offset through policies which will not involve a major break with existing political and economic arrangements. This is perhaps the dominant view of decision-makers and their advisers in the South itself, and dominant in a broad range of work associated with the activities of UNCTAD, the UN in its attempts to create a New International Economic Order (NIEO) and, most recently, in the two reports produced by the Brandt Commission. These essentially 'reformist' views refrain from challenging the positions of existing governments and of the MNCs, and assume that there is, in the last analysis, an essential mutuality of interests in the relationship between the rich world and the poor. They therefore reject revolutionary solutions involving the expropriation of capital and the overthrow of governments, but also argue that free trade and non-intervention will intensify existing structures of inequality and dependence. They therefore advocate the interventionist policies outlined in the second part of Chapter 2, and most especially the need for a much larger direct contribution by rich countries to the developmental needs of those in the South.

While the violent overthrow of corrupt regimes and degenerate capitalist structures may be essential in some places, this may be impossible or unnecessary in others where real policy interventions will have to be based on a dispassionate and rigorous examination of the real options embedded in the bodies of existing theory outlined earlier. Indeed, once in power even the most revolutionary movements have to come to terms with the intractable realities of poverty and scarce resources, and to adopt policies that will attempt to maximise returns from both domestic and international activities. Although it was once commonplace for Marxist regimes to reject market theory as an aspect of irrational capitalist exploitation, more and more of them are coming to accept its value in significant areas, and even to associate this with increasing collaboration with Western MNCs and financial markets.

Thus this part of the book will attempt an evaluation of the overall trajectory of development in the South in relation to a pattern of experiences and theories which is both complex and contradictory. Given the complexity of this experience, it will be impossible to give a detailed account of the actual process of change comparable to that provided for Britain in Chapter 6, or to deal with the development of the theoretical debate in anything but the broadest outline. Instead, Chapter 7 will attempt a brief summary of the experience of post-war growth and the changes in economic policy associated with it, and Chapter 8 an evaluation of the theoretical debate that has emerged out of it and, more especially, of the way in which this has been related to the integration of the LDCs into the official international economic agencies with which we have been concerned. In conclusion, we will consider the crucial and now critical role played by private banking capital in the relations between North and South since the 1970s, and the fundamental problems which this has created for the whole structure of international economic management and development.

7

Policies and Development in the Third World

The long boom, 1945–1971

At the end of the Second World War the majority of LDCs existed as direct or indirect dependencies of the leading industrial countries, tied into the autarchic monetary and trading blocs that had been established during the 1930s. Their economies were deeply integrated into the world system, but largely as raw material exporters and importers of manufactured consumer goods. Their needs and interests were defined for them by their colonial mentors who, for the most part, assumed that a natural harmony of interests existed between their 'comparative advantage' in the production of raw materials, as opposed to that in the production of manufactured goods in the industrial centres.[1] Thus, at the time of the Bretton Woods conference, the vast majority of the world's population lived in territories which were neither politically nor economically autonomous, so that the liberal vision of an open world system which dominated that meeting had even less validity in the reality of the Third World than it had in the First.

Yet a number of Third World countries were at least nominally independent when the war ended, and virtually all of the rest were to achieve the same status over the following twenty years. Although they tended to maintain many of the existing monetary and trading links with their former metropolitan countries, they were now free to join the international economic agencies in their own right, and to devise domestic and foreign economic policies designed to maximise their own interests rather than those of their erstwhile colonial mentors.

For virtually all of these countries the first priority became rapid industrialisation, an industrialisation which they saw as the only means of eliminating the poverty, ignorance and disease which they felt to be the most significant legacy of the colonial system. Though complex in its details, the development problem was therefore seen to be simple in its essentials: how to acquire the foreign exchange required to buy the Western capital equipment needed to sustain a rapid transition from primary to industrial production, and how to organise the domestic economy in such a way that conditions would be created in which these 'infant industries' would prosper and grow. The former would inevitably mean an even deeper integration into international trading and financial networks than before, the latter the need to create conditions that would enable domestic producers to compete effectively with their well-established foreign rivals. Thus successful development would depend directly upon an ability to manage the international dimension by overcoming the potential foreign exchange gap on the one hand, and guaranteeing efficient domestic production processes on the other. Domestically the success of this effort was to depend upon the adequacy of the state apparatus and the local and foreign private producers; internationally upon the financial flows emanating from the industrial countries together with the nature of the monetary and trading regime affecting the movement of commodities, capital and labour. We can now consider the way in which these problems were approached and growth stimulated or retarded, by looking at the nature of the economic policies adopted to deal with their external dependence, and the relationship between external flows, policy orientations, and the trajectory of development itself.

The political economy of colonialism had been based upon the integration of the LDCs into the world economy as suppliers of raw materials and as markets for Western consumer goods and the capital equipment for basic infrastructure. For the most part local manufacturing was discouraged, although not always altogether successfully.[2] At independence the commitment to industrialisation also included a more or less uncritical desire to base the new industry on the most advanced technology already developed in the West, so that the fundamental international economic problem was to find the foreign exchange required to import the necessary capital equipment. It was the expectation that their capacity to earn the requisite currency through exports would always prove inade-

quate (for the reasons set out in Chapter 2) which generated the
almost universal belief in the inevitability of a foreign exchange gap
which could only be bridged by protection of domestic output and
foreign aid.[3] Thus, according to Bienefeld:

> the wide and absolute gap in income and technology between
> today's industrialised and developing countries ... created a
> powerful and continuous tension between the almost unlimited
> number of internationally produced goods, which (apart from the
> ability to pay) the underdeveloped countries would find more
> useful and desirable than domestically produced goods, and,
> conversely, the small and restricted number of their domestically
> produced goods which can be sold on the international market.
> Indeed this tension is such a dominant characteristic of modern
> underdevelopment that the way in which a country seeks to deal
> with it must be regarded as a central feature of its development.[4]

In the more 'radical' countries like India, Indonesia and Ghana,
interventionism was seen as a manifestation of socialism, and
included a substantial degree of direct state ownership of the new
industrial capacity. But even in the less radical countries, state
power was used to provide favoured producers with monopoly
positions within the domestic market, privileged access to foreign
exchange for imported inputs, and often direct subsidies of various
sorts. Externally it involved continuous efforts to maximise the
inflow of capital, particularly through concessional official sources,
but increasingly from the private market as well; and also in the
majority of cases, strong attempts after the early 1960s to attract
private foreign investment through the creation of favourable conditions for the generation and repatriation of profits. This complex
of policies is now generally referred to as import substituting
industrialisation or ISI.

Politically this strategy could find strong allies, both domestically
and internationally. It involved, in the first instance, a diversion of
resources from the traditional raw materials-exporting producers to
a new industrial bourgeoisie, together with a tax on all consumers
now forced to use expensive domestic products in place of cheaper
foreign imports. While these sacrifices could be called for in the
name of nationalism, regimes could expect strong support from

both the new bourgeoisie benefiting from protection and a rapidly expanded bureaucracy created to administer the new economic machinery. For this class, both their new managerial positions and a wide range of unofficial payments stemming from the state's capacity to grant economic favours guaranteed consistent support for interventionism. For international capital the transition from colonial exchange to ISI probably produced more opportunities than costs. Some consumer goods producers in the advanced countries had been able to survive through their protected access to colonial markets, and would no longer be able to do so. But some of the more progressive were to be able to set up subsidiaries in LDCs behind protective barriers and exploit the opportunities created by the new regimes,[5] while the Western capital goods producers were now presented with significant new markets as industrial investment got underway. This whole process was further expedited through the growth of large-scale aid financing, which was primarily intended to provide the LDCs with the credit required to acquire the exports from the country which provided it and, more especially, the output of industries threatened with the emergence of surplus capacity.[6]

This alliance between capitalist and bureaucratic elements in more and less developed countries in support of ISI was a necessarily asymmetrical one, given the dependence of the latter on the technology, organisational skills and capital controlled by the former. Whether, as crude theories of imperialism would have it, the actual results (and more especially the failures) should be simply seen as the outcome of the dominance of international capital over economic decision-making in LDCs is a more problematic issue, which would have to take into account the problems involved in identifying a viable alternative non-Western route to industrialisation and the clear involvement of a wide range of Third World interests in their formulation and execution. Some of these issues will be taken up later; here we will be more concerned with the relative successes and failures of the ISI strategy and, more especially, with the reasons for the fundamental re-evaluation of the whole strategy in the 1960s.

Growth in the 1950s, and more especially in the 1960s, was uneven but not unimpressive. According to Little, it 'accelerated in all regions except South Asia, and possibly Africa' in the 1950s, when few figures are available;[7] in the low-income countries it increased by 3.6 per cent, and in the middle-income countries by 5.7 per cent between 1960 and 1970.[8] This can be compared with growth of 4.7 per cent in the industrialised countries, and was sufficient to produce improvements in per capita income which were faster than those in 'any comparable period before 1950 and [which] exceeded both official goals and private expectations'.[9] Industry grew more rapidly than growth as a whole (by 6.7 per cent in low- and 7.6 per cent in middle-income countries), and significantly increased its share of exports.[10] Total foreign private investment from the OECD countries was $57.6 billion between 1956 and 1970, averaging $2.66 billion between 1956 and 1960, $3.18 between 1961 and 1965, and $5.68 between 1966 and 1970.[11] Of this, about a half originated in the USA by the end of the period, more than a half was invested in raw material production, just over a quarter in manufacturing and the rest in public utilities and services.[12] Inflows of official development assistance totalled $86.2 billion between 1956 and 1970, the corresponding five yearly averages being $4.08 billion, $6.04 billion and $7.1 billion respectively.[13]

Alongside these trends was a rapid but uneven growth in LDC export earnings. These grew by 3.8 per cent per annum between 1950 and 1959, with non-oil exporters only growing by 2.1 per cent. But between 1960 and 1969 total exports grew by 6.6 per cent, those of non-oil exporters by 6.2 per cent. This improvement was almost entirely due to the expansion in manufactured exports, since these (starting from a very low base) grew by 15 per cent, while raw material exports grew more slowly.[14] Despite this export growth, LDC balance of payments on current account were always in deficit, averaging about $4.4 billion between 1960 and 1966, and about $7 billion between 1967 and 1970.[15] Yet such 'development deficits' were only to be expected from capital-importing countries, and were well covered by the aid and long-term capital flows already described. Thus, although particular countries were often seriously troubled by a balance of payments constraint, it would be wrong to argue that there was anything that could be described as a general balance of payments crisis until 1974.

These figures compare very favourably with the historical experience of both the LDCs and even of the DCs during their transition to industrialisation, and strongly suggest that many countries were able to benefit directly from the favourable conditions created by the post-war boom and decolonisation. Given the significant advances in growth rates, trade and industrialisation, it would be wrong to accept a crude characterisation of the North-South relationship as no more than an imperialistic transfer of surpluses from periphery to centre. Although the terms of trade moved slightly against LDCs from the mid-1950s to the late 1960s,[16] this was not sufficient to offset a substantial growth in export earnings stemming from increased exports of raw materials and more especially of simple manufactures. The 'export pessimism' which served as the fundamental presupposition of the protectionist thinking behind ISI could now be strongly questioned by liberal theorists whose market-oriented views were soon to displace those of the interventionists as the official orthodoxy.

Yet these generally favourable developments in no way suggested that existing policies had solved the development problem, because they concealed large inequalities in performance and the emergence of serious structural dislocations in many places. The reasons for these problems, and more especially the theoretical and policy conclusions to be derived from them, are very complex and the subject of serious and unreconciled intellectual dispute, but there can be no doubt that they had demonstrated that fundamental rethinking of the policy theory inherited from the 1940s and 1950s would be essential if a viable process of even development was to be established. What were the most important problems that emerged during this period, and what were the most important theoretical responses to them?

Firstly, at the level of the world economy, the relatively small excess of LDC growth rates over those of the DCs, combined with rapid population growth in the latter countries, meant that the 'gap' between them continued to widen, as it had done over the preceding 100 to 150 years. As a result, 'the per capita income of the developing countries as a proportion of that of the developed countries stayed fairly constant, at around 7 to 8 per cent', while the gap in GNP per capita between OECD and LDC countries widened from $2,191 in 1950 to $4,839 in 1975 (in constant 1974 dollars).[17] This growth in relative deprivation at the international level was associated with a serious increase in internal inequality and even of absolute impoverishment of the poorest groups in many countries.[18] Thus the moral/political problem associated with the development of an integrated international economic community characterised by rapidly increasing real inequalities of income continued to intensify, making it impossible for the South to share the rather complacent assumptions as to its value which were by then characteristic of attitudes in the North. Further, it also meant that the global problem of uneven development, and more especially of underconsumption in the South, had only been very partially relieved, leaving it to emerge as a critical problem for the equilibrium of the global system in the 1970s as soon as OECD growth rates slowed down.

Secondly, the 1950s and 1960s also saw a sharp increase in the inequalities within the South itself, with the NICs and oil exporters significantly outperforming the rest. Thus while the average growth rates for the least developed countries in the 1960s was 4.6 per cent, with almost half of them achieving per capita growth rates of 1 per cent or less, growth rates of the six countries usually characterised as NICs were between 7 and 10 per cent and per capita increases varied from 3 to 7.5 per cent.[19] More generally, although there was no necessary correlation between 'initial income level and subsequent growth rate', the 'absolute disparity between the richest and the poorest developing nations increased by a factor of about three'.[20] The role of MNCs can be shown to have strongly reinforced this tendency towards uneven development, as suggested by Chapter 4. According to an authoritative UN report, they 'tended to concentrate in a few developing countries', with 43 per cent of the stock of direct investment concentrated in some seven countries, and a further 30 per cent in another thirteen.[21] Thus, far from diminishing, the tendency towards uneven development accelerated during this period within the South itself, blurring the distinction between LDCs and DCs at the top end of the scale, but greatly intensifying it as between the low-income and middle-income LDCs. By 1972, therefore, a new structural problem had been identified:

It has become more and more clear that measures designed to help developing countries as a group have not been effective for these least-developed countries. They face difficulties of a special kind and intensity; they need help specifically designed to deal with their problems.[22]

Thirdly, despite relatively favourable growth rates, serious structural problems had emerged in a number of important ISI countries, which demonstrated that their momentum could not be sustained unless changes in policy were introduced. The very high levels of protection, the subsidisation of capital-intensive industrialisation out of traditional export earnings, and the difficulties associated with close administrative control of the allocation process, produced a number of structural imbalances which were to have serious economic and political consequences. The balance of payments remained in chronic deficit as a result of the excessive costs of capital-intensive capital goods imports and the large transfers of resources from traditional exporting sectors required to finance them. Employment growth was constrained by the nature of the new technology, while inequalities intensified for the same reason. Inefficiency and waste grew as the capacity of the state apparatuses proved unequal to the task of regulation and allocation required of them by the interventionist and centrist nature of the policy; the lack of effective political supervision and control of the bureaucracy produced corruption of a gross and debilitating kind. The resulting imbalances between supply and demand produced chronic inflation, which further worsened income distribution and undermined efficiency.[23] Politically these results engendered profound disillusion with the role of particular regimes and, indeed, of the state machinery itself. As a result, military intervention became commonplace and was often initially accorded considerable public support.

Now there is nothing intrinsic to these policies which suggests that they must lead to the above results, since, as we saw in Part II, their general principles were no different from those applied with considerable success in the advanced industrial countries during the immediate post-war reconstruction period. Equally, however, there is no guarantee that they will lead to a successful outcome unless they are applied with intelligence and administered by a state apparatus capable of imposing an effective discipline on the producers responsible for creating the new domestic industrial output. More especially, it will only be capable of doing this if it is willing, perhaps even forced through external political controls, to impose a similar discipline on itself by controlling the worst excesses of corruption and enforcing adequate standards of administration. It took the experience of the 1950s and 1960s in these countries to demonstrate that the principles of ISI had been taken to unsustainable extremes. Levels of protection had been raised in some cases to the point where they engendered large-scale smuggling and domestic costs for the production of domestic commodities so far out of line with the cost of equivalent imports that there could be little doubt that the resources would have been better used elsewhere.[24] Perhaps more important, the interventionist thinking implicit in ISI was a direct descendant of the Western social democratic tradition which itself presupposed the existence of a developed administrative machinery constrained by a functioning process of democratic accountability, however imperfect. But as Lal says:

Despite their trappings of modernity, many developing countries are closer in their official workings to the rapacious and inefficient nation states of 17th or 18th century Europe, governed as much for the personal aggrandisement of their rulers as for the welfare of the ruled.[25]

It would be foolish to pretend that he is wrong.

Thus we are fully justified in asking whether the failures in question were the result of the misapplication of the principles of ISI, or the *excesses* of protectionism and administrative control, rather than of interventionism *per se*. In an important critique of the new liberal orthodoxy, Bienefeld notes that although particular instances of political intervention are 'frequently a mistake', nevertheless 'there is no doubt that the conditions which justify it do exist':

They arise whenever the divergence between national and international levels of efficiency is such that an unqualified application of the competitive principle would demand a degree of social or political change which was either unattainable or undesirable for social or political reasons, or simply because it impaired the economy's long-term competitiveness. Furthermore, such conditions are more likely to apply: when the efficiency differential to be bridged is very wide; when the technological level of the weaker economies is such that they must seek to attain competitiveness primarily by means of lowering their labour costs; when the global economy is far removed from full employment and especially when this is also true within the leading economies; when the transfer of technology as between different types of economies is relatively inhibited; and when there are significant dynamic economies to be derived within particular nations by an intensive, nationally coherent and forward looking allocation of investible resources.[26]

But the liberal critique of ISI did not depend primarily upon a rigorous demonstration of the non-existence of these conditions, but upon another crucially important historical experience of the period – the very rapid growth rates and successful industrialisation experienced by a limited number of mainly small Third World economies which adopted a programme of *export-oriented indus-trialisation* (EOI) with considerable success. At the end of the 1950s these had come to the end of the initial phase of ISI, since they could no longer expand the production of non-durable consumer goods for the domestic market which was now saturated, and had to choose between moving into the production of durable consumer goods and the simpler producer goods for the domestic market, or into an expansion of manufactured output for the world market. If the work of the ISI theorists was to be believed, the latter could not expect to succeed because the output of Third World industry would not be able to compete on equal terms with established producers or world markets. But, placing their faith in the comparative advantage to be derived from their low-cost labour, they opted for exports and were quickly rewarded with very rapid growth. Manufactured output and exports increased dramatically, as did industrial employment. Once full employment had been achieved, wages also began to grow, so that 'the distribution of income seems not to have worsened, even to have improved ... during the period of most rapid early transition growth'.[27] The predictions of both structuralist and Marxist theory had apparently been falsified, so it is hardly surprising that this experience quickly became the most significant single piece of evidence put forward by liberal theorists in their opposition to their radical critics. Thus, according to Little, perhaps the most influential of the new liberal school, the dependency theorists' assertion of a necessary connection between integration into the world capitalist system and underdevelopment was effectively disproved 'by the performance of the "baby tigers"'.[28]

Given the immense theoretical and ideological significance of this experience, we have therefore to look very carefully at what was involved and what has been inferred from it. There can be little doubt that the policies adopted by the smaller NICs were closer to

the teachings of liberal orthodoxy than those of the extreme prac-
titioners of ISI. According to Ranis:

> Any enhanced orientation towards international markets on a
> competitive basis required a reduction in protection, the adop-
> tion and maintenance of more realistic exchange rates, interest
> rates closer to shadow levels, and the continued avoidance of the
> temptation to depress domestic agriculture's terms of trade
> artificially.[29]

Interestingly enough, MNCs do not appear to have been leading
actors in export promotion during this period, being primarily
concerned with the exploitation of the domestic market opportunities provided by ISI in the larger LDCs. Indeed, it can be argued
that the new strategy was the result of pressure from *domestic*
manufacturing bourgeoisie created during the earlier import substitution phase, but now concerned to escape the constraints on
further expansion imposed by the size of the national market.[30]
Equally important, the reduction of subsidies for the import of
capital-intensive producer goods associated with EOI also appears
to have led to the adoption of a much more 'appropriate' labour-
intensive technology for the new export industries, and, with more
favourable treatment of agriculture, to have led to a more balanced
growth overall. This combination of expanding manufactured and
raw material exports, together with adequate food production for
the domestic economy, all but eliminated the balance of payments
constraint, while its reduction of the 'import licensing systems,
overvalued exchange rates, [and] official low interest rates for
favoured borrowers'[31] greatly reduced the subsidies which had
previously gone to a small segment of the most favoured industrial-
ists. This, as a perceptive World Bank critic of ISI had pointed out,
had meant that its policy had never been one oriented to the needs
of the poor, but necessarily involved 'some form of "subsidized
capitalism" [involving] a transfer of resources from a poor taxpayer
or consumer to an investor who is usually a man or a group of men of
means'.[32] Associated with the rest of these policies was a relative
liberalisation of interest rates and the creation of a freer domestic
credit market. This was also given great prominence by McKinnon
and Shaw, two influential monetarist theorists who could now
attribute the greater part of the failure of many developmental

experiments to 'financial repression' – the imposition of rigid ceilings on interest rates by central governments which they felt had inhibited the growth in domestic savings.[33]

This liberal case was therefore clearly one which rested on both the good growth performance of the NICs and on their relatively successful distributional record. Since this body of theory had become the new developmental orthodoxy by the end of the 1960s and was to dominate policy thinking, especially in the international agencies, in the 1980s, it will be best to consider events during that period before producing a systematic critique of its empirical base, assumptions and relevance at the end of the chapter.

The crisis years, 1971–1984

The relatively positive performance of the Third World economies in the 1950s and 1960s was, of course, closely associated with the long boom in the industrial countries which had meant expanding demand for raw materials, full employment and trade liberalisation, stable exchange rates, and regular expansion of aid and private capital flows in absolute if not in relative terms. But the security and dynamism of the 1960s was to give way very dramatically in the 1970s and 1980s to a new phase of structural dislocation, reduced growth and uneven development which has yet to be brought under control. We must now consider its most important effects on the LDCs, and more especially on the way in which it has influenced their relationships with the international agencies and industrial countries and the theoretical debate through which these relationships have been understood. Before doing this, however, it should be useful to provide a brief overview of the most important development in the international context during the period.

The American repudiation of their Bretton Woods undertakings in 1971, and the collapse of the fixed exchange rate system in 1973, clearly indicated that the stability of a quarter of a century had come to an end. Almost immediately, oil prices were increased fourfold, pushing the structure of international payments into extreme disequilibrium. The oil exporters were suddenly able to transfer a substantial surplus to themselves, leaving the LDCs and DCs with very large deficits. For the first time in the post-war period output failed to increase, and only the creation of mechanisms for large-scale international lending prevented the development of a deep depression. After 1975 the strongest of the industrial countries were able to restore their balance of payments to equilibrium, but the LDCs were only able to survive by accumulating a growing burden of debt. Indeed, this 'privilege' was also very unevenly allocated, with the more advanced countries being able to borrow very freely, but the poorest hardly at all. For them the recession turned into a real depression, with imports being severely cut with drastic consequences for investment, growth and consumption.

Oil prices then declined in real terms until 1978, and with them the scale of the overall deficits in the system. Yet for those who prefer to believe that the problems of the last decade have been entirely created by the ability of the OPEC countries to exploit their monopoly power, the balance of payments figures of the period repay careful examination. The deficits of non-oil LDCs (NOLDCs) increased from $11.5 billion in 1973 to $45.9 billion in 1975; they then declined to $28.6 billion in 1977, but rose again to $35.8 billion in 1978, *before* the next major oil price increase, and at a time when the OPEC countries' surpluses declined from $31.9 billion to $5 billion.[34] Clearly, the imbalances within the international economic system now transcend those between an oil cartel with near monopoly power and the rest, and were directly related to the growing relative weakness of the NOLDCs in relation to the rest of the global system.

As if this were not enough, the collapse of the Iranian government at the end of 1978 and the consequent drastic reduction in its oil supplies produced a further escalation in oil prices and deficits. Only renewed borrowing on an even larger scale prevented a deep depression, and here again the poorest countries received very little, with devastating results:

Output per capita fell during the 1970s in 15 countries of Sub-Saharan Africa. In other Sub-Saharan countries and in some of the poorest ones of other regions, production barely expanded faster than population growth. In food production . . . the figures were even more alarming: no growth between 1970 and 1980 in per capita terms in the low income countries as a group: food production falling behind population growth in 31 of these countries. The 'least-developed' countries also registered declines in gross domestic investment, manufacturing output, export purchasing power and import volume during most of the 1970s. World Bank projections for 1980s for all of Sub-Saharan Africa, except the oil-exporting countries, range from stagnation in per capita GDP to a 10% decline.[35]

In the industrial countries the recession which began at the end of 1979 lasted into 1983 and was then not followed by a sharp increase in output, as had been the case in 1975 when governments had used expansionist policies to counteract increased unemployment. Now, obsessed with the need to end the inflation which had become chronic, they almost universally adopted tight monetary policies with high interest rates and reduced public spending. Unemployment and reduced growth resulted, with the structural dislocation intensified by the impact of a massive dose of industrial restructuring to incorporate the new technology based upon dramatic improvements in electronics and automation. As a result there was a sharp fall in raw material prices, which meant that in real terms they 'were lower in 1982 than at any time since World War II'.[36] For those not fully initiated into the complexity of neoclassical trade theory, the post-war development of raw materials prices, as reflected in Figure 7.1, must certainly suggest that the Prebisch assertion of their long-term tendency to decline deserves more attention than it has been given in recent years.[37]

This decline, combined with the increased interest rates in the industrial countries, also imposed heavy costs upon the more advanced LDCs which had been able to borrow on a large scale. By 1982 many of these were unable to meet their commitments, were forced (*de facto*) to default on their debts, and this threatened both the stability of the international banking system and the viability of their own hitherto healthy growth rates. The problems of the banking system and the relation of the debt crisis to the overall development of the global system are significant and technical, and will be dealt with in Chapter 9. Here it is important for us to note that it has forced several major industrialising countries (most of Latin America and Nigeria in particular) into austerity measures which must have a strongly deflationary effect upon the level of activity of the world economy as a whole. Thus, in 1983, the World Bank's authoritative *World Development Report* examined the likely results of average growth rates of only 2.5 per cent in the industrial countries between 1985 and 1995, and found them

Figure 7.1   Composite commodity price index, 1948–82

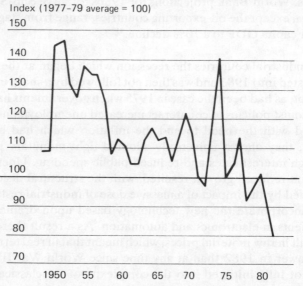

Index (1977–79 average = 100)

The graph shows non-oil commoditity prices as measured by the price of manufactures imported by developing countries. The commodities are coffee, cocoa, tea, maize, rice, wheat, sorghum, soybeans, groundnuts, palm oil, coconut oil, copra, groundnut oil, soybean meal, sugar, beef, bananas, oranges, cotton, jute, rubber, tobacco, logs, copper, tin, nickel, bauxite, aluminum, iron ore, manganese ore, lead, zinc, and phosphate rock.

SOURCE: World Bank, *World Development Report*, 1983, p.11

'alarming', leading to falling incomes in many countries, stagnation in others, increases in inequality, growing protectionism and reduced international trade and financial flows, and, in all probability, the endangering of 'social stability and governments' ability to devise and implement rational economic policies'.[38] Although they also assume the possibility of far more favourable outcomes associated with policies designed to restore growth in the OECD countries to higher levels, it is difficult to be optimistic about this possibility at this stage.

Against these negative tendencies, however, we have to set some important positive achievements. Growth rates overall did not fall significantly from the levels attained during the 1970s, and were higher than those in the industrial countries, where they fell from

5.1 per cent to 3.0 per cent. Exports, mainly from the more developed countries, also expanded rapidly during the 1970s, with the developed countries expanding their imports from LDCs 'from $48 billion in 1970 to $424 billion in 1980, or from $32 billion to $171 billion if oils and other fuels are excluded'.[39] Between 1970 and 1979 the manufactured exports of the top ten NICs increased by 26 per cent p.a., those of the next sixteen, a new group of 'second-tier' countries, expanded by no less than 37 per cent.[40] Perhaps more importantly, given the numbers involved, India and China, following relatively inwardly oriented policies, were able to sustain positive growth rates and an external equilibrium.

This review of the development experience suggests two things in relation to the general problem of uneven development. Firstly, this can no longer be identified with a simple cleavage between a 'developing' metropolis and an 'underdeveloping' periphery, since the most dynamic Third World economies have been growing far more rapidly than any but the most successful industrial countries, and their exports are now a real threat to those of the DCs in many sectors in world markets. Secondly, it suggests that the most extreme manifestations of uneven development are now intensifying within the Third World itself, as between a small number of dynamic growth centres and a large area where growth has been negligible or even negative. Thus the contradictory viewpoints outlined at the start of this section are a clear reflection of an equally contradictory reality in which a variety of experiences present to each a concrete justification for the views they are attempting to assert. Before attempting a general overview, however, some account should be taken of two important theoretical developments which occurred in response to the decline in the influence of traditional ISI theory and the resurgence of liberalism.

In the early 1970s a new critique emerged which was based on a rejection of the traditional assumption that development must involve an uncritical appropriation of the most advanced capital-intensive Western technology. On the Left this took the form of a demand that the emphasis be placed, in Thomas's words, on the creation of 'domestic production and domestic resources use for domestic needs'.[41] In its radical socialist version, this requires a break with capitalist market relations and structures in the domestic economy, and especially with foreign private capital, and with a process of 'de-linking' from the established trading patterns in the world economy to ensure the survival of domestic production based upon 'appropriate' technology and production structures. Although involving a move to a far higher level of self-sufficiency, this view would not involve a reversion to autarchy, but would require close control over international exchanges.[42] In less radical guise, though clearly influenced by the Marxist critique of traditional developmental literature, these themes were also taken up in a number of country studies by the International Labour Office (ILO) and in *Redistribution with Growth*, published by the World Bank in 1974. Here a guarded critique of the negative effects of some forms of MNC investment in the 'formal' (large-scale) sector of the economy was presented, and an assertion of the positive contribution to be made by the hitherto neglected group of small-scale indigenous enterprises using a far more local supply of inputs and labour-intensive methods. Although this view stopped short of any recommendation that the activities of MNCs be directly curtailed, it did call for a much expanded role for the small-scale 'informal' sector based upon increased support from the state.[43]

Secondly, by the middle of the decade the crisis in the world economy had provoked an increasingly critical response from representatives of Third World countries to the failure of the Western countries to respond to their problems, some aspects of which will be considered in more detail in Chapter 8. The campaign for a New International Economic Order originating in the UN, the demand for increased concessions in relation to aid and trade organised through UNCTAD, and the demand for a rapid increase in the proportion of global industry located in the Third World presented by the UN Industrial Development Organisation (UNIDO), were direct descendants of the arguments that had produced the original ISI formulation in the 1950s (sometimes produced by the same authors). All of them came together in the Brandt Report at the end of the 1970s, which, in essence, re-asserted the need for an expansion in managed resource transfers from North to South, for an actively planned industrialisation in the South, and for an active role for the state in the development of welfare services and other infrastructure. In response to the successes of the NICs, it now placed far more emphasis on industrial exports and on the need to open Western markets to Third World products, but still retained a strong 'dirigiste' element in that it failed to accept the whole critique of the role of the state to be found in the new liberalism. This is hardly surprising, since the critique originated for the most part from the political and intellectual establishment associated with the international institutions and the state system. This material has occasioned a broad ranging academic and political debate, and will not be directly confronted here.[44] Instead, we can now conclude this chapter by attempting an overall evaluation of the general theoretical debate in relation to the experience reviewed in the preceding pages.

Conclusions

This account of post-war development in the Third World has been mainly concerned with the relationship between the structures and options created by the international system and domestic economic policies and performance, viewing each as directly and organically linked with the other. An adequate evaluation of this interaction between domestic and international political and economic forces requires an assessment of both sides of this complex totality – an understanding of its impact on domestic growth, distribution and political autonomy within poor countries on the one hand, and of its implications for the stability, dynamism and openness of the world economy on the other. A detailed examination of these questions, and more especially of the second, must await the final chapter; here there is only space to draw attention in a preliminary way to the most general issues which arise out of the material that has been presented.

We have argued throughout this book that, in an increasingly open and inter-dependent system, the viability of the totality depends in the long term upon the ability to sustain an above average performance in its weakest members, thereby engendering a process of *even development* in the system as a whole. Given this perspective, the performance of the Third World, where the poorest peoples are concentrated in the poorest countries, becomes of more than average interest. Although the *dynamism* of the system as a whole might well be imparted by its dominant centres in the industrialised world, its *success* must be judged by the extent to which that dynamism enables the poor to catch up with the rich, rather than simply allowing the rich to extend further their control over the world's resources.

Testing this requirement against the post-war developmental experience, we can see that the level of achievement has been enormously uneven. In aggregate terms, the Third World can be said to have performed very effectively throughout the long boom up to 1974, and the more successful countries to have done even better between 1974 and 1982, when their growth rates comfortably exceeded those of the recession-hit industrial economies. Thus it is perfectly possible for orthodox theorists to claim that there is strong evidence to deny the extreme Marxist assertion that capitalism can do no more than 'underdevelop' the Third World, and that the only possible route to progress is via socialist revolution.[45]

Many Marxists would probably agree that the crude 'dependency theory' association between capitalism and one-sided surplus extraction cannot be sustained, [46] but whether the experience we have reviewed serves as an adequate basis for assuming that orthodox policies, widely promoted as a basis for domestic and international economic management, have in the past, and can in the future, provided adequate guidance for a process of even development, is a far more open question. What the experience we have reviewed has actually demonstrated is a capacity for great dynamism at certain favoured points in the Third World, combined with stagnation and, increasingly, actual regression in many others.

Thus, outside the favoured regions located in a few Latin American and East Asian countries, and relatively recently in India, per capita incomes grew at only 1.2 per cent from the 1950s to the 1970s, 'and unfortunately not at all over the past decade'.[47] Less easily documentable, but more significant from a social and political point of view, is the worsening of inequalities between classes and regions even within many of the more successful countries. While it may be the case that the most successful of the small NICs, notably South Korea and Taiwan, have managed to secure relatively favourable income distribution, this is certainly not generally the case, as the *Redistribution with Growth* study showed.[48] The World Bank also points out that 'in India, with the major exception of West Bengal, the states with the highest income levels in 1960 have grown fastest since then', while in Brazil about a third of the population lives in the north-east where, in 1979, 'average per capita income . . . was about 40 per cent of the national average'.[49] Perhaps most important of all, the dynamism of the whole system which has allowed positive growth to take place in the Third World, however unevenly, has clearly been interrupted during the last decade and more especially during the past five years. There is strong evidence that this downturn is being experienced far more intensely in the poorest countries than in the richest, and that almost none of the strong performers are being spared its effects, in large part because of the impact of the debt crisis to be taken up in Chapter 9. Unless the unevenness of the experience up to now and, most especially, the present impasse can be shown to be surmountable through the vigorous pursuit of liberal domestic and international economic policies, there can be little doubt that the already weakened structures of international economic co-operation will be further undermined.

But even if we are to accept at face value the assertion that real long-term development has occurred in many parts of the Third World and can continue to occur even more widely (and there is some evidence that a further group of industrial exporters is now beginning to emerge)[50] the attempt to present this as the *result* of application of orthodox domestic and international policies, as the liberals do, is highly questionable. For orthodox theory the successes of the NICs, identified with the application of liberalised trade policies, are evidence that full integration into the increasingly open international capitalist economy, multinationals and all, can serve to generate dynamic growth and, in the long run, full employment and an equitable distribution of income. For structuralists and Marxists, however, serious questions arise as to the genuineness of the liberal credentials of these countries and, more especially, as to the general applicability of the aggressive export-oriented strategy they have pursued.

Indeed, considerable evidence now exists to demonstrate that the Taiwan and South Korean cases, far from being typical examples of liberal, market-oriented policies, have been based on close state control over the domestic allocation of resources and over foreign trade as well.[51] What appears to be the case here is that the liberal theorists, in their eagerness to demonstrate the validity of orthodox theory, have mistaken a limited tendency towards *liberalisation* for the elimination of a highly centralised and protectionist policy orientation. While it is true that some of the worst excesses of old-style ISI have been eliminated, what remains is a system based upon close controls designed to favour domestic industry against foreign in both home and overseas markets. As Wade puts it in an important new work on Taiwan, 'it is as though the only significant feature of a tariff reduction from 60 to 50 per cent is the 10 per cent liberalising decline, not the 50 per cent that remains'.[52]

It is perhaps true that Hong Kong and Singapore do correspond very closely to the orthodox model and have been remarkably successful, but to base a theoretical model for the Third World on the achievements of two city states whose position and resources give them quite unique advantages is hardly convincing. If the development problem is to be solved, it has to be dealt with in the large poor countries and regions of Asia and Africa, not in the tiny, strategically significant areas whose input into the international system will always be inconsequential. In the really important examples of successful industrialisation, and this is even more evident in the large Latin American NICs like Brazil than in the smaller Asian cases, what has happened is not a reduction in the commitment to state intervention and external controls, but a decision to attack the export market rather than focus almost exclusively on import substitution. Although the successes involved have been very real ones, demonstrating high degrees of technical and organisational competence in many LDCs, they have been achieved through methods which do little to disprove the fundamental propositions of the structuralist school, and have taken place during a very favourable historical period in circumstances that are most unlikely to be sustained.

A number of conditions must be met if we are to be able to assert that liberal market-oriented strategies should dominate the development process, as orthodoxy does. These include, firstly, that there is clear evidence that liberalisation will not seriously undermine the position of small and medium-sized domestic producers, thus leading not to a more efficient allocation of productive capacity, but to unemployment and de-industrialisation. Secondly, liberalisation and low-wage export expansion in LDCs must not worsen unemployment in developed countries and lead to intensifed protectionism, heightened international competition between LDCs, and falling prices. Thirdly, the flow of concessional and commercial credit to LDCs required to sustain their existing economic capacity and increase investment must not be significantly reduced as a result of public spending cuts in developed countries, and the debt crisis in the private sector. Finally, the recession, worsening terms of trade and balance of payments now afflicting the whole of the Third World, with a few limited exceptions, must be overcome without a disintegration in the structures of international economic control of the sort which occurred during the last great depression in the 1930s. A general discussion of these problems in the light of all of the evidence presented in this book will have to await the last chapter. Here we can merely register some hopefully pertinent and certainly pessimistic impressions.

After 1973 one country did make a qualitative leap in a liberal direction, controlled by a new military dictatorship and a group of American-trained economists. In the 1970s the Chilean experiment was greeted as a major 'success', despite a huge increase in unemployment, because it brought down the rate of inflation, expanded some mainly raw material exports, and generated strong growth from 1977 to 1980. But this process was associated with serious de-industrialisation and largely financed by almost unlimited access to foreign credit (which had been denied to the Allende regime). Imports expanded dramatically (those of consumption goods rose from \$76 million in 1970 to \$903 million in 1981 in constant 1977 dollars) as did income inequalities. When the credit ran out in 1982, the whole edifice collapsed into an unprecedented crisis with GDP down by 14.3 per cent, unemployment at 30 per cent in March 1983, and inflation in the month up to 25 per cent.[53] These results are entirely consonant with the assumptions of the structuralist/Marxist approach, but we have yet to see any serious examination of their implications from the theorists responsible for them.

Associated with the belief that liberalisation will not lead to de-industrialisation in LDCs is the equally optimistic assumption that it will not lead to massive import penetration and unemployment in DCs. This in turn suggests the irrationality of the 'new protectionism' and its tendency to retard the flow of labour out of backward industries into the growth areas characterised by high technology. Yet the empirical basis for these assertions is very weak. It can, indeed, be established that the growth of Third World manufactured exports to DCs produced only a very limited reduction in employment in a very small number of sectors in the 1970s.[54] Yet this, of course, ignores the fact that these flows were not determined by 'market' forces, but by the close controls still exercised over access to Western markets, notably through the Multi-Fibre Arrangement. With a strong manufacturing base now established in the existing NICs, and an unlimited supply of free trade zones available to runaway multinationals with minimal wages and no trade unions, the possibility of unlimited growth in a wide range of manufactures is now a real and growing threat to the position of the organised working class in the West. Exploiting modern technology provided by MNCs and very low wages, exporters from the large labour surplus countries could soon swamp the markets of any DC willing to give them open access.[55] And to assume that there will be real opportunities for new jobs for the workers thrown out of traditional manufacturing industries in the DCs entirely ignores the massively capital-intensive nature of the new technology and the size and intractability of the existing unemployment problem in the West. Hence there must be a further intensification of protectionism if LDCs mount a generalised attack on Western industrial markets, which can only be seen as irrational if we accept a series of theoretical assumptions made by orthodox theory that are patently unrealistic in modern conditions of rapid technical change. In these circumstances export-oriented industrialisation as a *general* strategy for the South will be both technically and politically impossible.

We have already seen that the flow of official aid to LDCs has slowed down significantly during the 1980s, and there is little evidence of any improvement in the short run. The Brandt Commission's plea for an increased transfer of real resources to the South received no encouragement at the Cancun conference, and the best we can hope for is that existing flows (whose real value can, in any event, be seriously questioned)[56] should maintain their present level in real terms. When this is set against the massive loss of resources to the middle-income LDCs arising out of the debt crisis, we can see that prospects for growth are very slim indeed. Serious declines have been experienced in a number of important countries, and we have yet to discover how this process is to be successfully reversed without stringent controls over external trade and financial flows.

The stability, dynamism and capacity for international economic management created in the world economy since the war have certainly provided LDCs with some real advantages. Their ability to rely on growing export markets, flexible monetary arrangements, and relatively easy access to credit and technology has enabled them to perform far better than they did before the war or, indeed, than their industrialised predecessor did during their early developmental phase. Yet although many doomsday prophecies have already been falsified, it would be naive to believe that the foundations sustaining the present liberal international order are embedded in firm and unmovable ground. As we have seen, one crisis has followed another since the American repudiation of the gold-convertibility system in 1971, and it would be foolishly optimistic to assume that anything that has happened in the past two years has resolved these fundamental problems. Thus plans predicted firmly on the continuation of these conditions are built upon faith rather than rational calculation. We may hope that they will work out, but it would be wise to anticipate that they may not.

Finally, there is nothing in this account of the relative success of a number of dynamic zones in hitherto backward parts of the system which denies the Marxist view of capitalism as engendering a crisis-ridden process of combined and uneven development requiring the constant replacement of old processes and producers with new ones. What it does assert, however, is a constant tendency towards the concentration and centralisation of capital involving the marginalisation of backward areas and populations and the intensification of inequalities. We have seen that old industrial regions are not immune to the destructive effects of this process, and that new growth poles can always emerge, given the right conditions. But to jump from this to an assertion that an uncontrolled *laissez-faire* capitalism can create a stable growth path for the poorest peoples in the poorest countries appears to be dangerously close to pure fantasy, and a fantasy, moreover, which has a powerful hold on the thinking of some of the most influential theorists in the policy-making process.

From a Marxist perspective only an orientation designed to bring the market mechanism under the direct control of a rational social planning process can serve to guarantee both equity, growth and the autonomy of the direct producer.[57] Although few Marxists would be satisfied with the socialist credentials of the systems that have already broken decisively with capitalism, they can point, in many parts of the Third World, to experiences which belie the assertion that central planning must produce manifestly irrational allocations leading to stagnation, inequalities and corruption.[58] In countries like China, very adequate levels of growth have been associated with price stability, full employment and welfare provision to the poorest far superior to those in other LDCs with far higher average per capita incomes. This experience and the negative effects of the

insecurity and aggression engendered by the uncontrolled operation of the competitive principle, are entirely ignored by the
disciples of the new orthodoxy. For anyone concerned to establish a
genuinely dispassionate view of the development debate, however,
they should be given a great deal more weight.

8

The LDCs and the Official Agencies

Integration into the international system, 1945–1971

Most LDCs were externally controlled at the end of the war and therefore excluded from the international debate which led to the establishment of the IMF, World Bank and the GATT. Those that were involved, however, brought to it a commitment to the need for 'Structuralist' interventions even stronger than those put forward by the weaker industrialised countries like Britain and France at the time and considered in Chapter 3. Indeed, as Little puts it, the development establishment was in favour of planning trade, and much else, by direct controls, and also in favour of direct governmental initiatives in manufacturing investment.[1]

An immense distance therefore existed between the Southern view of the approach to international economic regulation and that of the USA, which, as we have seen, had been indelibly stamped upon the agencies into which the newly independent countries would eventually come to be integrated. Considerable conflict was therefore inevitable, and soon to lead to the consolidation of the LDCs into a political bloc with a common (though not identical) orientation to the problems of international economic policy and institutional change. This was to keep the problems of uneven development and the need for controlled resource transfers and interventionist policies at the centre of the international economic debate thereafter. Almost all non-communist LDCs joined the IMF and the World Bank at independence, most joining the former on the basis of Article XIV status which, it will be remembered, allowed them to retain non-convertible currencies until they considered their external trading positions to be strong enough to eliminate such restrictions.[2] This, as Little points out, produced 'one law for the rich and one for the poor',[3] and enabled them to retain controls over their own currencies, while, at the end of the 1950s, being able to rely on the convertibility of those of their major trading partners in the advanced countries. During the 1940s and early 1950s the balance of payments situation of most LDCs was relatively strong, since they had ended the war with substantial reserves, and raw material prices increased substantially during the Korean war. During these years, therefore, little use was made of IMF resources (only $419.8 million being drawn between 1947 and 1955), and it took 'little specific interest' in their particular problems, which were treated as if they 'were no different from those of developed countries'.[4] In the second half of the 1950s, however, their terms of trade deteriorated and the demand for financing increased sharply (£2,205.3 million being drawn between 1956 and 1963) and the problem of the restrictive nature of the IMF's response became an issue for the first time.[5] But it was only in the 1970s that this problem reached crisis proportions and produced a generalised critique of its adjustment policies which will be looked at below. Nevertheless, in response to increasing pressure on behalf of LDCs in other international agencies, some concessions were made: total quotas were increased (from $8,750 million in 1955 to $15,976 million in 1965),[6] and funds were set up to provide for the compensatory financing of export shortfalls and of buffer stocks under acceptable commodity agreements,[7] although very little use was made of them.[8] Finally, as we saw in Chapter 5, the LDCs were eventually included in the Special Drawing Rights scheme at the end of the 1960s organised by the IMF. This provided them with a limited form of unconditional credit, but did not meet their demand that it serve as an effective mechanism for resource transfer by being 'linked' to the provision of aid.

The World Bank, as we have seen, was originally set up on highly conservative principles, having to acquire all its resources from private capital markets and therefore to lend on non-concessional terms. Initially it was mainly concerned to lend to the industrial countries for 'reconstruction' projects, then to LDCs for infrastructure and public utilities. By 1959 it had lent $1.3 billion to LDCs and $1.6 billion to developed countries; its lending to the latter then declined rapidly, with net flows (disbursements minus repayments and charges) becoming negative after 1961.[9] LDCs in the 1950s were very dissatisfied with both the level of Bank lending and its non-concessional nature, so a campaign developed mainly within the UN for the creation of a multilateral lending agency which would perform this function under UN auspices. Despite initial opposition, the lending surplus countries were eventually converted to this proposal, but, by insisting that it be brought under the control of the Bank, were also able to ensure that they would be able to dominate its operations through its weighted voting system. As a result, the International Development Association (IDA) was set up as a Bank subsidiary, funded by grants from the industrial countries and able to lend on very concessional terms (usually for 50 years with a less than 1 per cent annual service charge) to low-income as opposed to middle-income countries. Lending began in 1961, and had totalled $3.4 billion by 1971, when IDA loans had come to represent about 25 per cent of total bank lending.[10]

The LDCs were even less satisfied with the GATT than with the structure of the Bretton Woods organisations, and very few joined during the 1950s. During the negotiations for the never-to-be established International Trade Organisation during the 1940s, they had pressed for an organisation that would assist them in their import substitution strategies.[11] Instead, after the collapse of the original ITO recommendations embodied in the Havana Charter in the USA, they were presented with the GATT as an inherently liberal mechanism for the negotiation of reciprocal trade concessions. This, according to an Indian spokesman in 1965, stripped them of real political and economic bargaining power, because they were not in a position to give the reciprocal concessions required in negotiations.[12]

These difficulties led to the establishment of a GATT committee in the 1950s under Gottfried Haberler (a leading free trade theorist) to consider the reasons for the tendency for LDC trade to lag behind that of the developed countries. This did not find any 'general tendency towards discrimination against the exports of less developed countries per se', but did identify many factors impeding their growth.[13] As part of an attempt to overcome these problems, the GATT Agreement was amended in 1964 to make it possible for developed countries to give preferences to imports from LDCs without contravening the most favoured nation principle which precluded the granting of preferential treatment by one country to another.[14] This meant that the LDCs could enter the 'Kennedy Round' tariff negotiations conducted through GATT between 1964 and 1967 in the hope of obtaining privileged access to industrial country markets. In the event the DCs were to insist on some degree of reciprocity being maintained in negotiations, although the LDC concessions 'were not equivalent to those exchanged among developed countries'.[15] Looked at from a liberal point of view, the GATT arrangements could now be seen as relatively favourable to LDCs in that they would benefit from the general tendency towards liberalisation now accelerating among the DCs without having to take equivalent action themselves.[16] However, the end result certainly failed to come up to their expectations: agricultural protection in the developed countries continued unaffected, tropical products were 'not generously treated', the growth in the relative importance of non-tariff barriers to LDC exports, which were not covered by the agreements continued, and

> even after the Kennedy round tariffs levied by developed countries on goods imported from LDCs were still generally higher than those on trade among developed countries, and levels of effective protection remained high.[17]

Finally, the special controls on cotton textile exports from LDCs (potentially the most important sector for them) established in 1962 and subsequently to become the Multi-Fibre Arrangement in 1973, continued unaffected. Hence the commodities of greatest interest to the LDCs were effectively excluded from the concessions, and in important areas LDC exporters had to face higher tariffs than did their DC counterparts.

Further LDC hostility to the GATT also led to pressure within the UN system for the creation of a trade-oriented agency which, operating on the basis of a non-weighted voting system, would be dominated by their interests and could serve as a counter-weight to the GATT in the international economic debate. These demands were pushed within the UN in the late 1950s by the LDCs and the Soviet bloc (which had resurrected the demand for the establishment of the ITO) and led in 1962 to an agreement to hold a conference on trade and development in 1964. The agenda for this conference was set out by Prebisch himself,[18] and incorporated the whole of the 'structuralist' critique of liberal theory outlined in Chapter 2. At this conference, despite consistent opposition from the USA, agreement was reached for the establishment of a permanent secretariat to work on the issues involved in providing 'solutions to the problems of world trade in the interests of all peoples and particularly to the urgent trade and development problems of the developing countries',[19] and regular conferences have been held thereafter, to discuss these issues.

The original impetus for the setting up of UNCTAD came from the group of seventy-seven developing countries which has since retained its capacity to formulate general principles around which LDCs have organised their interventions in the international economic debate. Still known as the 'Group of 77', it now contains well over a hundred members. Within UNCTAD the communist bloc has generally pressed for more effective international interventionist machinery comparable to that envisaged in the Havana Charter, while the LDC position on many issues has also secured some support from other developed countries. However, UNCTAD has never been given the responsibility for the actual management of any aspect of the international economic system equivalent to those accorded the IMF, World Bank and the GATT (although at the end of the 1970s it was attempting to organise an Integrated Programme for Commodities which has yet to take effective shape), and its conferences and publications have generally been treated as little more than an important forum in which to explore the conflicts of interest which separate LDC from DC views about the management and development of the international economy.

Thus UNCTAD clearly represents an attempt by LDCs to create an agency capable of developing policies and programmes designed to deal with the uneven development of the world economy through conscious redistribution and direct controls. In it they have achieved their goal of overall control secured through their superior numbers, always denied them in the IMF, World Bank and the GATT, and this has ensured that its debates take place within a framework dominated by structuralist rather than liberal theory.[20] Yet this could do nothing to reduce the 'breadth and depth of the gulf that separated Northern and Southern views of aid and trade policy', nor to overcome the Western (and Soviet) unwillingness to 'commit itself to increasing its aid to poor countries, except in expressions of goodwill that implied no necessary commitment'.[21] Thus, the working arrangements at UNCTAD have had little effect upon the transfer of real resources from North to South. There can be little doubt that any significant concessions on monetary and trade policy or on financial flows are reserved for the international agencies over which the industrial countries have effective control, or through bilateral bargaining between individual states.

Thus we can see that the LDCs came to be integrated into the international economic system on a different basis from the DCs, though not on terms over which they themselves had been able to exert very much direct influence. As a function of their commitment to interventionism examined in Chapter 7, they had insisted on retaining control over their currencies, the right to maintain quota and tariff restrictions on imports, and expected access to some flows of capital from bilateral and multilateral official sources on non-commercial terms. This means that they were effectively excluded from the tendency towards liberalisation gaining ground in the industrial countries from the late 1950s onwards. Instead they had taken on the powers required to develop an interventionist international economic policy based upon a theoretical commitment to policies of import-substituting industrialisation (ISI) discussed in Chapter 7.

Dealing with crisis, 1971–1984

During the 1970s, as in previous years, the LDCs were able to exert little influence over the development of the international system, and can hardly be said to have benefited much from it. The ending of dollar-gold convertibility and the introduction of freely floating exchange rates in 1971–73 greatly increased the instability of the system within which they had to operate. Most LDCs were still using unconvertible currencies and had been able to devalue at will themselves, so that the changes had little effect on their own freedom of action. However, most of them did not follow independent exchange rate policies, but tied the external value of their currencies to that of one of the advanced countries, usually the USA. With internal freedom and external stability they had obtained the best of both worlds; now their external purchasing power would be influenced by uncontrollable changes in foreign currency valuations stemming from the requirements of the industrial countries rather than from their 'own domestic or balance of payments needs'.[22] Perhaps more important, all held most of their reserves in dollars, so that they suffered a real loss in spending power as the value of the dollar fell between 1971 and 1979, and this also made it far more difficult for them to manage their foreign exchange reserves in an optimal way.[23] Their losses were then retrieved after 1979 as the dollar appreciated in response to tight US monetary policies, but these also involved large increases in international interest rates which more than offset the gains in the value of their reserves in the case of all of the more developed LDCs which had by then accumulated large debts.

In trade, the GATT-sponsored Tokyo Round tariff negotiations (1973–1979) were organised for the first time on the basis of a formal recognition of the principle of 'non-reciprocity' as between developed and less developed countries and recognised 'tariff and non-tariff preferential treatment in favour of and among developing countries as a permanent legal feature of the world trading system'.[24] But little of a positive kind has emerged from this formal commitment. The final cuts in industrial tariffs were some 30 per cent for the industrial countries, but this related to an average tariff of only 10 per cent and therefore would mean changes that would be 'insignificant in terms of the competitive pressure they [would] exert on domestic producers of manufactured goods'.[25] As Baldwin further notes, these reductions would be far less important than the competitive impact of the exchange rate changes occurring under the floating rate system. Against this, the negotiations did nothing to stop or reverse the growing tide of non-tariff barriers in a number of key areas and very largely directed against exports from Japan and the NICs. Agricultural trade has always been excluded from GATT negotiations, thereby leaving very heavy levels of protectionism in farm products, expecially in Europe, entirely unscathed. Textiles, always the most important area of manufacturing growth in the early stages of industrial development, continue to be rigorously controlled under the Multi-Fibre Arrangements, while steel, an important area for the more developed NICs, is increasingly protected in Europe and the USA.[26] The Group of 77, speaking for the great majority of LDCs, therefore found little to applaud in the Tokyo Round, but instead felt that the developed countries 'had failed to respond to the interests and concerns of the developing countries', and instead:

Observe with concern that certain important products, including tropical products, of export interest to the developing countries, and products from several industrial sectors in which they have the capability, the advantage and potential for growth, have been virtually excluded from the tariff concessions made by developed countries; and that no attempt to tackle the problem of tariff escalation has been made,

Note with disappointment that in the 'Special and Priority' sector of tropical products the results fall far short of those achieved on a general basis and that offers in some cases were made conditional upon reciprocity and remain unimplemented,

Express profound dissatisfaction that there has been no multilateral solution to the problem of quantitative restrictions faced by products of developing countries, and that restrictions in many important sectors such as textiles have not even been discussed,

Note with grave concern that no safeguards code has emerged as part of the final package so far which might protect the interests of developing countries and ensure their uninterrupted growth, and that the lack of success in this area is mainly due to the insistence of a few developed countries to secure unfettered freedom to make selective safeguard action which would enable them to discriminate against developing country exports.[27]

In the 1980s the recession finally produced a major retardation of the growth in trade which has been so prominent a characteristic of the whole post-war era: 'Exports grew by only 1.5% in 1980, stagnated in 1981 and declined by an estimated 2% in 1982 . . . Among developing countries, only a handful managed to increase their exports, mainly in manufactures'.[28] At the end of 1982 a ministerial conference of the GATT signatories was convened to examine and reinforce 'the functioning of the multilateral trading system . . . for the benefit of all nations'.[29] But the conference confined itself to calls for continued research and discussion on disputed issues, failed 'to make even a verbal commitment to the notion of successful resistance to domestic protectionist pressures', and therefore brought matters to a state in which 'the survival of GATT itself is in question'.[30]

For a group of fifty-eight of the poorest LDCs, negotiations for preferential treatment also took place through their direct association with the EEC, which produced two conventions (Lomé I and

II), signed in 1975 and 1979. These gave them preferential access to Community markets for most of their products, with limited funds for commodity price stabilisation and with privileged access to aid. But these 'concessions' mainly related to the promotion of non-competitive raw material exports, and did little to reduce the EEC's highly protectionist orientation to temperate agriculture, semi-processed raw materials and labour-intensive manufacturing where barriers have been heightened.[31] However strong their desire to take advantage of whatever they were offered, these countries came out of Lomé II negotiations feeling that they had left both their 'expectations of Europe, and Europe's own potential for meaningful co-operation . . . largely unfilfilled'.[32]

In a situation where the developed countries are setting themselves so resolutely against opening their own markets to LDC imports, it is hardly surprising that the LDCs themselves have yet to be convinced of the advantages of free trade in their own. Some Western commentators now claim that the weakness of the LDC bargaining position stems in part from their insistence on the principle of non-reciprocity, which makes it impossible for them to offer concessions to DCs in exchange for increased access.[33] But it seems highly unlikely that they could ever be in a position to offer enough to offset the almost irresistible protectionist pressures now stemming from the labour-intensive industries in DCs put at risk by low wage imports from LDCs. There is no prospect of any substantial growth in employment in competitive capital-intensive industries in these countries, where unemployment is already unacceptably high, because of the recession and the labour-saving nature of the new technology involved. In these circumstances liberal economists who base their theory upon the equilibrium economics of a world characterised by constant returns to scale may complain about the irrationality of workers who demand protection, but they can do nothing to demonstrate that these countries could adjust to the explosive growth in low wage competition that would result from free trade without 'dangerously divisive and destabilising' consequences.[34]

In this context of intensifying recession and bad temper, the role of UNCTAD became primarily that of providing a forum within which disagreements could be organised and ventilated. Its primary objective in the 1970s was to organise a comprehensive policy programme to deal with commodity trade, including the establishment of a Common Fund to finance international commodity agreements (ICAs). But the results have been minimal, as the Helleiner report claims:

> At the time the UNCTAD resolution on the Integrated Program-me for Commodities was adopted in 1976, developing countries had considerable hopes that it would lead to constructive action; but despite agreement in 1980 to establish the Common Fund, subsequent achievements have been very limited ... Exporters are not particularly interested in ICAs in periods of high prices, any more than importers are in periods of low prices. Only one new ICA with price-stabilisation provisions (that for natural rubber) had been negotiated since the IPC was agreed. Moreover, the agreed size and functions of the Common Fund are much smaller than in the original conception. The negotiation of new ICAs with price-stabilisation provisions will continue therefore to be extremely difficult.[35]

The liberals argue that the LDCs have been quite wrong to under-value the work of the GATT, where they might be able to negotiate real, if limited, gains provided that they were willing to offer something by way of reciprocal concessions, instead of placing all their emphasis on pointless confrontational politics 'under the big top of UNCTAD'.[36] Yet the fundamental question implicit in their demand for non-reciprocity has yet to be answered: can the existing tendencies towards balance of payments disequilibrium, uneven development and crisis be effectively overcome without major changes in the existing pattern of global resources allocation, and if not, what real concessions are the still dominant industrial countries going to be willing to make in order to initiate them? This question was equally forcibly posed and largely disregarded in the demand for expanded international resource transfers and market access for LDC exports in the UN proposals for a New International Economic Order in the mid-1970s and in the Brandt Reports at the start of the 1980s.

More concretely, perhaps, the flow of external resources into LDCs continued to increase during the 1970s, although its compos-ition changed dramatically. Aid flows grew rapidly in the first half of the 1970s (from $9.14 billion in 1971 to $20.95 billion in 1975), stabilised for the next two years, then jumped to $28.10 billion in

1978 and peaked at $37.33 billion in 1980, then fell to $34.24 billion in 1982. OPEC contributions increased from $2.03 billion in 1973 to $8.75 billion in 1980, and fell to $5.51 billion in 1982.[37] Overall contributions grew by about 4 per cent p.a. in real terms over the 1970s, but now appear to be stagnant; as a percentage of GDP, however, they have stagnated at around 0.35 per cent since the end of the 1960s, roughly half of the recommended 0.7 per cent level and well below the 0.53 per cent level achieved at the start of the 1960s.[38]

Over the same period direct private investment increased in 1971 from $3.31 billion to about $11.00 billion in 1982, but private bank lending, the major growth area, increased from $3.30 billion to $29.00 billion in 1981, $21.0 billion in 1982, and private export credits from $2.71 billion to approximately $9.00 billion.[39] Thus there has been a clear shift towards private non-concessional forms of finance over the past decade, mainly directed towards the middle-income LDCs, and necessarily generating a rapid increase in the long-term servicing costs for the countries involved, the consequences for whom will be considered in the next chapter.

What, then, were the implications of the continued expansion in MNC investments implicit in the growth in direct investment? During the 1950s and 1960s, as we have seen, the MNCs were closely associated with the attempts at ISI in a few of the larger LDCs, though not, at that stage, very closely with the beginnings of export-oriented industrialisation.[40] During the 1970s, however, the concentration of foreign investment in a very limited number of countries continued, but MNCs now came to increase their contribution to manufactured exports, though not usually by any more than domestic producers. During this decade countries with per capita incomes above $1,000, accounting for about 25 per cent of the population of the non-socialist developing world, 'received 65% of the foreign direct investment'; countries with incomes below $380, containing 60 per cent of the population, 'received less than 5% of the flow of foreign direct assistance in 1978–1980 compared with 14% in 1970–1972'.[41]

Although much MNC investment is still directed towards domestic markets, they do now make an important contribution to exports, especially in sectors 'where market barriers are substantial', and their international links give them an important potential 'for overcoming protectionism',[42] and also in the exports of labour-intensive components for incorporation in final products mainly produced in the advanced countries.[43] There appears to be no conclusive evidence demonstrating that foreign capital has a better or worse record than domestic capital with respect to exports – their presence neither 'necessarily contributes to strong export performance', but then 'neither does that presence impair export performance if the trade and macroeconomic environment is favourable'.[44] Indeed, in the favoured growth centres like Taiwan and Korea, where relatively full employment has been achieved, it is probably the case that they have contributed positively to output growth, to some expansion in exports, and have been important channels for new technology and therefore for the creation of a relatively high wage sector.

Yet this contribution is still confined to a relatively limited number of favoured countries and individuals. In all developing countries they are estimated to have created no more than two to four million jobs,[45] and no figures exist which allow us to compare these tiny totals with the number of jobs in traditional industries destroyed as a result of their inability to compete.[46] Furthermore, their contribution to exports has often been made at the expense of a considerable growth in imported inputs, and in the outflow of capital, so that the net effect of their activities on the balance of payments is often negative. There can also be little doubt that their profit rates in LDCs often are well above those in the industrial countries:

> In 1978–1980, developing countries made almost half the recorded payments of foreign investment, but received less than a quarter of the reported foreign direct investment inflows and a negligible amount of investment income. Developing countries reported total payments on foreign direct investment averaging some $12.8 billion annually during 1978–1980, compared with an inflow of some $8 billion of such investment.[47]

Associated with these tendencies was a further expansion in interfirm trade, and a corresponding increase in the capacity of MNCs to manipulate their external relations through transfer pricing, thereby evading the effects of government restrictions on their activities, and exerting significant pressures on the autonomy of governments in relation to the policy-making process.[48] Thus the developments of the last decade, despite the very real achievements of a few countries, have done nothing to suggest that the tendency of MNCs to reinforce uneven development and undermine the sovereignty of nation-states, outlined in Chapter 4, has been modified in any significant way.

Finally, in this review of the relationship between international structures and the Third World, we must consider the role of the IMF and World Bank, both of which have played a crucial role not only through the provision of funds, but also in relation to the international debate on the fundamental principles of economic policy. Here we are obliged to return to some of the policy issues raised in Chapter 7, and to show how these relate directly to the nature of the relationship prevailing between the LDCs and the structure of the international agencies.

Whatever we may think about the economic achievements of the LDCs over the past decade, no one is likely to deny the seriousness of the exogenously produced balance of payments problems that they have had to confront since the first oil price increase at the end of 1973.[49] The deterioration in their oil trade balance between 1974 and 1980 has now been succeeded by a general deterioration in their terms of trade, and in particular by a rapid escalation in the costs of servicing their debts, so we can see that the problem will not be reduced in the short term. Indeed, the deterioration has been so continuous and so serious that there can be little doubt that it can only be described as 'structural' or 'fundamental' in its nature, especially when compared with the much more favourable conditions that had prevailed during the previous twenty-five years. Looking back at the discussion of the requirements for the creation of a viable international economic system presented in earlier chapters, it will be remembered that an essential element was to be the creation of an effective international mechanism capable of overcoming a structural disequilibrium of this sort. More concretely, the Bretton Woods institutions were specifically created to perform this role, so in examining the way in which they responded to the deficits of the past decade, we can also evaluate their adequacy as agencies for international economic management.

The debate at Bretton Woods identified a real tension between a weak-country assertion of the need for a generous deficit financing facility to enable them to expand their way out of difficulty, as against a strong-country belief in the need for deflationary adjustments to policy designed to restore them to surplus in the short term mainly through their own efforts. The final compromise in 1944 put most of the emphasis on 'adjustment' rather than 'financing', since the USA at the time was not willing to make the contributions to the IMF that would have enabled it to operate a more generous approach. For countries with a 'fundamental' balance of payments disequilibrium, therefore, the IMF was to become a lender of last resort, whose limited resources could only be tapped in exchange for the surrender of considerable control over the important areas of economic policy-making. In these circumstances (prevailing at present in no less than thirty-nine countries) the conception of national sovereignty ceases to have any strong meaning, and the IMF comes closest to exercising the role of 'world government' which, it was argued in Chapter 1, is a necessary concomitant to the liberalisation and integration of the world economy. Has this role been exercised in a manner conducive to the effective resolution of the crisis in the external economic relations of the Third World?

Prior to 1974, as we have seen, American deficits served to finance the international trading system, and no fundamental disequilibrium existed for most LDCs. The crisis initiated by the oil price increase changed this situation, leading to a very large demand for credit, but one, it was assumed, that would be largely provided by the private banking system. During these years it could therefore, though with decreasing confidence after 1973, be assumed that countries which came to the IMF for help would be doing so because they had mismanaged their domestic economic affairs, rather than because there was any significant lack of liquidity available in the global system. In this context there did not seem to be any problems involved in the outcome of the Bretton Woods compromise described in Chapter 3 which had defined the IMF as a *monetary* rather than a *developmental* institution, and thereby specified its role as one of providing short-term balance of payments financing, rather than long-term developmental investment. This, together with the limited funds at its disposal and the liberal trading principles written into its constitution, meant that it was forced to approach the problems of the deficit countries in a very conservative way, mainly by imposing policies on them which would reduce demand in the short term. During the years of global expansion it was argued, and often proved in reality, that well administered policies of this kind would only reduce growth temporarily, and quickly restore both external balance and economic prosperity through the creation of an 'export-led boom'. It could also be asserted, with some justice, that the existence of a balance of payments deficit would eventually enforce a reduction in domestic consumption and thus an adjustment programme involving some degree of austerity, whether or not the IMF was involved. In these conditions, in the absence of IMF-provided credit, deflation would have to be even more severe, so that the Fund's intervention, far from intensifying the problem, was actually improving the situation.

Yet once the boom was over, these arguments could not be asserted with the same degree of conviction, since deficits could no longer be mainly attributed to domestic mismanagement, while the recession made it far more difficult to believe that exports could be easily expanded. Any rigorous enforcement of stringent adjustment policies might now turn the recession into a depression, so that powerful claims could be made for the need for a substantial increase in financing.[50] This was dealt with at the time mainly through a substantial increase in private bank lending, but the LDCs now began to demand the creation of a mechanism for the transfer of real resources to them, and for increased access to unconditional concessional assistance, preferably through an additional issue of SDRs 'linked' directly to their need for aid.[51]

The IMF then made a real but very partial response to these pressures. The major Third World demand for a 'link' between SDRs and aid was rejected, but a new fund with low conditionality, the 'Oil Facility', was created with some seven billion SDRs to deal with what was seen as an essentially short-term problem, while access to an earlier fund, the Compensatory Financing Facility, created in 1963 to deal with short-term shortfalls in export earning, was increased. Hence lending, which had averaged 1.36 billion SDRs between 1971 and 1974, averaged 4.15 billion between 1975 and 1977, with more than three-quarters derived from the low conditionality funds. Thus the number of conditional loans made during these years did not match those made during the 1960s, although total lending was substantially higher.[52]

The experience of those countries that were forced into conditional borrowing was so negative that it induced intense political opposition to the terms of IMF interventions, and made it increasingly difficult for it to sustain the myth of technical neutrality. This problem was most intense in countries like Portugal, Tanzania and

Jamaica under Manley, which were attempting to operate redistributive social democratic policies involving extensive state intervention in domestic and foreign economic policy. Here IMF demands involved cuts in spending and wages and the use of devaluation rather than further protectionism to deal with the external
problem, all of them shifting resources from the poor to the rich and
substituting market controls for state intervention. It was also
noticed that the Fund had refused to support the Allende regime in
Chile, but been remarkably generous with its military successor.[53]
Hence an international conference on the monetary system organised by Tanzania and Jamaica in 1980 could argue that its programmes constituted a 'form of political intervention' in favour of
policies subordinating the state to 'the free play of national and
international market forces', and systematically favouring 'the
more conservative sectors of society and traditional centres of
power'. More generally, it was also asserted that the generalisation
of deflationary policies across a wider number of deficit countries
would be bound to intensify the tendency towards global recession,
while the severe treatment meted out to deficit countries had to be
'contrasted with the complete freedom of action of those industrialised countries which have been in surplus for most of the last three
decades', and which were 'free to solve their own short-term
problems by exporting deflation and unemployment, and even to
adopt protectionist measures against Third World exports'.[54]

The response of the Fund to these criticisms has again been real
but very limited. On the one hand, it has liberalised access to credit
by continuously increasing quotas (29 billion SDRs in 1971, 39
billion in 1978, 60 billion in 1981 and 90 billion in 1983), increased
the General Arrangements to Borrow from 6.4 billion SDRs to 17
billion in 1983, created two new facilities during the 1970s which
increased the amount of aid that could be borrowed and the period
that it could be held, and issued twelve billion additional SDRs
between 1978 and 1980, though without conceding that the allocation should be made to LDCs in greater proportion than their IMF
quotas, and thus conceding the demand for the 'link'. While repayments actually exceeded lending between 1978 and 1980, the latter
increased from 2.4 billion SDRs in that year to 4.9 billion in 1981,
8.0 billion in 1982 and 11.3 billion in 1983. In addition, in 1981 and
1982 non-oil LDCs used some 418 billion SDRs to deal with

balance of payments problems. Thus, while the main emphasis in the late 1970s was on private recycling, the re-intensification of the balance of payments crisis in the 1980s has led to a renewed emphasis on the provision of credit through official channels.

Yet this time, with the exception of the increases in SDR allocations, the expansion in access has been closely linked to highly conditional funding. Almost two-thirds of the Fund's lending between 1981 and 1983 has taken this form, thus strongly emphasising its central political role as guardian of the policies to be adopted to deal with the crisis. The exercise of this role is closely tied to the activities of the private banking system, since the middle-income countries usually go to the IMF only after having exhausted their access to the private credit market.

Thus the IMF's political and economic significance can hardly be exaggerated, since it is the only international mechanism which formally and legally allows external policy controls to be imposed on countries which might otherwise be tempted (or even forced through lack of resources) to default on their debts or to adopt restrictive policies which would undermine the openness and integrity of the international monetary system. How adequate are the criticisms of these policies outlined earlier?

In a recent essay, Guitan, a Fund theorist, sets out the changes that have emerged in response to the recognition in 1980 that the 'payments imbalances prevailing in the international economy were structural in nature and therefore not amenable to correction over a short period of time'.[55] While he notes that earlier policies put all the emphasis on short-term measures to restrain excess demand through fiscal and monetary measures, current policies involving longer adjustment periods had now come to recognise the need for an emphasis on 'resource utilisation and therefore on production' (pp. 87–8). Given access to more time and money, programmes can now be defended against earlier claims that they had simply emphasised reduced consumption and deflation and thus retarded growth, since they now incorporated 'foreign borrowing strategies that directly enlarge the amount of resources to the member', thus allowing 'higher levels of expenditure ... as well as higher growth rates over the medium term' (p. 88). Yet when the fine print is examined, these concessions to 'financing' do not leave orthodoxy far behind, since the domestic adjustment policies associated with them are much the same as before:

> They normally include public sector policies on prices, taxes, and subsidies that can contribute to eliminate financial imbalances and to promote efficiency in public sector activities, interest rate policies that foster the generation of domestic savings and improve intertemporal resources allocation, exchange rate policy that helps to control absorption and the external accounts but is also a powerful tool for development; and incomes policies that keep claims on resources from out-stepping their availability. (p. 88)

Here, again, we see the emphasis on the elimination of direct forms of state intervention, tight controls over public spending, and incomes policies to control wages. Moreover, the rejection of direct controls over imports in favour of devaluation to control inflows is still a cardinal principle, with the whole of the protectionist case rejected almost out of hand when deficits have to be eliminated:

> Simply restricting international transactions cannot be considered as an adequate adjustment strategy, because restrictions do not act on the causes of the difficulties but only repress and usually aggravate them. (p. 77)

This is a view that is strongly reasserted in the IMF's 1983 Annual Report.[56]

The critique of the orthodox theory upon which these prescriptions are based was developed in Chapters 3 and 7, where it was argued that reliance upon liberal orthodoxy would be counterproductive in a world dominated by the monopoly power of established countries and companies, and by high and rising unemployment. As the IMF now admits, the key problem in deficit countries is to create the investment opportunities required to increase the production needed to close the gap between domestic production and consumption. What is questionable is its assumption that some additional foreign credit plus devaluation should be enough to bridge the discrepancy in the capacity to produce between the poorer LDCs and the established producers in the DCs and, increasingly, in the NICs themselves. Rigorous analysis exists which suggests that, with under-utilised capacity, and with domestic costs of production very strongly and unevenly dependent upon the cost of imported inputs (both generally characteristic of LDCs), the impact of an undifferentiated devaluation on the supply of exports will be 'very low',[57] while current price stabilisation policies based on reducing demand will 'often depress the level of activity'.[58] Hence, if domestic resources are to be fully utilised, policy interventions designed to 'distort' prices become essential for the reasons summarised by Beinefeld quoted earlier (Chapter 7, footnote 26). Such intervention can vary from the use of a differential devaluation suggested by Schydlowsky,[59] through the demand for significantly increased resource flows, radical import substitution, and finally socialistic self-reliance, which was outlined in Chapter 7.[60]

Efficiently conceptualised and implemented with the necessary discipline, all of these options can provide viable alternatives to the traditional monetarist policies now put forward as unavoidable. However, as we have seen, the commitment to liberalisation written into the IMF's constitution and deeply embedded in the thinking of its highly competent officials, excludes them from its frame of references and thus forces it to impose the restrictive and highly conservative policies that it does. For as long as its liberal assumptions are accepted, its claim that it is offering no more than purely technical advice to which there is no viable alternative is a correct one. Once these are questioned, however (and, as we have seen, there are good theoretical grounds for doing so) it becomes evident that its interventions have the effect of imposing a very particular kind of economic policy on its client countries, and one, moreover, of a highly conservative ideological kind.

Equally significant, the implications of the IMF policies cannot only be judged in relation to their impact on particular economies at a time when they are being imposed on a large and growing number of countries. The search for balance through domestic deflation and increased exports makes sense in a world in which demand is growing, but not in one in which it is stagnant and all countries, the strong surplus producers included, are attempting to increase exports in order to ease the situation of hard-pressed domestic firms. We saw in Chapter 2 that viable global adjustment depended on increased exports from deficit countries being met by increased imports from surplus ones, but it is clear that the latter are refusing to adopt the expansionary policies required for this to occur. Instead they are deflating to deal with inflation and promoting exports and protecting against imports to deal with unemployment, thus exporting the costs of their adjustment programmes to the weakest countries in the system. The IMF can and does complain about this pattern of essentially anti-social behaviour, but, without a viable scarce-currency clause, neither it nor the deficit countries can do anything about it. Indeed, to the extent that IMF interventions in deficit countries tend to weaken demand and increase the supply of exports, they can only exacerbate an already serious global problem.

The 'asymmetry in the adjustment process', as this inequitable mechanism is called in the textbooks, is a function of the weakness of the political structures created at Bretton Woods, where the strong created a framework which served to discipline the weakest countries in the system but left their own autonomy virtually untouched. This weakness makes it impossible for the IMF to deal effectively with the crisis within the framework of the liberal pre-suppositions within which it operates, and negates the first principle of legitimate political control – that the strong and wealthy rather than the poor and weak should be seen to be making the main contribution to the sacrifices required to stabilise a disintegrating system. Up to now, the availability of substantial amounts of credit to stronger LDCs at least has served to conceal the worst effects of this inequality from view, but this, as we shall see in Chapter 9, is no longer the case. The worsening of the crisis has now drawn the IMF deeper into the role of crisis manager, while effectively removing the external conditions that helped to sustain the restrictive role which its limited resources and conservative frame of reference imposed upon it. In these circumstances the effects of its interventions could become increasingly counter-productive, with potentially disastrous effects on the world economy.

Alongside the IMF, the World Bank, its sister institution, also expanded its activities during the 1970s. During the 1960s its lending had stagnated under very conservative leadership, but when Robert McNamara took over it became a far more dynamic force. McNamara, a somewhat shell-shocked veteran of the US war in Vietnam, had clearly come to recognise the crucial importance of the developmental problem if other countries were not to go the same way, as his many speeches clearly show. Not only did he recognise the need for greater lending, he also appointed a radical team to the Bank's research department, which, from the early

1970s, began to press for policies committed not only to growth, but also to redistribution.

Following closely on the analysis presented in earlier International Labour Office country studies,[61] the Bank brought out *Redistribution with Growth*[62] in conjunction with the Institute of Development Studies at Sussex University in 1974. This recognised the existence of a two-sector economy in LDCs, with the bulk of the employment opportunities being found in the 'informal' sector characterised by small-scale operation, simple, often domestic technology, and widespread exclusion from organised marketing structures and the benefits of public investment. Whereas most orthodox theorists treated this sector as dominated by 'traditional values' and economic inefficiency to be eliminated through a dynamic expansion of the 'formal' large-scale sector, the *Redistribution with Growth* approach accepted that its members operated as rational economic maximisers in a hostile environment making a major contribution to welfare and political stability. This view, subsequently extended in the so-called 'basic needs' approach, mainly developed by the ILO,[63] implied a fundamental redirection of policy involving a much smaller emphasis on foreign trade and foreign capital and much stronger emphasis on employment creation and human capital formation.

Some of the more general implications and weaknesses of this analysis will be considered in the final chapter in relation to the other views discussed already. Here it is perhaps sufficient to note that, although of considerable ideological importance given the immense influence exerted by the World Bank, it does not appear to have moved very far out of the research department into the areas where the operational decisions are taken. Furthermore, other, and perhaps more influential, theorists associated with the Bank have clearly retained their full commitment to the orthodox liberal export-oriented strategy discussed earlier.[64] The overall approach to development policy displayed in the Bank's very important country studies carried out before any country becomes eligible for large-scale lending, strongly emphasises this orientation.[65]

Before completing his work at the Bank, McNamara accepted a further initiative, with the introduction of a programme designed to provide long-term balance of payments financing, rather than project aid,[66] but it now seems that this relatively expansionary and innovative period has come to an end. McNamara was replaced in

1981 by Clausen, a traditional banker, and this change was associated with the advent of Reaganism in the USA. Despite the devastating effect of the recession on the position of the poorer countries and especially of the poorest peoples in them, the Americans have reduced their committment to IDA funding, held up negotiations and curtailed the level of activity to a serious degree. Thus, although IDA disbursements as presented in Table 8.1 show a sharply rising trend in the 1980s, this is a reflection of decisions made earlier, since the quantity of new loans is stagnating, and the funds available to IDA are very likely to fall in real terms.[67] The *Redistribution with Growth* group at the research department has been disbanded and the research department is under the control of Anne Krueger, a leading exponent of the liberal export-orientation school. Thus it is highly unlikely that the Bank will be in the forefront of any radical effort to alter the structure of an increasingly inequitable situation in the immediate future. Indeed, this liberal view has strongly influenced its response to the crisis in Africa, as exemplified in a recent special World Bank study.[68]

Table 8.1   **World Bank and IDA lending 1966–82 ($million, annual averages)**

	1966–70	1971–75	1976–80	1981–83
World Bank	753	1361	3172	6068
IDA	265	545	1249	2180

SOURCE: World Bank, *Annual Reports.*

We can see that there has been some attempt by the official agencies to respond to the crisis by expanding the resources available to the Third World, but this has not occurred on a scale commensurate with the problem. Further, their interventions are still heavily influenced by their role as guardians and managers of an essentially liberal international economic order and hence take too little account of the inequalities built into the structure of a competitive trading system which constantly undermine the viability of the weaker sections of the Third World. Thus their role has been a fundamentally conservative one whose inadequacy is being increasingly exposed by the progressive deterioration in the relationship between the private international banking system and its leading Third World clients, to which we can now turn.

9
Private Banks, LDC Debt, Global Disequilibrium

> Though foreign loans are indispensable for the emancipation of the rising capitalist states, they are yet the surest ties by which the old capitalist states maintain their influence, exercise financial control and exert pressure on the customs, foreign and commercial policy of the young capitalist states.
> (Rosa Luxemburg, *The accumulation of capital*, 1913, p. 421)

> There are 10 countries in the developing world that are crucial to the future success or failure of world capitalism. Between them, they contain 13% of the world's population, they produce 8% of its gross national product, and they account for $355 billion, or 47%, of developing countries debt. Watch them closely, for they are all market economies, and some of them are in great danger.
> (*Euromoney*, October 1983, p. 64)

By 1982 national governments had borrowed more than a trillion dollars from the private international banking system, and a number of them could no longer meet the obligations they had accumulated. What had once appeared to be a very successful resort to the market mechanism to deal with the problem of structural balance of payments deficits along Keynesian lines, had instead produced a debt structure which had come to threaten the stability of the capitalist system itself.[1] This has locked a number of important banks into a symbiotic relationship with about a dozen of the most advanced LDCs which could threaten many banks' long-term survival if the countries concerned are unable to improve their external performance dramatically. It has produced a situation in which many countries are having to reduce their imports, thus cutting consumption and domestic investment and also destroying jobs in the industrial exporting countries. It has also forced the leading international agencies and the governments of the main industrial countries to evolve large-scale rescue packages that involve a direct interference with the market mechanism, and which puts very large amounts of public money at risk. Thus what we are concerned with here is nothing less than the relationship between private and public economic power at the highest level and in its most developed form – a relationship which has hitherto enabled the system to manage its most severe contradictions but which is now in deep crisis. To understand why this should be so it will first be necessary to show why the market has grown so quickly and why its organisation makes it particularly vulnerable to exogenous disruption.

According to the Bank for International Settlements, the size of the 'eurodollar' or 'eurocurrency' market grew in gross terms from $131.8 billion in 1972 to $1,686 billion in 1982; with inter-bank lending eliminated, the corresponding figures were $91 billion and $1,020 billion.[2] These figures are, however, a substantial underestimate of the overall growth in borrowing, since they exclude short-term debt, the activities of the Middle Eastern banks which are now extensive, and most military debt. According to the World Bank, total private and official LDC debt rose from $91 billion to $462 billion between 1972 and 1982, but the addition of short-term borrowing would push that figure up to well over $600 billion.[3] This debt is highly concentrated, with 65 per cent going to the thirteen largest borrowers,[4] but almost none of the private credit to the poorest countries. Since the crisis in 1982, the IMF has also become a large lender, and by early 1984 had almost $9 billion outstanding.[5] By the early 1980s the major banks, the most important being those in the USA, Britain and Germany, had lent sums to LDCs far in excess of their capital assets and could therefore very easily be technically bankrupted if these debts ceased to 'perform'.[6] Despite the problems involved, the whole enterprise has been and continues to be an immensely profitable one – in 1976, for example, Chase Manhattan earned 78 per cent of its profits on its international operations.[7]

The reasons for this massive expansion in debt have to be considered in relation to both demand and supply. Why do the countries concerned need to borrow, and why do the banks have the money to lend? We have already seen in earlier chapters that the

developing countries as a whole (and this chapter will confine itself
to this aspect of the problem, since this is where the difficulties have
arisen) can be expected to be net importers of capital and therefore
substantial borrowers on international credit markets. Furthermore, by the end of the 1960s a number of the more successful
countries had become successful exporters and had increased the
speed at which they were industrialising so that they could now be
expected to graduate from concessional official aid to independent
operators on the private market. But in addition, the oil price
increases of 1973/4 and 1979, together with the worsening external
environment produced by the recession, led to a rapid widening of
balance of payments deficits: those for non-oil LDCs increased
from $11.3 billion in 1973 to $46.3 billion in 1975, fell to $28.9
billion in 1977, but then rose to $107.7 billion in 1981 and were still
an estimated $68 billion in 1983.[8]

In this situation the choice was to borrow or to cut back imports,
and hence consumption and development, to levels which would
have threatened economic and political stability and almost certainly turned the international recession into a deep depression. While
most of the poorest countries were forced to take this course since
they were not credit-worthy enough to enter the private market
place, the middle-income countries as a group became major
borrowers and were therefore able to sustain the highly positive
growth rates described in the preceding chapter. This process was
greeted with widespread acclaim at the time as a vindication of the
market mechanism, which, in the case of international banking, was
operating in an almost completely uncontrolled form, since the
system was almost wholly unregulated by national authorities.[9] As
the Bank for International Settlements (BIS) put it, the 'functioning
of the world economy and the international financial system has
since 1974, and in particular following the successive oil shocks,
depended on the role of the intermediary played by international
banks'.[10] It was widely assumed at the time that this would not
create serious long-term problems, since interest rates were low and
even negative, and the deficit problem was expected to be a
temporary one.

On the supply side the banks were able to finance their activities
by using the US deficit and the OPEC oil surpluses at different
stages of the period from the late 1960s, when the market first
began to expand rapidly, to the present, when it has begun to

contract. This expansion of surpluses, however, coincided with the recession, and thus with limited demand for credit from the large-scale corporate sector – normally the bankers' largest customer.[11] Thus, unable to lend to domestic investors on a sufficient scale, the banks were forced to lend to LDC governments in amounts that would not have been made available in other circumstances. During these years the BIS was constantly expressing its concern with the lack of 'prudence' in banking behaviour, but, in a highly competitive industry in which profits could only be made by finding large-scale borrowers, it is difficult to see how else the bankers could have behaved.

What we are dealing with here, therefore, is a global system for resource transfers from and to governments and private enterprises, mediated by a structure of private financial organisation whose primary concern is its own profitability and whose activities are determined by market competition alone. The future of depositors, borrowers, of the banks themselves and, in the last analysis, of the capitalist system as a whole, is, therefore, tied to the adequacy of this mechanism, a mechanism which, although controlled by the market, has profound political implications. Here neither political nor economic variables can be understood in isolation from each other, nor, given the scale of the transfers involved, in isolation from the functioning of the world economy itself. Any failure in this system will therefore have fundamental implications for the stability of the banking system, for the political and economic viability of the borrowing countries, and for the future dynamism of the world economy. To deal with these problems we must look at the technicalities involved, at the reasons why that system has been brought under pressure, at the effects of that pressure on banks, debtor countries and the world economy, and at the adequacy of the measures that have been implemented to deal with them.

In any banking system, interest rates provide the major source of profit to the banks and of costs to the debtor, but are only partially determined by the direct relation between lender and borrower. The banks borrow from depositors or other banks at a rate generally taken to be the London Inter-Bank Offer Rate (LIBOR), and lend them at LIBOR plus a 'spread' (which is that part of the interest rate accruing directly to the bank) negotiated with the final borrower. LIBOR will be determined at any point in time by the general interest rates prevailing in the industrial countries and more especially in the USA, spreads by the credit-worthiness of the borrower and the intensity of the competition between banks for customers. Most loans are now made on a variable interest rate basis, where rates are renegotiated every six months to take account of the changes in LIBOR.

Over the last decade, however, this system has produced some problematic results, since monetarist policies in the leading countries have pushed interest rates up to record levels despite the large supply of funds on the market. Thus LIBOR has fluctuated dramatically during these years, having been 5 per cent at the end of 1976, 19.7 per cent in March 1980 and 9.6 per cent in January and 11.7 per cent in May 1984.[12] Although *nominal* rates have tended to fall since the early 1980s, they have actually increased in *real* terms as a result of falling inflation and especially of falling raw material prices. On the other hand, the large supply of funds combined with sharp banking competition has kept spreads very low: for 'prime' borrowers they have gone down as far as 0.33 per cent and even LDC governments have been paying less than 1 per cent. Thus, despite the fact that the final borrowers have had to pay a great deal for their money, the banks have been operating on small margins which could lead them into difficulty. Most loans are organised on a consortium basis with many banks contributing, where the 'lead' bank carries out the operation and is paid substantial fees for the effort. This provides them with a large proportion of their income, but this option is not open to the smaller banks which have to live by spreads alone. Thus the interest rate system has tended to penalise final borrowers by imposing huge and variable interest rates on them (a 1 per cent increase in LIBOR adds $3,160 billion to the current account deficit of the ten largest borrowers), while still leaving the banks, and especially the smaller ones, operating on margins that are dangerously thin.

Secondly, maturities (the repayment period) are also directly affected by competition, and the conditions prevailing during the 1970s led the banks to borrow short and to lend long. Thus, with money which might have to be repaid at a week's notice covering debts extended for six to eight years, the banks could find themselves caught in a 'maturity transformation problem', where a large-scale withdrawal of deposits forced them back to the market to find new and more expensive deposits. In this situation, with very thin spreads, profits very quickly turn into losses, as the bankrupting in 1974 of Franklin National, a large US bank, clearly demonstrated.[13] For borrowers, long maturities are a distinct advantage, especially when inflation is eroding the real cost of the debt, as was the case in the late 1970s. But here problems arise out of a bunching of repayments at particular points in the future where external circumstances (like a change in the oil-price) might adversely affect the balance of payments. This problem can be greatly worsened where borrowers resort to short-term credit to deal with an immediate short-fall, as was recently the case with several large debtors. In this case debt service ratios (the ratio of foreign exchange earnings to all debt payments) can reach unsustainable levels – in 1983, for example, those for Argentina, Brazil and Mexico were estimated at 174 per cent, 149 per cent and 141 per cent respectively[14] – and rescheduling becomes inevitable.

Thirdly, the banking system is highly integrated, since much of the money involved is raised on the inter-bank market with smaller banks borrowing from larger ones, rather than directly from depositors. Thus a bank failure anywhere in the system is bound to threaten profits, and therefore confidence in the whole edifice, since 'in a banking crisis, banks would have difficulty collecting funds due to them from a failing bank, while the failing bank or its liquidators would insist on funds due to it from other banks'.[15] In 1974 the German Herstatt bank was closed leaving $30 million in inter-bank credits unpaid; in 1982 Banco Ambrosiano Holdings in Luxembourg closed owing some $450 million to eighty-eight other banks; and the Mexican default in August 1982 put $6–7 billion worth of inter-bank loans at risk received by Mexican from foreign banks. Thus although the system is regulated through individualistic competition, its structure is highly collective, so that individual acts of irresponsibility or illegality (which occurred in the Herstatt, Ambrosiano and Franklin National cases) constitute a threat to the integrity of the market as a whole.[16]

Finally, despite its immense importance and vulnerability, the eurodollar market has operated almost entirely outside any system of effective political control. Domestic banking, especially after the crisis of the early 1930s, has been subjected to close supervision from central banks involving the enforcement of 'prudent' ratios between reserves and liabilities, the monitoring of banking practices and the creation of an official 'lender of last resort' capable of guaranteeing deposits if banks failed. This has been of the greatest importance in guaranteeing public confidence and therefore bank-ing stability, since one of the greatest problems in banking is the possibility that deposits will be withdrawn from fundamentally sound banks in response to short-term difficulties, thus pushing them into bankruptcy.

The eurodollar market has grown up outside this context. In London, its largest centre, *external* transactions are kept separate from domestic ones and not subjected to Bank of England scrutiny, while a number of other centres have been created in small Third World countries like the Bahamas and the Cayman Islands from which the banks, far more powerful than the host governments, are able to operate very much as they please. In the 1960s the leading American banks, closely regulated at home, moved into these 'offshore' havens on a large scale, and in the age of convertible currencies and electronic communication, have been able to use them to transfer resources from branch to branch at will. Since 1981 US bank regulations have been modified to allow their own banks to set up domestic International Banking Facilities (IBFs) with the same freedom as their branches enjoyed abroad in order to capture a part of this large market, so that the relaxation of controls has been increasing rather than declining, even into the 1980s.

But even within this highly permissive environment the interna-tional structure of the banks' operations gives them further free-doms. Banks, like other MNCs, have been able to exploit the possibilities of transfer pricing by moving funds from one branch to another at prices which are not market-related and which therefore enable them to declare their profits wherever this is most advan-tageous, and, it would seem, to avoid the effects of domestic regulations where these do subject them to irksome constraints.[17] In the mid-1970s the BIS set up a special committee (the 'Cooke Committee') to monitor the system and ensure that 'prudential' standards were maintained, but, in the absence of a global political authority with powers of enforcement behind it, in the face of compliant national governments anxious to attract as much banking business to their shores as possible, and dealing with international firms able to exploit their global reach, creative accounting techni-ques and the most advanced electronic technology, it is difficult to see how they can hope to bring this system under effective control. What we are dealing with here, therefore, is something close to a paradigm case of the effects of unregulated market competition on a large and complex resource allocation process. The outcome does not make happy reading for the proponents of this mode of social organisation for reasons that are related directly to the uneven development manifested in the world economy over the past decade. Before considering the implications of these results, however, it is first necessary to say something about the requirements of the banking system itself.

A viable banking system involves a transfer of resources from a saver to an investor at a rate of interest which can subsequently be covered from the increased output generated by the new productive capacity so created. Where this occurs, an increase in net indebtedness does not imply a fundamental problem, since repayments will be covered by increased income, and borrower, lender and depositor will all have benefited from the relationship.[18] Where the borrowing is only used to sustain current consumption or investment with a rate of return lower than the rate of interest, however, the accumulation of debt will soon produce a burden of repayments which will lead to bankruptcy in a private firm and to increased taxation and reduced consumption and investment in a national economy.[19] Banking will then have changed into *usury*, and the system will soon collapse.

In the case of the international banking system, moreover, these conditions have to be met in a specific way. Loans are made and must be repaid in foreign exchange, so that the system can only survive if the country concerned can sustain a large enough increase in exports (or reduction in imports) to cover the additional repayments. Thus the general effect of the expansion of international banking is to tie the LDCs concerned ever more firmly into an export-oriented strategy rather than one involving greater national self-sufficiency, and also to make the relationship involved particularly vulnerable to adverse changes in the international economy. Unless borrowers can develop adequate new investments in *internationally competitive production processes*, whether directly financed by the loans involved or indirectly in response to the new infrastructure so created, the process must soon be halted. It was because growth in the industrial countries from the early 1970s had reduced the demand for credit among large corporations there that the bankers were forced to extend loans to LDC governments which were not covered by the economic guarantees and legal safeguards which would have existed in the private sector.

As we have seen, the growth of the eurodollar market has been a direct response to the uneven development of the global economy since the late 1960s. At that stage it was a function of the escalating American deficit; since then this element has varied in importance and has been joined by the oil surpluses of 1974 to 1977 and again from 1979 to 1982. These have both created a demand for foreign credit to fund balance of payments deficits and generated the savings at other points in the system to allow the banks to perform the function. Despite the absence of any official mechanism for this purpose along the lines envisaged by Keynes at Bretton Woods, the private banking system was able to meet the need and to allow the wealthier LDCs to increase their indebtedness by more than 25 per cent each year up to 1982. The banks felt that their loans were guaranteed by the ability of the governments concerned to repay them out of their general foreign exchange earnings, and therefore failed to subject individual loans to close scrutiny.[20] The governments between 1974 and 1980 were able to rely on rising prices to offset the real cost of their accumulated debts plus increasing general and export growth. According to the World Bank:

> In the 1970s economic growth averaged 8% a year in the East Asian and Pacific area and 6% a year in Latin America and the Caribbean ... Export growth was likewise exceptional for some of these countries in the 1970s; average annual growth of merchandise exports from the Republic of Korea was 23% a year, for Mexico it was 13.4%, Chile 10.9%, Argentina 9.3%, Brazil 7.5%.[21]

But even this growth, based on easy access to credit and rising prices, was insufficient to match the growth in debt servicing obligations, and the implementation of an anti-inflationary strategy based upon high interest rates became general in the industrial countries. Demand and raw material prices fell sharply, while servicing charges increased equally quickly. Inability to pay soon led to an avalanche of rescheduling – the sums involved increased from $4.9 billion in 1979 to $27.9 billion in 1982.[22] In that year the three largest borrowers, Mexico, Argentina and Brazil, defaulted in quick succession and the bubble had burst. It was now evident that far from having solved the crisis of capitalism as the optimists had assumed, the growth of international lending had merely postponed and intensified it, as Marxist theory would suggest.[23]

In the second half of 1982, therefore, the system was confronted with a crisis at least as serious as any that had occurred since the war. The main threat was a fully fledged repudiation of debt by any of the major borrowers since this could have been followed by others and put the existence of the leading banks at risk. The main safeguard against a debt repudiation is usually the loss of access to new loans and the threat of legal action resulting in the sequestration of a country's foreign assets by the creditor banks, but as early as 1982 the main borrowers were paying out far more than they were receiving and, once the crisis had struck, would only be borrowing in order to repay earlier debts for a long time to come. Thus, on the basis of purely financial considerations, they must have been sorely tempted to refuse to pay and may well only have been restrained by the threat of legal actions by the banks. From the start of 1982 onwards debt negotiations took place in a context in which virtually the whole of these countries' foreign exchange earnings would be mortgaged to meet the immediate debt commitments, and in which they were now transferring billions of dollars to the advanced industrial countries. In the eighteen months from the start of 1982, Amex estimates that about $47 billion left the twenty-four major LDC borrowers in net outflows, while some $25 billion was exported from Mexico by private individuals, mostly to the USA.[24] Indeed, the most recent BIS report suggests that this has been a more general and longer-term problem, since 'the external position in Latin America appears to have been severely aggravated by private-sector capital outflows' which they estimate to have totalled 'around $50 billion' between 1978 and 1983.[25] Far from the Third World being in receipt of development finance from the Western countries, it has therefore now become a major net exporter of capital. The economic and political consequences of this situation are complex and far-reaching both at the level of the system as a whole and in the debtor countries concerned. Let us now consider them in that order.

Having allowed the banks to make their profits where they could for fifteen years, the international authorities were then forced to mobilise immense amounts of resources in 1982 to rescue them from a catastrophic collapse. In the absence of an effective lender of last resort capable of guaranteeing the deposits of the threatened banks, the agencies most closely involved – the BIS, the IMF and the US government – were forced to substitute for this role by extending sufficient credits to the borrowers to make it possible for them to meet their commitments. The decision to ignore the normal working of the market mechanism and allow the imprudence of the bankers to go unpunished was quite deliberate. As BIS put it, they had to make a fundamental choice between 'preserving the normal functioning of the markets' and thus letting

> those countries which are unable to repay interest and principal be declared in default, and leave the resulting losses to be borne by the imprudent lenders. In this way both borrowers and lenders would think twice before again engaging in such imprudent credit arrangements.[26]

This was a solution, it should be said, which would have involved far lower costs for the borrowers than the one that was eventually arrived at. Alternatively they could intervene to rescue the system by mobilising official support for it, a decision they took with great expedition, because 'a problem of worldwide proportions had emerged', there was 'no world government' to limit the damage it might cause; the crisis was the outcome of a combination of eventualities which made it impossible to know 'which of the countries is likely to be unable in the future to service its debt'; and debtors, as sovereign countries, were not private corporations with assets that could 'be taken over by the creditors or sold off to another country'.[27]

The inadequacy of the political structures surrounding the functioning of the global economy was never more apparent nor more clearly recognised, and those agencies which did exist, and notably the BIS and IMF, were then forced to take on an active redistributive role despite the *laissez-faire* theory which had always dominated their thinking. The agencies, the leading industrial countries and the banks worked out a co-ordinated rescue package in association with the debtors to stave off the immediate threat of default, and to provide for a longer-term adjustment programme. The BIS, working in close touch with the US government, immediately guaranteed emergency credits of $1,850 billion to Mexico, $1,450 billion to Brazil and $500 billion to Argentina, and made these conditional on continued lending by the private banks, despite the fact that none of them would voluntarily have been willing to do so. For the longer term, additional credits were tied to a willingness to accept IMF conditionality and the adjustment programmes associated with them. This has meant the very large increases in IMF quotas discussed in Chapter 8, introduced in record time despite strong domestic opposition in the USA, and an ongoing and deeply problematic involvement by the IMF in the design and implementation of massively unpopular austerity programmes in the debtor countries.

Having thus had to deal with the crisis created by tying the recycling process to a purely commercial mechanism, a number of established authorities are now calling for a far more extensive recycling mechanism to deal with the problems of resource transfers, with the BIS, for example, concluding its analysis of the problem by asserting that 'any longer-term scenario that did not call for sharply increased resources to be put at the disposal of *both* [the IMF and the World Bank], well beyond what may be needed in any case in the short run, is virtually inconceivable'. Here the Bank in particular is to be given the role of providing the resources needed to finance the long-term 'deficits corresponding to development needs', which the BIS now recognises cannot be adequately met through domestic investment effort, private investment or bilateral aid all of which, it feels, 'tend to reinforce the prevailing trend towards protectionism and the fragmentation of the world economy'.[28] Thus the crisis, having forced an unplanned and unintended resort to greatly increased *official* recycling to avoid a general collapse, has now produced a renewed recognition of the need for a far more adequate, politically controlled global redistributive mechanism than exists at present. We can therefore conclude this chapter by looking at the medium-term prospects of the measures that have already been taken, and at the longer-term implications of the problems of global economic management which the debt crisis has so clearly exposed.

For the present programme to hold together, the costs of existing debts must fall and/or the level of LDC exports must rise. Although the latter depends to some extent on the domestic economic efficiency of the borrowers, both depend far more directly upon events in the industrial economies, where interest rates and LDC export markets are mainly determined. At present most commentators hope that sustained growth combined with low inflation in these economies will keep interest rates down, stabilise raw material prices and expand markets for LDC manufacturers. A 1 per cent fall in LIBOR together with a 1 per cent increase in industrial country growth rates would reduce the deficits of the ten main borrowers by more than $6 billion and perhaps bring the problem under control over time.[29] In 1983 it began to seem that the worst effects of the recession were over, as growth rates began to recover, led by the growth of the US deficit.

Thus, although conceding that the approach 'seems rather precarious, vulnerable to accidents, and to changes in what lawyers call material adverse circumstances – and very hard on the nerves, a senior banker was recently 'not persuaded that the market mechanisms, supplemented by IMF programmes and official support, could not themselves develop and adjust, given time, ingenuity and the will to succeed'.[30]

Yet it would be foolish to take such claims at face value, especially given the immense vested interest that all bankers have in sustaining confidence in a system which has the inherent stability of a house of cards. A dispassionate look at the situation suggests instead that the long-term prognosis is no better than it was in the early part of 1982, when officialdom as a whole appeared to have no idea that a major crisis was only weeks away.

Firstly, there is little indication that the *real* costs of debt servicing are going to fall soon. Rescheduling has involved a sharp reduction in immediate repayments, but at the cost of much larger total repayments arising out of sharply increased spreads and the cost of servicing debts over a much longer period.[31] Thus, far from the banks suffering serious losses, *if* the present strategy holds, these changes will ensure that they will greatly increase their profits. Perhaps most significant of all, in 1983/4 it became clear that the effects of a large US budget deficit and tight monetary policies were not only increasing imports, but also forcing up real interest rates and the value of the dollar, thus significantly increasing debt servicing costs at a time when raw material prices were at historically low levels,[32] and when many manufactured exports from LDCs were meeting greater protectionist barriers in the US market. Thus Minford was able to demonstrate that these policies have enabled the USA to draw in a large flow of foreign resources to finance growth, and that the LDCs' '"debt crisis" can be laid squarely at the door of US fiscal policy'.[33] This has not only created immense economic problems for the debtors, but also exposed the inequitable nature of an economic system in which the richest country can secure substantial benefits by unilaterally imposing substantial resource transfers upon a number of much poorer ones. This has created an immense and justified resentment among the debtor nations and led to increasingly co-ordinated action, in particular in Latin America, designed to overcome these problems. In May 1984, for example, Brazil, Mexico, Argentina and Colombia formally announced that:

> We do not accept being pressed into a situation of forced bankruptcy and of prolonged economic paralysis.
> We consider it indispensable that the international community initiates, without delay, a concerted effort aimed at defining actions and co-operation measures which would permit a resolution of these problems, particularly in the interrelated sectors of commerce and international finance.[34]

Here, in remarkably clear relief, we can therefore see again that the resolution of the conflicts of interest generated by the functioning of the global economy requires political solutions at the international level for which the existing machinery is entirely inadequate. Although the international agencies have been able to limit the worst effects of the crisis, they have been entirely unable to stop either the banks or the American government from following policies which first created and are now intensifying it. Indeed, their main political input has been to impose adjustment policies on the major debtors which have substantially reduced domestic consumption and are now greatly intensifying political tensions.

Secondly, it would be optimistic to rely on sustained growth in the OECD countries, since there are already signs that the US budget/balance of payments deficit will not be sustained after the next presidential election, and this is likely to lead again to increased interest rates and falling demand. Furthermore, protectionist pressure against LDC exports of manufactures is hardly likely to fall, and this will inhibit both their domestic growth and increased export earnings. The Americans, for example, have recently increased protective barriers against the import of Brazilian steel. Thus history is repeating itself. In the 1920s there were mass defaults on American overseas investments, not least because 'all this lending had taken place without any assurance that the USA would be prepared to accept interest and amortization payments in the form of goods and services'.[35] Thus, not only will the debtors have to find increased income with which to meet their existing obligations, but they will also find it more and more difficult to sell their goods in foreign markets and earn the foreign exchange required.

Thirdly, although the current supply of official and private credit is far larger than it would have been without strong political intervention, this has only very partially offset the fundamental change in the overall functioning of the credit system that became fully visible in the first half of 1982. By then it had ceased being a mechanism generating a new flow of resources to deficit countries and begun to work sharply in the opposite direction. Thus, having temporarily resolved the problem of uneven development in the late 1970s, it is now strongly reinforcing it, with devastating consequences for the viability of the system as a whole.

These consequences are being most strongly felt in the LDCs concerned, where the effect of the IMF adjustment programmes they have had to accept has been a deflationary reduction in imports, rather than an increase in exports, with Mexico, for example, cutting imports by £14 billion in the year after the crisis. This, of course, must have a serious effect on consumption, with the worst suffering, in the presence of an IMF programme, inevitably being felt by the poorest.[36] Equally important, it must also have significant effects on economic activity, making it virtually impossible to maintain existing capital equipment, let alone lead to investment in new capacity. Thus, although we noted earlier that debts can only be repaid through the creation of new productivity, there has been sharp regression in all of the countries involved in stringent adjustment programmes, so that their real capacity to deal with the problem has actually been reduced.[37] Lending money merely to keep debtors afloat while destroying the productivity of their economic system is surely the classic definition of what constitutes usury rather than rational economic intervention.

Fourthly, the problem is not confined to the debtors, since, as we have seen, it was the buoyancy of their credit-led growth in the 1970s that served to do much to offset the recessionary tendencies then. Now this process has been reversed and their inability to import is cutting markets and jobs in the developed countries. Thus Morgan Guaranty notes that the USA loses 25,000 jobs for each cut of a billion dollars in its exports and has heavy 'yet poorly recognised' loss of sales to LDCs:

Inability to service debts has deprived many LDCs of access to credit, forcing them to cut back imports and hurting US exports. Relative to the 1981 position, the entire deterioration in the 1983 year-to-date US merchandise balance – $21 billion – is paralleled in the trade balance with non-OPEC developing countries and the Eastern bloc. The incidence of deterioration correlates with credit difficulties . . . first half 1983 data show that other industrial-country exporters have experienced similar declines.[38]

Hence it is clear that at least 500,000 jobs were lost in the USA in 1982/3 as a result of the debt crisis, and a great many more in the rest of the industrial countries. Unless the present pattern of net transfers from the South to the North can be quickly reversed, therefore, it will continue to impose a strong deflationary pressure on what is in any case a weak recovery process in the world economy as a whole.

Fifthly, the accumulation of LDC debt and problems arising out of the need to write off loans to domestic companies bankrupted by the recession has now pushed the banking system to the point where its stability is seriously threatened. A large number of smaller banks have failed in many countries, especially after 1981, but most significantly, the 'unthinkable' finally occurred in May 1984 with the failure of Continental Illinois, one of the largest of the American banks. Carrying a number of 'non-performing' domestic loans and with a very heavy exposure in Latin America, it lost the confidence of its depositors and only survived as a result of an infusion of some $7.5 billion 'provided jointly by the federal authorities and the [other large] commercial banks'. By the end of July two rescue attempts had been made and failed, and a third had been announced under which 'the Federal Deposit Insurance Corporation, America's banking watchdog, is expected to take 80%' of its equity, thus effectively leading to 'the nationalisation of the nation's sixth largest bank'.[39] Not long after this failure strong rumours surfaced predicting the failure of Manufacturers Hanover, America's third largest bank, which had the largest overseas exposure, but these subsequently disapppeared. But although the crisis was contained in the short run, these developments mean that the stability of these formerly utterly safe institutions can no longer be guaranteed, that it will be immensely expensive if others have to be rescued, and that it will clearly no longer be possible for them to perform the international financial recycling role which they performed on such a large scale between 1974 and 1982.

Finally there is little evidence to suggest that greatly increased concessional flows are likely to be forthcoming in the immediate future, despite the authoritative nature of the calls being made for them. The recent increase in IMF quotas will all be absorbed in repayments to Western banks and will have no effect on productive capacity in LDCs. Mainly as a result of US opposition, the present replenishment of IDA will fall far short of what already exists and of what is required to sustain the present programme. Restrictive fiscal policies are also constraining the growth of bilateral aid spending, as we have seen. Thus there is little sign of an adequate political response to the need for additional flows from Western countries, as the refusal to respond to the Brandt Commission at the Cancun conference clearly demonstrated. As a result, a major reflationary element which kept the global economy growing in the 1970s has now gone into reverse and the programmes devised to stabilise the situation can do no more than moderate the most immediate short-term effects, while actually worsening the underlying problem.

Both the attempt and the failure to deal adequately with the economic crisis generated by the debt problem must have profound long-term political consequences for the management of the world economy as a whole. This has exposed both the need for an effective global redistributive mechanism to offset the negative effects of uneven development, and the dangerously inadequate nature of the market-directed structures that emerged to deal with it at the end of the 1960s. We can therefore conclude this chapter by looking at some of the more important political issues involved, issues which have largely been ignored during the settlement of the present problem, but which will have to be resolved if the integrity of the system is to be maintained.

Firstly, for an open and integrated world economy to exist it must be able, as we have argued earlier, to create structures which ensure that all of its elements, and especially the poorest of them, benefit from the way in which it functions. Yet the private recycling mechanism operating since the oil price increase in 1974 has contributed virtually nothing to the development of the least developed countries, and therefore served as a significant factor in the growing gap between their productive capacity and that of the two dozen countries that it did serve. Although these countries are now having to retrench in order to meet their debts, they are doing so from a position of much greater strength than would have been the case otherwise. The poorest countries, however, as we saw in Chapter 7, have in many cases suffered real regressions in per capita incomes over the same period, and are now having to cope with the recession and low raw material prices from a resource base which is actually deteriorating. It is difficult to discuss the consequences of this process in the dispassionate language normally expected of social scientists: it has meant an intensification of conditions of life of the utmost degradation for millions of people, conditions which should be intolerable in a world with the technical capacity finally to eliminate them. No system which claims to be built on co-operation and rational social organisation as opposed to pure repression can hope to sustain its long-term ideological legitimacy if these inequalities are allowed to persist.

Secondly, the impact of externally induced adjustment policies on the standard of living of the bulk of the populations in the worst affected debtor countries is subjecting their already fragile political systems to intense stress. No doubt externally supported regimes prepared to intensify repression could be created to deal with these problems, but the costs and risks are high. Not even the most complex and lavishly funded repressive apparatus in the Third World was able to rescue the Shah of Iran in 1978, nor an American war the capitalist regime in South Vietnam. It is clear to everyone in these countries that their sufferings are the direct result of the need to repay loans to foreign banks which even respected bourgeois organisations like the BIS recognise as having been irresponsible and ill-conceived. The BIS may feel that the banks must be baled out in order to rescue the international capitalist system, but it is not self-evident that the workers and peasants of Latin America, who are actually having to pay the bill in the last analysis, will agree with this. The possibility of a powerful populist movement built around a demand for debt repudiation and national economic autonomy is therefore going to grow each day the austerity programmes remain in place. Unless some mechanism can be found that will enable these classes to be reintegrated into a growth process capable of reversing the losses they are suffering now, both the political and economic integrity of the financial system will be threatened.

Thirdly, the possibility of a wider banking collapse can no longer be ignored. If the political situation destabilises further in any of the major debtors, and it is already very difficult in several of them, this will further expose the fragility of the relationship between assets and liabilities in the banking system and could always lead to a crisis of confidence. Further, as I have argued elsewhere,[40] and was also the case with Continental Illinois, the stability of the banking system can be threatened not merely by losses in the eurocurrency markets, but also in their other dealings like domestic lending, foreign exchange dealing and operations on the bond market. In all of these areas the system is much less stable than it was before, and although this always creates the possibility of large profits, it also creates the possibility of equally large losses. Thus, even though the national authorities are unlikely to allow banks like Lloyds or Chase to go to the wall, the cost of rescuing them could be immense, and the effect of doing so on the overall problem of economic management correspondingly disruptive.

Finally, we can also see how everything in this chapter reinforces the political analysis presented in Chapter 2. There we argued that a global process of exchange based on a market mechanism cannot be treated as an apolitical entity capable of virtually administering itself on the basis of arms-length negotiations between sovereign nation states in a context of global agencies committed to pure *laissez-faire*. Huge redistributive flows have been needed to stabilise and equalise world economic development since the end of the war, and the growth of the private eurocurrency system in the 1970s did nothing to change this. For reasons outside their control, the bankers were pushed into a recycling process which was already unsustainable over the long run, whose dangers were pointed out very early,[41] and which collapsed dramatically in 1982. Confronted with the real consequences of *laissez-faire*, even its most ardent exponents immediately withdrew and mobilised massive amounts of official resources to rescue the economy, thus demonstrating in action, if not in words, that capitalism as a system cannot survive without a political mechanism which provides it with effective and rational social control.

These *ad hoc* interventions have served to stabilise the crisis in the short run, but not to provide the system as a whole with a mechanism that can operate both effectively and legitimately in the long run. To do this we will need a major restructuring at both the global and the domestic levels, and a restructuring that will require a much more effective political mechanism to bring the market under social control and ensure that it ceases to create crises which threaten economic stability and, indeed, civilisation itself.

Conclusion: Out of Anarchy?

the avoidance of unemployment or under-employment, through the achievement and maintenance in each country of useful employment opportunities for those willing and able to work and of a large and steadily growing volume of production and effective demand for goods and services, is not of domestic concern alone, but is also a necessary condition for the achievement of the general purposes and objectives of the Charter, including the expansion of international trade, and thus for the well-being of all other countries.

(*Havana Charter for an International Trade Organisation*, Article 2, 1, 1948)

The correction of maladjustments in the world economy of the magnitude of those which confronted the world after the last war and will again confront it at the end of this war cannot be left to market forces. The necessary adjustments will have to be carefully planned if we are to avoid a repetition of the international economic chaos of the interwar period.

(H. W. Arndt, *The economic lessons of the nineteen-thirties*, 1944, p.297)

Non-intervention in the market cannot apply when there is no more market. (C. G. Langoni, former Governor of the Central Bank of Brazil, *Euromoney*, October 1983, p. 20)

Amidst the carnage of the First World War Lenin saw global capitalism as a system of monopoly competition and imperialistic nationalism which had become 'a shell which no longer fits its contents ... which must inevitably decay ... [and] will inevitably be removed'.[1] He anticipated a general socialist transformation which, in the event, was to be initially confined to his own country. Elsewhere the capitalist system lived on, but in circumstances which could only serve to confirm rather than negate his diagnosis. The Versailles settlement, correctly viewed by Keynes as a recipe for disaster, imposed burdens on the weaker areas which made it impossible for them to rebuild, while the overwhelming strength of the USA, compounded by an irresponsible protectionism, caused it to appropriate an increasing proportion of the world's surpluses. The greater part of the world's population lived in colonial subordination, with industrialisation blocked by the self-interested policies of their occupying powers.[2]

This structure of intensifying inequality imposed intense deflationary pressures on the world economy and soon generated fundamental economic and political instabilities. Depressions in the early 1920s and again on a grand scale in the 1930s induced huge losses of production and an intensification of class struggle, pushing the system in the weaker countries to its outer limits. A choice between socialism and barbarism became inevitable in Italy, Portugal, Japan, Germany and Spain, and in each case the latter triumphed. Democracy was destroyed and the system rescued through the naked exercise of state power. Nor, given the already well developed internationalisation of the system and of the crisis, could the tide of barbarism be confined within national boundaries. The right-wing counter-revolution in the weaker countries was itself a response to the imposition of unacceptable costs on their economies by the operation of the global system. Right-wing nationalism turned effortlessly into militarism in an attempt to restore national prosperity by forcibly appropriating foreign resources. Indeed, far from external exchange becoming a mechanism for mutual benefit, 'under German leadership and example trade in a large part of Europe had been made an instrument for increasing war potential and a weapon to achieve political ends'.[3] Inevitably the tensions arising out of this escalating pattern of mutual hostility and beggar-thy-neighbour competition again engulfed the world in war. The failure to replace the 'decaying shell' after the First World War had, by 1945, left fifty million dead in Europe and Asia and a legacy of military advancement which, in the form of the nuclear arsenal, now threatens human survival itself.

In 1984, however, it is very tempting to look back over those brutal years with considerable complacency. In the late 1940s the ultra-left confidently expected another fundamental economic crisis, an upsurge in the class struggle and the political transformation anticipated by Lenin.[4] George Orwell, one of the most perceptive critics of his time, portrayed a totalitarian world in a state of permanent war in 1984. Yet, as we have seen in the earlier parts of this book, the crisis of the late 1940s was triumphantly overcome and a system of military and economic co-operation created which served to contain communist expansion and underpin a period of sustained growth which was to last for more than twenty-five years. Within the industrialised countries the competitive power and prosperity of Europe and Japan were restored in conditions which allowed for the political and economic incorporation of virtually the whole working class. Within the Third World decolonisation provided for the incorporation of the new national bourgeoisie and, even though it has generally been impossible to create stable democratic institutions in most countries, rapid economic development has occurred very widely and a basis for rapid industrialisation has been created in a number of places. These developments have depended on and given rise to an expansion in international trade and exchanges of all kinds of an entirely unprecedented magnitude, suggesting that humanity has finally been able to organise its global affairs in such a way as to make trade 'the principal guarantee of the peace of the world',[5] rather than an instrument of war and international aggresssion.

These achievements, and such they certainly were, have required the creation of a system of international economic co-operation that was almost entirely absent before the war. This has involved the development of a flexible and powerful mechanism for international payments and credit flows, a set of international agencies designed to regulate the disputes between states and co-ordinate economic policies for the nation state system, the emergence of a group of multinational companies capable of taking modern production processes to the most backward countries, and a structure of military surveilllance which has, like the Pax Britannica of old, guaranteed the free movement of the factors of production and, to a large extent, the sanctity of property rights. These concrete developments have been rationalised and justified through the development of a technically sophisticated theory of free trade – a hegemonic ideology asserting the benefits to the weak as well as the strong necessarily arising out of the liberalisation and extension of international economic co-operation and exchange. An ideology, moreover, which, while always used as a guiding principle, has never been mindlessly enforced where the circumstances prevailing in the weaker countries would turn it into a tool of economic dislocation or political exclusion.

This evolution of structures and theory has raised the level of global productivity and co-operation to levels undreamed of before the war and which Lenin would certainly have considered to be incompatible with the continued operation of the capitalist system. What we must now consider is whether they have, in fact, resolved the tensions that have always lurked below the surface within that system, and thus produced a regenerated 'shell' still capable of providing us with the framework required for a further period of stable and equitable growth. This book has been built around an attempt to illuminate the relationship between theory and practice; more precisely, that between the different theories of the international economy and its actual performance in the post-war period. We can therefore now approach this fundamental question by reviewing the evidence presented in the substantive chapters in the light of the major theories outlined in Chapter 2. This will suggest that the present crisis cannot be resolved without a radical restructuring of both political and economic relationships and enable us to conclude by looking in a very preliminary way at what this must require of us.

Let us start with some agreements. Liberals, Keynesians, structuralist and Marxists would accept that a stable world economy would require balance of payments equilibrium and, to achieve it, the *even* development of productive resources involving adequate growth in weak as well as strong economies. Secondly, that the actual world economy has been and still is characterised by a very high degree of inequality in productive capacity, is highly and increasingly interdependent, and must sustain the conditions required for this interdependence if there is not to be an uncontrollable loss of welfare and political stability. What is at issue, therefore, is the nature of the economic and political structures best able to generate even development in an interdependent world; a growth process that will not merely maximise global output, but ensure that the greatest gains are made in the weakest rather than the strongest areas. How then, do the claims of the various bodies of theory we have looked at measure up in the light of the experience of the past forty years?

For liberals, with their belief in free trade and market regulation, the first half of the period can only be seen as one characterised by a range of 'distortions' stemming from interventionist policies in direct contradiction with the basic principles on which their theory was built. Here, in the industrial world and its colonial empires, the domestic economy was subject to close controls and the external one dominated by protectionism and capital movements mainly organised by public authorities. We have seen how central a role the Marshall Plan and US military spending played in the industrial world; in the colonies the role of aid programmes and of development planning was equally significant. But the liberals could also argue that this 'Second best' system was merely a response to the dislocations caused by underdevelopment and war, and was designed to be self-liquidating. The most important structures set up to mediate international economic relations, as we have seen, incorporated a short-term commitment to controls on the assumption that they would create the foundations on which a fully developed liberal system could be created in the long term.

Here they can certainly point to many substantial achievements. The economies of Europe and Japan were rebuilt and their external relations liberalised; there has been decolonisation and rapid growth in the Third World, and it has been argued that the countries that have followed liberal teaching most closely have been the most successful; the role of the IMF, the World Bank and GATT, all built firmly on liberal capitalist principles, has been consolidated at the centre of the system; more recently, liberal monetarist theories of economic management have effectively displaced Keynesian interventionism as the dominant approach to both domestic and external economic management. All of this has finally consolidated the intellectual achievements of a neoclassical tradition which appeared to be entirely discredited at the end of the war.

In 1984 it is this view that exerts the most pervasive influence over domestic and international economic policy-making, and which therefore is of fundamental political importance. In this view the recent difficulties experienced by the world economy are no more than temporary problems arising out of a failure to take market principles to their logical conclusion by allowing monopoly power to continue to exert a decisive influence over resource allocation in a number of areas, notably in the Western trade union movement (thus keeping wages too high), in the oil-producing cartel (thus leading to fundamental international imbalances) and in the American government's ability to maintain a budget deficit which is also leading to serious domestic and international distortions. If these arguments continue to be accepted, the political response to the crisis will simply involve an extension of present tendencies – notably the attack on the bargaining power of the working class through mass unemployment and legal controls over trade unions, the further reduction in the ability of governments to exert any direct control over domestic and external economic relations, and an ever heavier use of the market mechanism to ensure an adequate flow of real resources into, and growth of productive capacity within, the weaker countries in the system.

Yet despite the persuasiveness of some of this case, a great deal of the evidence in this book points towards conclusions that can only be made intelligible through the use of Keynesian and structuralist arguments. There can be little doubt that the major successes of early post-war rebuilding were the outcome of a general recognition of the need to 'supplement and in part replace the market mechanism by direct control and planning' identified at the end of the war by Arndt in a Chatham House study.[6] During this period the USA and, in a far more minor role the UK, at the centre, together with the governments of the other colonial powers, accepted that the need to 'avoid a repetition of the international economic chaos of the inter-war period' would entail 'a conscious policy designed to ensure the requisite changes in the productive structure of the various national economies... a measure of control of the volume and directions of international trade and investment... [and] the need for international co-operation [and] supra-national economic authorities'.[7] The US and UK deficits, based on overseas aid and heavy defence expenditure, provided the capitalist world with military security and an adequate supply of liquidity; protectionist policies in the weaker industrial and the newly independent countries allowed the development of rapid industrial growth; rapid expansion in Western aid flows and markets undermined Soviet influence and tied most of the Third World into the Western alliance, thus halting communist expansion. All this was clearly an achievement of conscious planning informed by Keynesian and structuralist thinking; the evidence presented in the body of the text suggests that an early reversion to market forces would have resulted in a major collapse in 1947 and a return to 'economic chaos', as Arndt had predicted.

The lessons of the 1960s and 1970s are clearly more ambiguous, but by no means encouraging from a free trade perspective. From the mid-1960s liberalisation and instability have grown in equal measure. The deficits of the USA and UK, once a necessary element in the overall economic recovery, have become a major source of instability in the system and have not responded in a stabilising way to the effects of greater competition. Equally, the trading surpluses of the strong countries, and of West Germany and Japan even more than the oil cartel, have not disappeared in response to full employment and rising costs as Hume's analysis predicts, but have continued to impose deflationary pressures on much of the rest of the system. The successes of the NICs, looked at more closely, are seen to be the outcome of strongly interventionist rather than liberal policies, and almost certainly not generalisable to the rest of the Third World without an immense disruption of productive capacity in advanced countries where structural unemployment is already unacceptably high and shows no sign of coming down. The inability of weaker sectors in Western economies to reduce import penetration in these conditions of very high unemployment has led to a rapid and unco-ordinated growth in protectionism, largely directed at the exports of Third World countries which need them most. The use of a private banking system to recycle the surpluses that emerged in the system from the late 1960s, originally greeted as a triumphant vindication of the market mechanism, has now produced a debt crisis which threatens many countries with intense deprivation and political instability, and the Western banking system with something not far short of collapse. Finally, and most tragically, the failure to devise any adequate response to the needs of the poorest peoples in the poorest countries of Africa and Asia, peoples clearly lacking in the economic and political structures required to compete on equal terms in the international market place, is producing economic collapse, devastating suffering and a moral crisis which must soon undermine the legitimacy of the system as a whole.

We can now attempt to make sense of these problems through the application of Keynesian/structuralist theories by viewing them as the outcome of the inadequacy of global demand management and of the weaknesses imposed by pre-capitalist structures on the economic and administrative capacity of LDCs. The policy prescriptions flowing from this diagnosis would then be of a relatively limited and reformist kind. They would almost certainly include: a substantial new allocation of SDRs with a significant proportion going to LDCs;[8] the implementation of more effective mechanisms for international economic management of a reformist social democratic kind in the weaker developed countries with the greatest emphasis on Keynesian reflation and managed devaluation; a substantial increase in concessional aid for LDCs, together with an improved structure of economic management, combining a balanced growth between exports and inward oriented industrialisation along the lines set out in the Brandt report;[9] and an emergency programme of virtually free resource transfers to the poorest countries to create the basic infrastructure and human capital required to get an autonomous capitalist development process under way.

Looked at from a Marxist perspective, however, many of these options would not be rejected, merely seen as entirely inadequate of themselves to deal with the underlying problem. Here the multiplying contradictions that confront us are not seen as the outcome of a lack of effective demand or of the temporary weakness of pre-capitalist formations in backward countries to be remedied by global recycling and limited state intervention. Instead they are viewed as the inherent outcome of the functioning of a system of market competition which, by combining private appropriation of surpluses, continuous technological progress and increasing returns to scale, must, without social control, inevitably lead to uneven development and crisis.[10] Reformist mechanisms of the sort already outlined may well serve to offset or displace the effects of this process, but not to reverse it. During the post-war period the undoubted successes of the long boom can be traced directly to the existence of effective mechanisms for large-scale resource transfers which depended directly on the exercise of state power – notably the US/UK aid and defence deficits and the subsequent expansion of private debt to the governments of both developed and less developed countries. They also rested very heavily on the building of a reformist social democratic consensus domestically, using Keynesian demand management to guarantee full employment and rising consumption. Yet there is no doubt that both of these mechanisms are no longer functioning in a stabilising manner, and that the response to this change on the part of the establishment has been to go back to the theoretical formulations of the 1930s which it was, until recently, treating as entirely discredited.

Now, with accelerated labour-displacing technological change occurring throughout the system mediated by a structure of multinational capital largely outside the control of national governments, huge quantities of functioning but no longer profitable productive capacity is being destroyed, putting millions out of work and imposing severe downward pressures on demand. To replace this capacity on the scale necessary to restore full employment would require more capital than can be mobilised in the short run, and is probably ecologically impossible in the long run unless we can ensure that new investment goes into activities which do not depend upon an excessive supply of non-renewable natural resources. Furthermore, it is very probable that present technical changes will shift the balance of advantage in a number of traditionally labour-intensive sectors away from Third World and towards the most advanced First World producers, [11] thus undermining many of the limited gains already made in export-oriented industrialisation. In these circumstances a further dose of free competition can only be expected to kill the patient. Hence, while it is true that socialist theory can be justly accused of paying far too little attention to the utility of competition in guaranteeing efficiency and consumer satisfaction in the micro economy, it can still point with undiminished confidence at the inherent inability of the mechanism to produce a rational, stable and equitable solution to the problem of economic interdependence at the macro level. If this is true then we must now look for a fundamental change in economic strategy and political structure designed not so much to destroy the global market mechanism, as to bring it under effective social control. We can now move towards the end of this book by considering in broad detail some of the implications of this point of view.

To suggest, as we have done, that socialists must initiate a process that would bring what is now an essentially 'anarchical' system[12] under effective social control is not to deny the commitment and the resources devoted by the establishment to the production of reforms intended to stabilise what is now generally recognised as a 'non-system'. Indeed much of this book has been concerned to evaluate the attempts to produce solutions to the problems of monetary, trading and financial instability which have induced a growing crisis of confidence among even the most powerful. If these attempts were to succeed and the apparent stability of the early 1960s restored, we could expect a return to the conditions that produced the political consensus and the corresponding 'end of ideology' at the time. The argument presented here would have been falsified and the need for a socialist programme could no longer be substantiated. From a bourgeois point of view, therefore, it is essential that these problems should be resolved through reforms which leave the essential features of global capitalism intact, since neither the capitalist class itself, nor the political agents who run the major governments, the international agencies or the central banks, can afford to live with a future in which the framework within which they operate is constantly threatened by economic disintegration and mounting political opposition. The lessons of the 1930s have not been entirely forgotten – the reversion to autarchy then, the direct result of the inability to sustain an equitable structure of integrated economic activity, meant a widespread loss of welfare and an intensification of international hostility which eventually led to war. The growth of interdependence since then would make the costs and dangers of a similar disintegration far worse.

Thus the attempts to restructure the system from above will continue, but the major purpose of this book has been to demonstrate that they cannot produce a viable response because of the fundamental contradictions that exist within the structure of the capitalist world economy. A real and systemic deviation exists between the real interests of each individual competitor in the market economy who must maximise profits and growth or perish, and the equilibrium conditions essential for the stability of the world community of producers. The former, manifesting itself concretely in the inexorable growth of the power of the global corporation and of the dominant national centres of productive capacity, leads directly to a process of concentration and centralisation of capital which constantly undermines the attempts by weak firms and regions to catch up and thus establish the essential tendency towards even development and balance of payments equilibrium. Accepting the individualistic principle as the fundamental requirement of capitalist market competition, the theorists of bourgeois internationalism have postulated an ideology of free trade which, as we have seen, entirely ignores these inexorable tendencies and is therefore entirely incapable of coming to terms effectively with their effects. As a result they have created a structure of international political regulation and intervention which requires even development for its stable functioning, but which presides over a set of processes that constantly intensify uneven development and balance of payments disequilibria. Their failure is therefore a structural one based upon what can only be described as a *necessary* 'false consciousness' leading inevitably to 'the logical impossibility of discovering theoretical and practical solutions to the problems created by the capitalist system of production'.[13] If this is so, the only alternative to a further degeneration must be some form of socialist internationalism based upon a generalised commitment to an end to anarchy by building a collaborative global mechanism capable of providing an effective counterweight to the tendencies towards international inequality that are now threatening the very survival of civilisation itself.

In a world dominated by capitalist structures and categories it would be naive to imagine, however, that some vast revolutionary project could be devised, put to an international proleteriat, and carried into effect through a universal uprising. The Left intelligentsia has no such project, nor, even if it did, could it find a working class unified or conscious or determined enough to put it into effect. At present most of the working-class movement has suffered a series of serious political defeats and is for the most part pessimistic and disunited. But it is also being forced to recognise more and more clearly that current strategies are essentially designed to resolve the crisis of profitability at their expense. Thus, presented with viable and comprehensible projects, their energies could now begin to be mobilised for radical social change, most especially in some Third World countries where the impact of the crisis is most severe. All that we can do at this stage, therefore, is to identify a set of demands which, while technically feasible, could also mobilise real political support, begin to displace the market mechanism from its central position in the international economy, and then provide stepping stones to yet further demands of a socialist kind.

We can start, perhaps, by reaffirming the basic proposition of this whole work. In the modern world of developed economic interdependence, the social planning required to overcome the instability that characterises the system as a whole must be international in scope if it is to pre-empt a return to autarchic nationalism which will

otherwise be inevitable as national groups struggle to defend themselves against the effects of international competition. These struggles, allowed to run their course, must inevitably generate real
losses in economic welfare and a dangerous escalation of international tensions and conflict. While capital is increasingly effectively
organised at the international level, labour very largely remains
wedded to national strategies based upon its earlier incorporation
into social democratic reformism organised by the nation state. This
orientation is still clearly visible in Left strategies like that put
forward by the British Labour Party in 1982, which moved decisively towards protectionism in an understandable reaction to the way
in which external forces had destroyed its policies in the past.[14]
Thus, without any effective international mechanisms capable of
sheltering national working-class fractions from the effects of the
international domination of capital, they will have no alternative
but to adopt divisive measures of this kind. Therefore it now seems
abundantly clear that if we cannot go forwards to an effective
system of social organisation based on the need for a fully interdependent world economy, we must go back to national planning,
which must necessarily limit the potential available to everyone.
Thus we can begin by restating Arndt's conclusions arrived at after
the last great capitalist crisis, the Second World War:

> Surely the obvious and the only answer ... is that there must
> indeed be planning of international trade and investment, and
> that there may even be 'discrimination', but that planning must be
> international wherever possible. In some respects international
> control may confine itself to agreement on rules of international
> good behaviour in economic matters. Such rules will have to
> make provision for such methods of commercial policy as coun-
> tries cannot reasonably be expected to forego; 'non-
> discrimination' will not do. Such rules could undoubtedly be
> devised. In many spheres, however, international co-operation
> will have to go beyond agreement on 'don'ts'. There will have to
> be direct planning of international economic intercourse. How
> far this will have to take the form of international cooperation,
> how far it will be possible to get countries to submit to suprana-
> tional authorities – these are important but secondary questions,
> provided the imperative need for planned international action is
> recognised and acknowledged. In the last resort, international
> good behaviour in the economic as in the political field will still

require the sanction and backing of power – and the will to use that power effectively in the general interest.[15]

It would take another volume to set out in detail the economic content of such a project. Certainly it would require a powerful financial mechanism of the kind envisaged by Keynes at Bretton Woods to recycle surpluses from strong to weak areas and thus enable us 'to offset the contractionist pressures which might otherwise overwhelm in social disorder the good hopes of our modern world', and by substituting 'a credit mechanism in place of hoarding ... repeat in the international field the same miracle, already performed in the domestic field, of turning stone into bread'.[16] This conception, implicit in virtually all subsequent reform proposals, has been presented in the Brandt Report as a demand for the development of 'automatic mechanisms' for the raising of such revenues on comparable principles to the taxes levied in welfare states where 'taxes are progressive in incidence, social expenditures are redistributive and the links between taxpayers and beneficiaries are indirect'.[17] This recommendation, radical though it may sound, is no more than a necessary response to the arguments set out here and in Chapter 2, which assert that in an interdependent community, where free exchange enables some to benefit greatly at the expense of others, political and economic stability requires an effective redistributive mechanism if inequality is not to widen to breaking point.

Secondly, it would require an effective mechanism that ensured that irresistable pressures were exerted on strong surplus countries to ensure that their continued expansion did not worsen the position of deficit countries. The scarce currency clause of the IMF Articles of Agreement was intended to perform this role but has never been invoked, while Article 4 of the ill-fated Havana Charter also attempted to impose an *obligation* on such countries to make a 'full contribution ... towards correcting the situation' by using methods 'which expand rather than contract international trade'.[18] The need to control the surpluses of the strong countries might well be entirely compatible with the requirements of orthodox trade theory, but the political failure to implement these provisions is no accident. The structural surpluses of the strong countries stem from the market domination of their leading domestic producers, which is derived from their increasing control over modern production processes. These producers *must* maximise their overseas sales and profits to survive. To ask them to do otherwise is to expect them to act in direct opposition to their principle of existence. Thus any effective control over the surplus countries must require a major shift in the international balance of political forces as this exists in the present structure of global economic management and control.

Finally, in a world of unequal economic power, where theory tells us that free trade is going to intensify uneven development rather than reduce it, internationalism requires the planning of production and exchange to ensure that gains are fairly distributed and contribute to a genuine equalisation of productive capacity world-wide. This would involve a willingness, as part of adjustment programmes for weaker areas, to accept and support policies which broke from the liberal principles that now dominate IMF thinking. These would have to take account of the need for countries to 'opt for strategies which emphasise national planning, systems of administrative budgeting (of foreign exchange, imports, investment and credit), the reform of traditional institutions, and an active role for the public sector'. Rather than use international leverage as the IMF does to undermine such policies, assistance should be given to help these countries 'overcome the difficulties and obstacles which such a development model necessarily encounters'.[19] Such a strategy would also have to take careful account of the arguments advanced in the new critique of development theory put forward in its moderate form in the World Bank's *Redistribution with Growth*, and in a more radical form in Clive Thomas's *Dependency and Transformation*, which suggests the need to ensure that resources go in large measure to structures capable of producing not merely output growth, but also full employment, an equitable distribution of income, and a sustainable utilisation of non-renewable natural resources.[20]

Such a strategy, involving large concessional transfers from surplus to deficit countries, the recognition of the need to impose direct controls over domestic and foreign economic exchanges to deal with structural balance of payments disequilibria, and the creation of mechanisms to impose effective adjustment policies on structural surplus and deficit countries, would involve a fundamental break with existing practice and inevitably invoke strong opposition from the powerful vested interests that dominate the present system. Yet to say that it would confront almost insuperable obstacles can be no excuse for inaction if the analysis presented in this book is accepted. What it does suggest is the need for serious attempts to produce viable technical solutions and effective political strategies to deal with it. In the pages that remain we can do no more than raise some of the technical and political issues which such a strategy would have to confront.

At first glance it would seem that it would be far simpler to find technical solutions to the first two issues outlined earlier than to the third. The need for an increased flow of official concessional resources to deficit countries is already widely recognised, mainly as a response to the threat posed to the banking system by the debt crisis. IMF quotas have been greatly expanded and could be yet further opened up; the SDR mechanism already exists, and influential authorities are calling for its extension and for it to be linked to the needs of LDCs. It would also take no more than an effort of political will to increase the resources at the disposal of the established multilateral and bilateral aid agencies which already exist, especially since token commitments already exist which would virtually double them simply by meeting the 0.7 per cent target that already exists. Again, pressure on surplus countries to adjust could be relatively easily increased through an amendment of the scarce currency clause in the IMF Articles of Agreement, and of the clauses in the GATT Agreement allowing weaker countries to protect their markets against imports from the stronger ones without breaking their rules. At present the only acceptable mechanism to deal with this problem is the undifferentiated and relatively weak weapon of devaluation, so that more and more countries are dealing with their problems by using hidden subsidies and administrative and other forms of control which constitute 'back-door' protectionism which breaks the spirit if not the letter of existing agreements. This undermines the credibility of the institutional structures through which international co-operation is organised and, because it occurs unilaterally and outside the negotiating structures, cannot be organised into a rational and legitimated response to the real problems of economic inequality which made the action essential in the first instance. What is required are mechanisms fully recognised by the IMF and GATT which could only be invoked after open discussion, and on the basis of agreed criteria that would impose clear obligations on surplus and deficit countries alike. Such a mechanism would therefore serve to consolidate international integration by giving the weaker countries adequate safeguards against exploitation, while enabling the adequacy of their policy responses to be closely examined at the international level.

Yet the technical simplicity of these solutions does very little to resolve the most serious problems that must be confronted if the present imbalances in the international economy are to be corrected. Both would do no more than create the *possibility* of an effective response in deficit countries, but would not guarantee the existence of the conditions needed to ensure one, since these, in the last analysis, would depend upon the creation of effective domestic structures and strategies capable of putting to use the resources and market opportunities provided. The problems of international inequality are a function of the problem of *production* – more precisely, of production in weaker areas whose lack of capital, entrepreneurial skills and social organisation makes it difficult for them to compete on equal terms with those that are already strong.

In the debate in the rapidly expanding literature on the solution to the balance of payments problem, a clear distinction is usually made between those who emphasise 'financing' as opposed to 'adjustment', the former relating to resource transfers, the latter to changes in policy and economic structures required to bring the economy back into balance. Radical demands made on behalf of deficit countries often call for a substantial increase in the former and the virtual elimination of the latter, thus implying that there are no major domestic obstacles to the initiation of a viable development programme, provided only that external conditions can be improved. Yet it is in fact very unlikely that an increase in resource transfers and markets for deficit countries will guarantee that they are effectively used. In the worst cases the leaders of corrupt and incompetent governments are more likely to appropriate than invest additional resources; in the better ones they will attempt to do so, but will be held back by the underdevelopment of their infrastructure and the inadequacy of their policy-making processes. Even in advanced deficit countries like Britain in the 1960s and 1970s, as we have seen, adjustment must involve complex trade-offs between welfare, defence spending and investment, and has a direct effect on the distribution of income between classes, which must induce complex political battles that cannot simply be suppressed in a democracy. Thus social democratic governments are very likely to encourage levels of consumption that repress investment and cannot be sustained over the long term.

In these circumstances an adequate flow of external resources will make it enormously easier to develop effective domestic policies, but will not, as the IMF theorists correctly argue, absolve governments of the need to take effective and sometimes unpalatable policy decisions. The demand for an increase in 'financing' cannot therefore be for entirely unconditional flows, since, in a world still characterised by unacceptable levels of scarcity and want, those who provide them are bound to wish to satisfy themselves that they are going to be put to positive use. Thus, what is at issue is not the problem of policy conditionality *per se*, but of the particular forms it should take.

Up to now conditionality has been almost exclusively associated with the restrictive monetarist policies favoured by the IMF and imposed on governments whatever their own prior political commitments and orientation. To move beyond this entirely unsatisfactory state of affairs, we have to be able to demonstrate the existence of alternatives which, without requiring the monetarist disciplines favoured hitherto, will also be able to elicit a rational and disciplined response to the need to build up self-sustaining and autonomous productive structures in deficit countries. This response would therefore have to accept the possibility of the use of socialist planning models, whether of the limited 'mixed economy' variants favoured by democratic socialists in still prodominantly capitalist countries, or of the statist variants already in operation in the centrally planned economies.

Yet this proposition, of course, raises even more problems than it resolves. A very powerful critique can and has been levelled at the old-style import-substituting policies practised in many countries under socialist labels and which in many cases served as little more than mechanisms for bureaucratic aggrandisement and the enrichment of multinationals at the expense of consumers and small producers of all kinds. Many socialists, in an over-reaction to the externally induced crises that many of them are confronting, are now calling for autarchic policies based on an almost complete 'de-linking' from the international economy. This, if carried to its logical conclusion, would almost certainly impose massive costs on populations by excluding them from access to the technological heritage created by human endeavour but now effectively monopolised by a small minority. Thus the demand that socialist planning be put back on the agenda in the central agencies of the international economic system has also to be accompanied by clear evidence that those who do so have more to offer than the negative critique of capitalist society that has almost exclusively preoccupied them in the recent past.[21] Yet to accept the claim of market theorists that their prescriptions can be accorded the sole claim to scientific rationality because of the failures of a few badly designed import-substitution programmes, or the successes of export-oriented strategies which, on closer inspection, can be shown to owe as much to planning as to the market, would be to negate the massive achievements of a history of interventionism stretching from the protectionism of the nineteenth century to the social democratic and communist planning of the twentieth. There is much to criticise here, but as much to celebrate, and we should never forget, as we are wont to do, the devastating effects of the market mechanism on the economic security of communities, on the welfare of individuals 'rationalised' out of jobs, and on the political stability of a world rent by the tensions arising out of the struggles induced by the uncontrolled need to capture markets and exclude competitors.

Secondly, to accept that an international agency like the IMF was to have the right to finance and supervise the implementation of radical adjustment policies of this kind in deficit countries would be to accept that it involved itself even more directly in the political debate there than it does at present. Had it backed the radical version of Manley's policies in Jamaica in the 1970s, or the Left Labour alternative in Britain at the same time, it would have been acting against the interests of powerful class forces both there and elsewhere. Thus, in a situation where difficult adjustments were being asked of both deficit and surplus countries, the debate over policy in the international economic agencies would inevitably become very much more contentious and political than is now the case, and the problem of sustaining a consensus would be very much more difficult.

On the other hand, the present attempt to preserve the myth of political neutrality and technical rationality merely serves to conceal the real conflicts that are being induced by the adjustment process in which one particular ideological tendency has been able to establish its dominance. If these monetarist solutions could be expected to succeed in the long run without imposing unacceptable costs on a broad range of interests in deficit countries, then the system could no doubt hope to survive for the foreseeable future in its present form. Yet this is almost cetainly not the case, as the balance of payments crises requiring intervention become more frequent and more serious. We already have a considerable history of anti-IMF riots and of lost elections; the scale of the adjustments now being asked of the large debtors like Mexico, Brazil and Argentina, designed to secure the future of some of the largest and wealthiest banks in the world, is clearly threatening to induce an Iranian-style political upheaval and a rejection of external obligations. Unless some means is found of making the IMF more receptive to less rigid policies, and of ensuring that an adequate political process could be developed through which they could be debated in a forum representing a far wider range of the interests affected, the 'loss of political legitimacy' already sapping its ideological position could well become terminal.

Thus, whatever the technical difficulties involved, it is essential that we now draw up a new political agenda to provide the basis for a movement away from the capitalist internationalism in the form of free trade being imposed upon us at present, to a socialist internationalism designed to create an effective basis for a planned redistribution of resources and a dynamic and sustainable process of even development. The capitalist system has created world history by developing the world market; we have now to bring it under social control before it destroys us all.

We can now conclude this work by looking briefly at the structures that must be captured and the forces that must be mobilised if this task is to be given the priority it demands.

However distorted and underdeveloped, a structure of global economic management already exists which incorporates most of the world's population. There are those who believe that these structures are so deficient that the only answer is demolition and the creation of alternatives; others of a more moderate persuasion would like to see new structures to supplement those already there.[22] This is a direct reaction to the inadequacies of the existing institutions and, more especially, of their weighted voting systems which give the strongest countries, and especially the now almost entirely reactionary USA, an entirely disproportionate influence. Yet to focus upon a campaign to create new structures because of the dominance of established interests in them is to risk an unnecessary duplication of functions (with corresponding inefficiencies and high level bureaucratic waste), and to encourage the illusion that the political battles that cannot be won inside these organisations can somewhow be by-passed. For as long as the present set of right-wing forces remain in control of the national governments of the industrial countries and of the structure of private multinational economic power, they will continue to dominate all of the agencies that are able to control real resources like the IMF and World Bank, and will reduce those which they cannot control, like UNCTAD, to impotence. This would apply as much to any new agency as to those that already exist, so it would seem to be more significant to identify what should be done to produce some real changes in the institutions that already exist, than to attempt to design new ones.

Given the political dominance of *national* governments at the present time, and the impossibility of creating any meaningful structure of direct democracy at the global level, it would be foolish to suggest that international agencies should be given direct authority over domestic economic policy. The limitations inscribed in the structures of the existing agencies are less a function of their scope and responsibilities (dealing as they do with money, trade and development finance) than of the limited resources at their disposal and the liberal ideological framework within which they have had to operate. Thus what we now require is an effective mobilisation of political forces at the national level designed to extend their scope, change their policies and expand the resources which they can mobilise. We would be deluding ourselves, however, if we were to assume that this could be done without confronting a number of very serious problems.

Firstly, it is evident that capitalist interests are far more effectively organised at the global level than are those of the working class, as a result of the internationalism of the structure of the MNC and of the domination of the leading agencies by the strongest industrial powers and by the *laissez-faire* ideology that they support. Working-class movements, mobilised economically in trade unions and politically in social democratic parties, have long been dominated by an almost entirely national organisation and orientation. Although both are tied into wider international structures, their eyes are turned firmly on to national governments and domestic employers, not least because they are often involved in struggles which involve them in antagonistic contradictions with groups of workers in other countries. Indeed, one can think of many occasions when workers have joined forces with weaker elements of national capital to call for protection against imports on which foreign workers depend for their jobs – capital and commodities can be exported and sold, labour and jobs (or the lack of them) are, for the most part, tied to particular national and even regional locations.

As a result, social democratic movements in the industrial countries in particular have characteristically assumed that political control over their national governments can be translated into the capacity to redistribute resources from capital to labour through welfare spending, full employment policies and the reinforcement of trade union structures. But, as we have seen, capital has now been able to use its control over the international economy to short-circuit this process by switching its resources abroad, allowing a balance of payments crisis to develop, and re-establishing its control under the aegis of an IMF-imposed 'adjustment' programme. The alternative, short of an effective mobilisation of international resources, is protectionism, some form of 'siege economy' and a reduction in international exchange, in the short term at least. In the absence of an effective alternative, this is likely to become a more and more attractive option, but the costs must be high in terms of reduced consumption, increased central direction and intensified competition with workers as well as capitalists in other countries. The imposition of such policies by democratic socialist governments is bound to lose them political support and increase the problems involved in building an effective class alliance over the long term.[23]

Secondly, in the Third World strong working-class organisations hardly exist, and the major political contradiction is still between nationally oriented interests and imperialism. It is not surprising that in this context the awareness of dependence on external forces is far more developed than it is in Western countries, and that a far more serious attempt has been made to respond to it. The Group of 77, as we have seen, has established a complex structure and has the ability to take joint positions and to operate as a reasonably coherent political force in the international economic debate. It is also no accident that the Brandt Report, with its strong Third World representation, has put forward the most far-reaching recommendations for international restructuring that we have seen since the 1940s.

Yet we have also to look very closely at the weaknesses that characterise this structure of political mobilisation. As official representatives of governments, the members of the Group of 77 speak for an assortment of political tendencies, stretching from the extreme Right to the extreme Left. Their demands are mainly for a greater flow of real resources to Third World countries and usually leave out of account any close analysis of the purpose to which they will be put. Given the reactionary nature of many of these governments, we know that they will often be neither economically rational nor likely to benefit those whose needs are greatest. This does not mean that the principle of the need for increased resources transfers has to be rejected, only that socialists would have to look very closely at the uses to which they were to be put and be willing to reject them where they were clearly to be used to sustain wasteful, inequitable or reactionary policies and programmes. There is therefore no automatic alliance to be struck between Western socialist movements and the governments of even the poorest Third World countries, a problem which reinforces the need for the development of effective interventionist policies discussed earlier and which must also have serious implications for the formulation of progressive aid policies by socialist governments.

Thirdly, as we have seen, international economic, and for the most part political, power is still firmly in the hands of the dominant capitalist interests and the dominant industrial countries, and this influence stretches deep into the policy-making process of most Third World governments. Serious attempts at social reform in these countries have therefore to contend with direct and indirect external pressures, of which the US-backed invasions of Grenada and Nicaragua are only the most recent examples. Thus, however effectively the anti-imperialist forces might organise in the Third World, their ability to sustain progressive domestic and foreign policies over the long term will be decisively influenced by the balance of political forces in the advanced industrial countries. Unless these can alter the orientation of their own governments and of the international agencies, the possibility of a progressive initiative stemming from the world level will never become a serious possibility.

We can conclude by doing no more than assert the need for a major initiative along these lines from the Left in the advanced countries, an initiative designed to take account of the international dimension now built firmly into the class struggle wherever it occurs, and one capable of building the structures required to enable the working-class movement to meet the challenges it involves without resorting to chauvinistic nationalism and economic autarchy. The trade union movement is beginning to strengthen its international structures and linkages in response to this challenge, and especially to that created by the 'global reach' of the multinational firms they must contend with. Writing now as a democratic socialist involved in the European movement, perhaps it is possible simply to list the political forces we can identify with and indicate the problems that will have to be resolved before an effective international alliance can be created.

The most obvious starting point must be within Europe, where it is possible to build upon a long history of socialist co-operation and more especially to organise effectively to deal with the challenge to socialist policies posed by the present structure and orientation of the EEC. In its present form this undoubtedly constitutes a serious obstacle to effective interventionist policies in member countries, since it institutionalises the principle of competition at both the domestic and Community level. Yet Gorz was undoubtedly correct when he argued many years ago that a socialist strategy based on the national resources of any one country would be far more problematic than one which was organised on a Community-wide basis.[24] Here we can at least identify one promising initiative in the form of the *Out of Crisis* programme devised by a group of socialist politicians and academics,[25] although without much evidence that it has gathered any degree of popular support.

Although signs of growth can be found in Europe, an almost complete vacuum still appears to exist in the USA where the weakness of the Left has allowed a pathologically dangerous right-wing regime to take control. It is difficult not to despair faced with this situation, but it is essential that we recognise that strong progressive elements exist in that country, and that no global strategy can succeed which failed to link up with them. It is difficult to interpret the implications of movements concerned with democratisation in Eastern Europe, but there can be little doubt that they have gained in strength in recent years, and that links which break through the barriers dividing Western socialists from those in the East are bound to be a central element in an effective strategy. Finally, although it would be wrong to cut off all links with Third World countries which remain under the control of essentially capitalist regimes, our main concern must be to strengthen those with genuinely progressive regimes where they do exist, and with progressive movements struggling for political and economic liberation where we can find them.

Thus, within a general commitment to international planning, we must find ways of unifying the working class without ignoring the very real conflicts of interest that separate movements in different countries, identify viable policies capable of resolving the current impasse without more exploitation or economic disintegration, and find ways of liberating the poorest from poverty and oppression.

Notes and References

Introduction

1. H. D. White, 'Preliminary draft proposal for a United Nations Stabilisation Fund', in J. K. Horsefield, *The International Monetary Fund, 1945–1965*, Vol. III, *Documents* (Washington: IMF, 1969) p. 37.
2. *Ibid.*, p. 38.
3. *Ibid.*, p. 40.
4. V. I. Lenin, *Imperialism* (Moscow: Progress Publishers, 1970) pp. 178–9.
5. G. Haberler, 'International trade and economic development', cited in G. M. Meier, *Leading issues in economic development*, 3rd edn (New York: Oxford University Press, 1976) p. 703.
6. M. de Vries, IMF survey. 7 January 1980.
7. G. Lukács, *History and class consciousness* (London: Merlin, 1971) p. 28.
8. *Ibid.*
9. K. Marx, *Grundrisse* (Harmondsworth: Penguin, 1973) p. 100.
10. K. Marx and F. Engels, *The German ideology*, ed. C. J. Arthur (London: Lawrence & Wishart, 1974) p. 78.
11. W. Hager, 'Germany as an extraordinary trader,' in W. Kohl and G. Basevi, *West Germany: a European and global power* (Toronto: Lexington, 1980) p. 15.
12. *Ibid.*, pp. 15–16.

Chapter 1

1. See L. Robbins, *Essay on the nature and significance of economic science*, 2nd edn (London: Macmillan, 1935) p. 16.
2. For the classic definition see M. Weber, *Economy and society*, eds G. Roth and C. Wittich (Berkeley: University of California Press, 1978)

p. 52. 'A ruling organisation will be called "political" insofar as its existence and order is continuously safeguarded within a given *territorial* area by the threat and application of physical force on the part of the administrative staff. A compulsory political organisation with continuous operations will be called a "state" insofar as its administrative staff successfully upholds the claim to the *monopoly* of the *legitimate* use of physical force in the enforcement of its order.'

3. For a good recent review of the orthodox arguments presenting international relations as an anarchical but ordered system in which 'modern states have formed, and continue to form, not only a system of states but also an international society', see H. Bull, *The anarchical society* (London: Macmillan, 1977) p. 24.

4. K. Marx, *Grundrisse* (Harmondsworth: Penguin, 1973) p. 84.

5. And this holds for both the *laissez faire* and interventionist states, whatever the claims made by the supporters of the former. As Gramsci notes, 'Thus it is asserted that economic activity concerns civil society and the state must not intervene in its regulation. But as in actual reality civil society and the state are identified, it must be settled that even liberalism is a form of "regulation" of a state kind, introduced and maintained by means of legislation and coercion, it is an act of will conscious of its own ends and not the spontaneous, automatic expression of an economic fact'. A. Gramsci, *The modern prince and other writings* (New York: International Publishers, 1957) p. 153.

6. Bull, 1977, p. 13. He excludes economic regulation from this list and, like many others in this tradition, takes virtually no account of the effects of economic interaction upon the political autonomy of particular governments.

7. G. Hegel, *Hegel's philosophy of right* (London: Oxford University Press, 1952) p. 219.

8. E. H. Carr, *The new society* (London: Macmillan, 1956) p. 82.

9. See H. Morgenthau, *Politics among nations*, 5th edn (New York: Knopf, 1973) and I. Claude Jr, *Power and international relations* (New York: Random House, 1962) for a general discussion of the implications of this conception.

10. N. Harris, *Of bread and guns* (Harmondsworth: Penguin, 1983) p. 45.

11. Bull, 1977, pp. 8–9.

12. J. M. Keynes, 'Proposals for an International Clearing Union', in H. Grubel, *World monetary reform* (London: Oxford University Press, 1964) p. 79.

13. T. Hobbes, *Leviathan* (London: Collins, 1962). For a clear formulation of the conditions which must be met for the Hobbesian formulation to hold, see C. B. Macpherson, *The political theory of possessive individualism* (Oxford: Clarendon Press, 1962).

14. R. Murray, 'The internationalisation of capital and the nation state', in H. Radice, *International firms and modern imperialism* (Harmondsworth: Penguin, 1975) p. 107. This article, together with Mandel's analysis cited below (note 19) constitutes the most effective

treatment of the problem dealt with in this chapter that I have yet found. Contrast this analysis with that found in Bull, 1977, notably in his treatment of MNCs on pp. 270–3.

15. *Ibid.*, p. 123.
16. I have dealt with the political implications of this requirement at length in *International money and capitalist crisis* (London: Heinemann, 1983) ch. 1.
17. Thus Czecheslovakia was in effect excluded from the IMF in 1955 for non-fulfilment of obligations, while Cuba withdrew in 1964 when threatened with the same fate. See J. K. Horsefield, *The International Monetary Fund, 1945–1965*, Vol. I, *Chronicle* (Washington: IMF, 1969) pp. 363, 549.
18. Henry Fowler in 1965, cited in H. L. Robinson, 'The downfall of the dollar', in *The socialist register, 1973* (London: Merlin, 1974) p. 405.
19. E. Mandel, *Late capitalism* (London: Verso, 1975) pp. 327–8. Mandel is here only referring to the needs of Western Europe, but the same argument applies with even greater force at the level of the world economy as a whole.
20. The phrase is again taken from Mandel, 1975, p. 328.
21. For a developed statement of a possible response of this kind see I. S. Abdulla, 'The inadequacy and loss of legitimacy of the IMF', *Development Dialogue*, 1980, 2.
22. Mandel, 1975, p. 330 ff.
23. *Ibid.*, p. 334
24. See Brett, 1983.
25. This leaves out of account the role of gold and silver, which I have dealt with in *International money.*
26. Note, for example, S. S. Kuznets's assertion that small countries 'can attain economic growth *only* through a heavy reliance on foreign trade', *Modern economic growth* (New Haven: Yale University Press, 1966) p. 302
27. A. Emmanuel, *Unequal exchange* (London: New Left Books, 1972) p. xiv.
28. H. G. Johnson, 'International trade: theory', *International Encyclopedia of the social sciences*, Vol. 8, p. 88.

Chapter 2

1. A. Smith, *An inquiry into the nature and causes of the wealth of nations* (Chicago: Encylopedia Britannica, 1952) p. 190.
2. D. Hume, 'On the balance of trade', in *Writings in economics* (London: Nelson, 1955).
3. D. Ricardo, 'On foreign trade', in *The principles of political economy and taxation* (London: Dent, 1973). For a modern presentation see G. Haberler, *A survey of international trade theory* (Princeton: Princeton University Press, 1961).

276   *Notes and References*

4. W. M. Corden, *Recent developments in the theory of international trade* (Princeton: Princeton University Press, 1965) p. 24.
5. For the classic statement of the gains from trade see J. S. Mill, *Principles of political economy* (London: Longman, 1900) Book III, Chapter XVII. A useful modern textbook is L. B. Yeager, *International monetary relations*, 2nd edn (New York: Harper & Row, 1976).
6. See J. B. Say, 'On the demand on market for products', in H. Hazlitt, *The critics of Keynesian economics* (Princeton: van Nostrand, 1960).
7. The classic reformulation of this argument in relation to the situation of underdeveloped economies is to be found in W. A. Lewis, 'Economic development with unlimited supplies of labour', *The Manchester School*, 22(2) 1954. The assumed relation between employment and wages is now usually explained through the use of the 'Phillips curve', developed in A. W. Phillips, 'The relation between unemployment and the rate of change of money wages in the United Kingdom', *Economica*, November 1958.
8. Here see H. G. Grubel, *International economics* (Homewood: Irvin, 1981); C. P. Kindleberger, *International economics*, 5th edn (Homewood: Irvin, 1973); J. E. Meade, *The theory of economic policy*, Vol. I, *The balance of payments* (London: Oxford University Press, 1951); B. Tew, *International monetary cooperation, 1945–1970* (London: Hutchinson, 1970); and for an introductory text H. G. Grubel, *The international monetary system*, 3rd edn (Harmondsworth: Penguin, 1977).
9. The classic essay here is M. Friedman, 'The case for flexible exchange rates', in *Essays in positive economics* (Chicago: Chicago University Press, 1953).
10. The official defence of the fixed exchange rate system can be found in the IMF's, 'The role of exchange rates in the adjustment of international payments', in M. de Vries, *The International Monetary Fund, 1966–1971*, Vol II, *Documents* (Washington: IMF, 1974) p. 11.
11. The classic discussion of this question is to be found in Meade, *The theory of economic policy*.
12. For a recent discussion of the issues involved see T. Killick (ed.), *Adjustment and financing in the developing world* (Washington: IMF/ODI, 1982).
13. The significance of this argument against what are now called 'mercantilist' policies for the long-term viability of the international monetary system is brought out very clearly by J. Williamson in *The failure of international monetary reform, 1971–1974* (London: Nelson, 1977). The quotation is from p. 170.
14. Both an early and the revised (official) versions of this are reprinted in J. K. Horsefield, *The International Monetary Fund*, Vol III, *Documents*. The latter version was published as an official White Paper, Cmd 6437, April 1943.
15. The argument is presented in outline in J. M. Keynes, *The general theory of employment, interest and money* (London: Macmillan, 1973),

chs 2 and 3; an introduction to the elements of the Keynesian system can be found in M. Stewart, *Keynes and after* (Harmondsworth: Penguin, 1967).

16. See J. M. Keynes, 'National self-sufficiency', *New Statesman and Nation*, Vol. 6, Nos 124 and 125, 1933.

17. For a description of his role see Horsefield, *The International Monetary Fund*, Vols I and II; and R. Harrod, *The life of John Maynard Keynes* (London: Macmillan, 1951).

18. See, for example, the literature on the question discussed in Chapter 8.

19. This argument is put forward in classic form in F. List, *The national system of political economy* (London: Longman, 1904, first published in 1832).

20. The major protagonist of this so-called 'terms of trade' argument is R. Prebisch, 'Commercial policy in the underdeveloped countries', *American Economic review*, Vol. 49, No. 2, 1959.

21. See, for example, A. Singh, 'UK industry and the world economy: a case of de-industrialisation', *Cambridge Journal of Economics*, Vol. 1, No. 2, 1977.

22. For a good recent formulation see R. R. Nield, 'Managed trade between industrial countries', in R. Major, *Britain's trade and exchange rate policy* (London: Heinemann, 1979). This position has now been adopted as official policy by the Labour Party in Britain; see Labour Party, *Labour's programme 1982*, pp. 20–3.

23. Here see T. F. Cripps, and W. F. Godley, 'Control of imports as a means to full employment and the expansion of world trade: the UK case', *Cambridge Journal of Economics*, Vol. 2, No. 3, 1978.

24. What follows is essentially a simplified version of the argument I have presented in *International money*, Chapter 3; an excellent treatment of the same problem (which I had not read when writing the above) is to be found in Mandel, *Late capitalism*, ch. 11. Here he provides a decisive critique of the still widely accepted 'unequal exchange' thesis put forward by A. Emmanual, *Unequal exchange*, and S. Amin, *Accumulation on a world scale* (New York: Monthly Review, 1974).

25. The major elements of this argument are set out in K. Marx, *Capital*, Vol III (London: Lawrence & Wishart, 1972).

Chapter 3

1. See in particular Horsefield, *The International Monetary Fund*, Vols I and II; R, Gardner, *Sterling-dollar diplomacy* (Oxford: Clarendon Press, 1956); R. Harrod, *The life of John Maynard Keynes* (London: Macmillan, 1951); T. Balogh, *Unequal partners* (Oxford: Blackwell, 1963).

2. These are reproduced in Horsefield, *The International Monetary Fund*, Vol III.

3. See, for example, the discussions contained in *Development dialogue*, 1980, No. 2.
4. For good historical accounts see K. Kock, *International trade policy and the GATT, 1947–1967* (Stockholm: Almqvist & Wiksell, 1969); and W. A. Brown, *The United States and the restoration of world trade*, (Washington: Brookings, 1950); and K. W. Damm, *The GATT: law and economic organisation* (Chicago: University of Chicago Press, 1970).
5. K. Kock, *International trade policy and the GATT*, p. 59.

Chapter 4

1. See N. Hood and S. Young, *The economics of multinational enterprise* (London: Longman, 1979) p. 47.
2. For the classic statement see, C. A. R. Crosland, *The future of socialism* (London: Cape, 1956).
3. I have developed this argument, and the critique of it, in chapters 2 and 3 of *International money and the capitalist crisis*; for an excellent review of the recent literature on the subject and the development of an 'eclectic theory' of the 'market imperfections' approach to the problem see J. H. Dunning, *International production and the multinational enterprise* (London: Allen & Unwin, 1981). In my view his examination of the factors leading to the dominance of MNCs is an excellent one, though I do not accept his assessment of the consequences of this tendency.
4. See S. Hymer, *The multinational corporation* (Cambridge: Cambridge University Press, 1979) and especially ch. 2.
5. R. Solomon, *The international monetary system 1945–1976* (New York: Harper & Row, 1977) p. 18.
6. A. McEuan, 'Slackers, bankers, marketers: multinational corporations and the pattern of US foreign direct investment', mimeo, p. 16; see also Hood and Young, *The economics of multinational enterprise*.
7. Hood and Young, p. 18.
8. *Ibid.*, p. 18.
9. McEuan, 'Slackers, bankers, marketers', p. 4; for a graphic illustration of this trend see Hood and Young, p. 20.
10. See US Dept. of Commerce, *Survey of Current Business*, 63(8), August 1982, pp. 14 and 31; in 1981 the corresponding figure for outward flows was 5 per cent, the lowest since 1945, and a record 31.8 per cent for inward flows (*ibid.*, 62(8) August 1982). Between 1980 and 1983 the gap between American private foreign assets and foreign assets in the USA declined from $140.3 to $119.5 billion, as American foreign investment increased by 14.9 per cent, and foreign investment in the USA by no less than 94.6 per cent.
11. Dunning, *International production*, p. 1.
12. McEuan, 'Slackers, bankers, marketers', p. 13.

13. G. Helleiner, 'Intra-firm trade and the developing countries', in R. Murray, *Multinationals beyond the market* (Brighton: Harvester, 1981) p. 53.
14. Economist Intelligence Unit, 'Multinationals and world trade', in *Multinational Business*, No. 4, 1981, p. 20.
15. *Ibid.*
16. Hood and Young, *The economics of multinational enterprise*, p. 25.
17. *Ibid.*, pp. 26−7.
18. G. M. Meier, 'Private foreign investment', in G. M. Meier, *Leading issues in economic development*, 3rd edn (New York: Oxford University Press, 1976) pp. 373−4.
19. For an excellent outline see R. Murray, 'The internationalisation of capital and the nation state', in H. Radice, *International firms and modern imperialism* (Harmondsworth: Penguin, 1975).
20. Here see the material in Murray, *Multinationals beyond the market*.
21. J. H. Dunning, *International production*.
22. C. Vaitsos, *Employment problems and transnational enterprises in developing countries* (Geneva: ILO, 1976) p. 1.
23. O. Sunkel, 'Transnational capitalism and national disintegration', in G. M. Meier, *Leading issues in economic development*, p. 696.
24. The crucial weakness of Dunning's approach is that he not only fails to take seriously the impact of MNCs on the weaker regions of countries where they did invest, but he also fails to consider the implications of their global activities for the weaker countries which can hardly hope to become favoured centres for investment in the forseeable future. It is always easier to take account of the implications of the *presence* of a phenomenon than of its *absence*, though the latter may have even more significant implications.
25. Hymer, *The multinational corporation*, p. 63.
26. *Ibid.*, p. 64.
27. Here see S. Langdon, 'Multinational corporations, taste transfer and underdevelopment', *Review of African Political Economy*, Vol. 2, 1975; and J. de Coninck, *Artisans and petty producers in Uganda*, PhD thesis, Sussex University, 1980.
28. The economic benefits of this process to capital and the corresponding tendency for it to intensify the 'agglomeration' on concentration of capital is clearly set out in R. Murray, 'Underdevelopment, international firms and the international division of labour', Society for International Development, *Towards a new world economy* (Rotterdam: Rotterdam University Press, 1972); I have also treated the problem at much greater length than is possible here in *International money*, ch. 3.
29. V. I. Lenin, *Imperialism* (Moscow: Progress Publishers, 1970).
30. According to the most recent US Dept. of Commerce report, direct investment income on US direct investment abroad was $37.1 billion in 1980 and $31.9 billion in 1981; against this the direct investment position abroad increased by $27.7 billion in 1980 and $11.8 billion in 1981. Almost all of this increase, it should be noted, was derived from

reinvested earnings, and not from new outflows from the USA. To income should also be added fees and royalty payments of $5.8 billion in 1980 and $5.9 billion in 1981. *Survey of Current Businesses,* August 1980, pp. 11–19.

Chapter 5

1. M. Kostecki, *East-West trade and the GATT system* (London: Macmillan, 1979) p. 3.
2. See R. Gardner, *Sterling-dollar diplomacy* (Oxford: Clarendon, 1956); for contemporary accounts see T. Balogh, *The dollar crisis* (Oxford: Blackwell, 1949) and C. P. Kindleberger, *The dollar shortage* (Cambridge, Mass: MIT, 1950).
3. Cited in Gardner, *Sterling-dollar diplomacy*, p. 200.
4. T. Balogh, *Unequal partners* (Oxford: Blackwell, 1963) p. 11.
5. J. Spero, *The politics of international economic relations*, 2nd edn (London: Allen & Unwin, 1982) pp. 40–41.
6. W. Hager, 'Germany as an extraordinary trader', in W. Kohl and G. Basevi, *West Germany: a European and global power* (Toronto: Lexington Books, 1978) pp. 6–8.
7. H. Patrick and H. Rossovsky, 'Japan's economic performance' in Patrick and Rossovsky, *Asia's new giant* (Washington: Brookings, 1976) p. 11.
8. See S. Tsuru, *The mainsprings of Japanese growth* (Paris: Atlantic Institute, 1977) ch. 3.
9. Here see R. Solomon, *The international monetary system, 1945–76* (New York: Harper & Row, 1977).
10. World Bank, *World development report 1982* (New York: Oxford University Press, 1982) pp. 112–13.
11. R. Solomon, *The international monetary system, 1945–1976* (New York, Harper & Row, 1977) pp. 186–7. The Managing Director of the IMF was told of the changes only ten minutes before Nixon went on the air to make the announcement!
12. In Robert Triffin, *Gold and the dollar crisis* (New Haven: Yale University Press, 1961); see also his *The world money maze* (New Haven: Yale University Press, 1966).
13. Good accounts of this period can be found in R. Solomon, *The international monetary system*; S. Strange, *International monetary relations* (London: Royal Institute of International Affairs, 1976); S. Cohen, *International monetary reform, 1964–1969* (New York: Praeger, 1970); B. Tew, *The evolution of the international monetary system, 1945–1977* (London: Hutchinson, 1977); and for the official IMF accounts see J. K. Horsefield, *The IMF, 1945–1966* (Washington: IMF, 1969), and especially M. de Vries, *The IMF, 1966–1971* (Washington: IMF, 1976).
14. See H. Robinson, 'The decline of the dollar', *Socialist Register*, 1973.

15. IMF, *Balance of Payments Yearbook*, various issues.
16. IMF, *International Financial Statistics*, various issues.
17. See, for example, J. Williamson, *The failure of monetary reform, 1971–74* (London: Nelson, 1977) pp. 20–1, 25.
18. For a good account see K. A. Crystal, *International money and the future of the SDR* (Princeton: Princeton University Press, 1978); the negotiating process is outlined in great detail in de Vries, *The IMF, 1966–1971* as I have already dealt with it at greater length in *International money and capitalist crisis*.
19. Group of 10, *Report of a study group on the creation of reserve assets* (Ossola Report), 1965, p. 59.
20. This demand was originally formulated in a report by a 'Group of Experts' for UNCTAD, *International monetary issues and the developing countries* (New York: UN, 1965).
21. O. Emminger, *Inflation and the international monetary system* (Basle: Per Jacobssen Foundation, 1973) p. 40.
22. Bank for International Settlements, *Annual Report*, 1979, p. 138.
23. See in particular Williamson, *The failure of monetary reform* and Solomon, *The international monetary system*, both members. The report itself is IMF, Committee on reform of the international monetary system, *International monetary reform* (Washington: IMF, 1974).
24. Williamson, *The failure of monetary reform*, p. 73.
25. The current deficit was about $30 billion in the first quarter of 1984 alone.
26. For a 'new classical' demonstration of the link between US policies and the overseas debt crisis, see P. Minford 'The effects of American policies', Mimeo, 1984.

Chapter 6

1. I am heavily indebted in this section for ideas and material from Steve Gilliatt and Andrew Pople which is treated more fully in T. Brett, S. Gilliatt and A. Pople, 'Planned trade, Labour Party policy and US intervention', *History Workshop Journal*, April 1982.
2. H. W. Arndt, *The economic lessons of the nineteen-thirties* (London: Oxford University Press, 1944) p. 102. This account provides a useful analysis of both the British case and of the development of the international economy during the inter-war period. Its general conclusions are powerfully argued and directly relevant to the current debate.
3. I have discussed these developments in British policy in *Colonialism and underdevelopment in East Africa* (London: Heinemann, 1973).
4. S. Strange, *Sterling and British policy* (London: Oxford University Press, 1971) p. 56. This study is a major contribution to the analysis of British policy and, so far as I know, the best general analysis of the nature of the link between external commitments and internal economic failures.
5. UK Committee on the working of the monetary system, *Report* (Rad-

282   *Notes and References*

cliffe Report) (London: HMSO, 1969) pp. 226–8.
6. *Ibid.*, p. 227.
7. See especially K. Kock, *International trade policy and the GATT*, 1947–67 (Stockholm: Almquist & Wiksell, 1969).
8. For an earlier version of this account see T. Brett, S. Gilliatt and A. Pople, 'Planned trade, Labour Party policy and US intervention'.
9. J. M. Keynes, 'Overseas financial policy in stage III', Cabinet Papers WP (45) 301, ff. 251–2; Cab. 66/65. This paper, read in conjunction with Keynes's paper for Bretton Woods (q.v.), provides us with a clear insight into the external policies required to complement the domestic policies implicit in the *General Theory*, which are often assumed to be absent from his work. They stand in sharp contrast to his earlier protectionism (see, for example, 'National self-sufficiency', *New Statesman*, 8 and 15 July 1933) and must form an important part of any complete assessment of his work.
10. H. Dalton, *High tide and after. Memoirs, 1945–1960* (London: Muller, 1962) pp. 74–5.
11. Cabinet Papers, CM(45) 57, 29/11/35; Cab. 218/4.
12. Dalton, *High tide and after*, p. 85.
13. Strange, *Sterling and British Policy*, p. 61.
14. The classic description of the debate in both Britain and the USA is to be found in R. Gardner, *Sterling-dollar diplomacy* (Oxford: Clarendon Press, 1956).
15. Close detailed analysis of the period will be found in Steve Gilliatt and Andy Pople's Sussex University PhD theses.
16. T. Balogh, 'The international aspect', in G. Worswick and P. Ady, *The British economy 1945–1950* (London: Oxford University Press, 1952).
17. C. J. Bartlett, *The long retreat* (London: Macmillan, 1972) p. 12.
18. *Ibid.*, p. 60.
19. *Ibid.*, p. 13.
20. Cabinet Minutes, CM 66(47), 31/7/47; Cab. 128/10.
21. UK, *Capital investment in 1949*, Report of the Investment Programmes Committee, July 1948.
22. G. Worswick, 'The British economy 1950–1959', in G. Worswick and P. Ady, *The British economy in the nineteen-fifties* (Oxford: Clarendon Press, 1962).
23. Bartlett, *The long retreat*, p. 24.
24. G. Cooke, *The life of Richard Stafford Cripps* (London: Hodder, 1957) pp. 361–2.
25. M. Nicholson, *The system* (London: Hodder & Stoughton, 1967) p. 313. It is worth noting here that the only period in recent British history when a comparable industrial performance has been sustained was the years from 1932 to the war *after* the replacement of free trade by Imperial Preference and the introduction of a policy of 'cheap money' based on a low exchange rate. 'Between 1932 and 1937 real national income increased by 20 per cent, industrial production by 46

per cent and even unemployment declined by 17 per cent while income
per head rose 18 per cent and industrial production per man year by 16
per cent', H. W. Richardson, *Economic recovery in Britain* (London:
Weidenfeld & Nicolson, 1967) p. 21. For comparative figures see C.
Kindleberger, *The world in depression, 1929–1939* (London: Allen
Lane, 1973) p. 280, which, incidentally, demonstrates that Germany,
the worst offender in terms of economic nationalism and central
controls, dramatically out-performed everyone else.

26. Strange, *Sterling and British policy*, p. 64.
27. Radcliffe Report, p. 228.
28. Keynes, 'Overseas financial policy', p. 14.
29. Gardner, *Sterling-dollar diplomacy*, p. 205.
30. *Ibid.*, p. 326.
31. Strange (*Sterling and British policy*, p. 60) denies this, claiming that
    Keynes greeted the American demand with 'incomprehension'. But we
    have seen that he himself had initiated the suggestion, and Gardner's
    evidence to the contrary is entirely convincing.
32. Gardner, *Sterling-dollar diplomacy*, pp. 326–7.
33. *Ibid.*, p. 327.
34. G. Patterson, *Discrimination in international trade* (Princeton: Prince-
    ton University Press, 1966) p. 70.
35. Strange, *Sterling and British policy*, p. 67.
36. *Ibid.*, p. 62.
37. Radcliffe Report, p. 264.
38. A. Shonfield, *British economic policy since the war* (Harmondsworth:
    Penguin, 1959); for the official justification for the system see Radclif-
    fe Report, pp. 265–6.
39. See, for example, W. B. Walker, 'Britain's industrial performance
    1850–1950', in K. Pavitt, *Technical innovation and British economic
    performance* (London: Macmillan, 1980).
40. In a very helpful review of the original article on which this section is
    based, John Saville does, however, miss this latter point (*Socialist
    Register*, 1984, pp. 308–10). Whatever its motives, the Labour gov-
    ernment of the 1940s was able to demonstrate that managed trade did
    not necessarily lead to low growth and inefficiency.
41. Strange, *Sterling and British Policy*; S. Pollard, *The development of the
    British economy*, 2nd edn (London: Arnold, 1969) chapter 8.
42. A few weeks before the outbreak of the war, Bevin, speaking for the
    Foreign Office, had told the Cabinet that 'our future relations with the
    US will largely be determined by the success of our collaboration with
    the Atlantic Treaty. Since it is the kernel of their policy it must be the
    kernel of ours' (Cabinet Papers, CP(50) 118 Lab. 129/141).
43. Details can be found in G. Worswick, 'The British economy,
    1950–1959', in Worswick and Ady, *The British economy in the
    nineteen-fifties*; Political and Economic Planning, *Growth in the British
    economy* (London: Allen & Unwin, 1960); and Bartlett, *The long
    retreat*. Three Labour Ministers resigned over these decisions, and

there can be little doubt that they were an important element in the fall of the government in 1951.

44. Bartlett, *The long retreat*, pp. 64–5.
45. An excellent statistical presentation can be found in R. Caves *et al.*, *Britain's economic prospects* (Washington: Brookings, 1968) p. 151.
46. In 1955, 'rejecting the reimposition of direct restrictions upon imports, and determined not to alter the exchange rate, the Government was left with no choice but to intensify the restraints upon demand at home' (Worswick, 'The British economy, 1950–1959', p. 35).
47. Pollard, *The development of the British economy*, p. 454.
48. The overall balance of payments figures, and those for official flows are taken from Caves, *Britain's economic prospects*, p. 151; those of private overseas investment from, A. Hazlewood, 'The export and import of capital', in Worswick and Ady, *The British economy in the nineteen-fifties*, pp. 197–8.
49. 'Memoranda of Evidence submitted by HM Treasury to the Radcliffe Committee', Radcliffe Report, *Principal Memoranda of Evidence*, Vol. 1., p. 117; and H. Macmillan, *Riding the storm* (London: Macmillan, 1971) pp. 342 and 722. Macmillan's account makes it clear that it was the desire to obtain these surpluses which lay behind the very restrictive policies being advocated by the Treasury at the time.
50. Treasury evidence to the Radcliffe Committee, p. 118.
51. These figures are taken from J. Tew, 'Policies aimed at improving the balance of payments', in F. Blackaby, *British economic policy, 1960–74* (Cambridge: Cambridge University Press, 1979).
52. There is a useful account of the way in which the Maudling strategy had to be financed 'at the expense of the balance of payments' in R. Bacon and W. Eltis, *Britain's economic problem*, 2nd edn (London: Macmillan, 1978) pp. 40–6.
53. H. Wilson, *The Labour government, 1964–1970* (London: Weidenfeld & Nicolson, 1971) p. 5.
54. *Ibid.*, p. 37.
55. *Ibid.*
56. *Ibid.*, p. 38; the ease with which this transaction was conducted compares favourably with the complications associated with the American loan in 1945, but its tendency to tie the government into the international system was entirely similar. This package was put together from contributions of $500 million from the USA and the rest from ten other banks, followed a loan of $1 billion from the IMF a few days earlier. See R. Solomon, *The international monetary system, 1945–1976* (New York: Harper & Row, 1977) p. 89.
57. Solomon, p. 90. Solomon was a senior official in the US Federal Reserve Bank at the time.
58. Bacon and Eltis, *Britain's economic problem*, pp. 50–1.
59. *Ibid.*, p. 51.
60. At the OECD Working Party Three discussion of Britain's proposed loan from the IMF, 'the French delegate is understood to have hinted

that next year's Budget should be approved by the Fund (IMF) and the OECD before submission to Parliament' (*Financial Times*, 30 November 1967).

61. W. Beckerman, 'Objectives and performance: an overall view', in W. Beckerman, *The Labour government's economic record, 1964–1970*, (London: Duckworth, 1972) p. 58.

62. Strange, *Sterling and British policy*, p. 74; this account, which seems entirely plausible, emphasises the limited nature of these moves, and the continuing inability of the authorities to recognise the real implications of the overall situation.

63. Blackaby, *British economic policy, 1960–74*, p. 323.

64. W. Eltis, 'Economic growth and the British balance of payments', in D. Aldcroft and P. Fearson, *Economic growth in 20th century Britain*, (London: Macmillan, 1961) p. 197 reproduces the table and provides a more detailed comment on its significance.

65. A comparative examination of the falling rate of profit into the early 1970s can be found in A. Glyn and B. Sutcliffe, *British capitalism, workers and the profit-squeeze* (Harmondsworth: Penguin, 1972).

66. Good accounts of the Heath administration can be found in A. Gamble, *The Conservative nation* (London: Macmillan, 1974) and C. T. Leys, *Politics in Britain* (London: Heinemann, 1983).

67. Calculated from A. Prest and D. Coppock, *The UK economy*, 8th edn (London: Weidenfeld & Nicolson, 1980) p. 45.

68. C. Brown and T. Sheriff, 'De-industrialisation: a background paper', in F. Blackaby, *De-industrialisation* (London: Heinemann, 1978) p. 251. An even sharper downward trend is shown for industrial and commercial profits by J. R. Sargent, in 'Productivity and profits in UK manufacturing', in R. Matthews and J. Sargent, *Contemporary problems of economic policy* (London: Methuen, 1983) p. 84.

69. Blackaby, *De-industrialisation*, pp. 11, 244.

70. Blackaby, *British economic policy*, p. 327.

71. Bacon and Eltis, *Britain's economic problem*, p. 56.

72. Notably in the work of Stuart Holland, an active member of policy-making committees at the time. See his *The socialist challenge* (London: Quartet Books, 1976).

73. According to Joel Barnett, Wynn Godley and Nicky Kaldor were calling for import controls at the start of 1975. *Inside the Treasury* (London: Deutsch, 1982) p. 62.

74. R. Caves and B. Krause, *Britain's economic performance* (Washington: Brookings, 1980) p. 58.

75. See Leys, *Politics in Britain*, p. 86.

76. Brown and Sheriff, 'De-industrialisation', p. 251.

77. Barnett, *Inside the Treasury*.

78. In 1975 reserves stood at $5.4 billion, total borrowing at $8.9 billion and OPEC deposits alone at more than $5 billion. Figures from Caves and Krause, *Britain's economic performance*, pp. 35 and 58.

79. Much of the detail here comes from S. Fay and H. Young, *The day the £*

nearly died (London: *Sunday Times*, 1978).

80. *Ibid.*, pp. 12–13. It does not seem to have struck Mr Yeo that in 1976 the Americans were also consuming far more than they were earning. But then the special role of the dollar protected them from the need to control their deficit as the British were being forced to do.

81. The text is reprinted in *The Times*, 16 December 1976.

82. Cited in Caves and Krause, *Britain's economic performance*, p. 75.

83. The rationale of the development of the Treasury's 'political economic' theory is set out in a very revealing article by J. Fforde, 'Setting monetary objectives', *Bank of England Quarterly Bulletin*, 23(2), 1983.

84. S. Pollard, *The wasting of the British economy* (London: Croom Helm, 1982) p. 62.

85. Figures from Matthews and Sargent, *Contemporary problems of economic policy*, pp. 148–9.

86. Fforde, 'Setting monetary objectives', p. 203.

87. *Ibid.*, p. 207. It is interesting to note that the Bank is quite willing to concede that much of the argument that was put forward was quite consciously designed to negate the democratic process, and also that it is now quite happy to admit this openly.

88. Pollard, *The wasting of the British economy*, p. 166.

89. Lord Richardson, Governor of the Bank of England, 'British economic policy over the last decade', *Bank of England Quarterly Bulletin*, 23(2), 1983, p. 195.

90. *Bank of England Quarterly Bulletin*, 23(1), 1983, p. 29.

91. J. M. Keynes, 'The International Monetary Fund', speech to the House of Lords, 23 May 1944, reprinted in A. Hansen, *The new economics* (London: Dobson, 1947); in particular he claimed that 'we abjure the instruments of bank rate and credit contraction operating through the increase in unemployment as a means of forcing our domestic economy into line with external factors' (p. 374).

92. S. Pollard, *The development of the British economy, 1914–1980*, 3rd edn (London: Arnold, 1983); and *The wasting of the British economy*.

93. Pollard, *The development of the British economy*, 2nd edn, p. 445.

94. *Ibid.*, p. 443.

Prologue to Part III

1. The Brandt Commission, *Common crisis* (London: Pan, 1983) p. 25.

2. The quotation is from D. Lal, *The poverty of development economics* (London: Institute of Economic Affairs, 1983); this, together with the powerfully argued *Economic development*, by I. M. D. Little (New York: Basic Books, 1983) constitutes an excellent outline of the optimistic liberal case which sees the future as a matter of learning from the 'four little tigers' (Hong Kong, Singapore, South Korea, Taiwan).

3. Lal, *ibid.*

Chapter 7

1. I have outlined the presuppositions of British colonial economic policy in *Colonialism and underdevelopment in East Africa* (London: Heinemann, 1973) ch. 3.
2. My *Colonialism and underdevelopment* also contains an account of colonial industrialisation in East Africa; for a liberal account of the growth of manufacturing in India in the 19th century, see Lal, *The poverty of development economics*, pp. 82 ff.
3. For a vigorous statement of the basis for the 'two-gap theory' see I. M. D. Little and J. M. Clifford, *International aid* (London: Allen & Unwin, 1965) p. 140 ff.; Little gives the reasons for a subsequent change of mind in *Economic development* (New York: Basic Books, 1983).
4. M. Bienefeld and M. Godfrey, *The struggle for development* (New York: Wiley, 1982) pp. 44–5.
5. An account of the development of the textile industry in the Ivory Coast by French capital can be found in B. Campbell, *The social, political and economic consequences of French private investment in the Ivory Coast, 1960–1970*, Sussex University PhD, 1973.
6. I have outlined this connection in pre-war Britain in *Colonialism and underdevelopment*, ch. 4; it is documented in the post-war period in D. Burch, *Overseas aid and the transfer of technology*, Sussex University PhD, 1979.
7. Little, *Economic development*, p. 277.
8. World Bank, *World Development Report*, 1978, p. 78.
9. D. Morawetz, *Twenty-five years of economic development* (Washington: World Bank, 1977) p. 12.
10. Manufactures rose from 1 per cent of exports to 8 per cent in low-income countries and from 5 per cent to 17 per cent in middle-income countries between 1960 and 1975 (World Bank, *World Development Report*, 1978, p. 88).
11. Figures from OECD, *Development cooperation*, various issues.
12. Information from UN, *Multinational corporations in world development*, (ST/ECA/190) (New York: UN, 1973).
13. OECD, *Development Cooperation*.
14. Little, *Economic development*, p. 280.
15. These figures have been derived from the summary tables found in relevant issues of IMF, *Annual Report*. The 'current account' used here includes only goods, services and private transfers and excludes official government transfers and long- and short-term private transfers. Balance of payments accounting is notoriously problematic, and accurate figures are very difficult to establish, so that they are given here only as approximations which probably capture the general trend.
16. LDC terms of trade declined by 7 per cent between 1955 and the late 1960s, while those of the DCs improved by 10 per cent. C. Frank and others, *Assisting developing countries* (New York: Praeger, 1972) p. 393.

288   *Notes and References*

17. Morawetz, *Twenty-five years of economic development*, p. 26.
18. The evidence is surveyed in Morawetz, and in A. Chenery and others, *Redistribution with growth* (London: Oxford University Press, 1974) ch. 1.
19. Figures extracted from World Bank, *World Development Report*, 1983, Tables 1 and 2. The six countries are Hong Kong, Singapore, Taiwan, South Korea, Mexico and Brazil. Figures for Taiwan are taken from G. Ranis, 'The NICs, the near NICs and the world economy', manuscript.
20. Morawetz, *Twenty-five years of economic development*, p. 17.
21. UN, *Multinational corporations*, p. 19 (I have taken the liberty of counting five very small Caribbean islands as one country in the first group).
22. OECD, *Development Cooperation, 1972 Review*, p. 103.
23. The case against structuralism is clearly presented in D. Lal, *The poverty of development economics*, I. M. D. Little, *Economic development*, I. M. D. Little and others, *Industry and trade in some developing countries* (London: Oxford University Press, 1970).
24. In some extreme cases it could be shown that the foreign exchange costs of the imported inputs involved 'were higher than the price of a comparable imported product'. World Bank, *Accelerated development in sub-Saharan Africa* (Washington: IRBD, 1981) p. 28.
25. Lal, p. 108
26. Bienefeld and Godfrey, *The struggle for development*, p. 33.
27. G. Ranis, 'The NICs, the near NICs and the world economy', manuscript, p. 12.
28. Little, *Economic development*, p. 262.
29. Ranis, p. 10.
30. I owe these points to Raphael Kaplinsky.
31. Ranis, p. 18.
32. J. H. Adler, 'Allocation of investment', in IBRD, *Some aspects of the economic philosophy of the World Bank* (Washington: IBRD, 1968) pp. 47–8.
33. E. S. Shaw, *Financial deepening in economic development* (New York: Oxford University Press), R. I. McKinnon, *Money and capital in economic development* (Washington: Brookings, 1973).
34. All figures from IMF, *Annual Report*.
35. OECD, *Development Cooperation, 1982 Review*, p. 27.
36. World Bank, *World development report*, 1983 (Washington: IBRD, 1984) p. 11.
37. For an excellent summary of the 'terms of trade' debate, and critique of the liberal position, see Bienefeld and Godfrey, *The struggle for developments*, p. 58.
38. World Bank, *World development report*, 1983, p. 35.
39. OECD, *Development Cooperation, 1982 Review*, p. 37.
40. *Ibid.*, p. 38. This report contains a useful analysis of the composition and experience of this new group of high performing countries.
41. C. Thomas, *Dependence and transformation* (New York: Monthly

Review, 1974).
42. These points were forcibly made by S. Amin at the Global Crisis conference organised by the British and Dutch Labour Parties in London in 1984.
43. See H. Chenery *et al.*, *Redistribution with growth* (London: Oxford University Press, 1974). The various ILO reports are listed and the implications of their views surveyed in G. Kitching, *Development and underdevelopment*, and also in Little, *Economic development*, ch. 11.
44. See, for example, 'Britain on Brandt', *IDS Bulletin*, 12(2), 1981; D. Seers, 'North-South: muddling morality and mutuality', *Third World Quarterly*, 2(4) 1980; D. Elson, 'Strategy: the Brandt Report', *Capital and Class, 16*, 1982.
45. See, for example, Little, *Economic development*, p. 262 ff.
46. See in particular B. Warren, *Imperialism, pioneer of capitalism* (London: Verso, 1980); C. T. Leys, 'African economic development in theory and practice', *Daedalus*, 111(2), 1982.
47. World Bank, *World development report*, 1982, p. 21.
48. Chenery *et al.*, *Redistribution with growth*.
49. World Bank, p. 25.
50. The evidence is presented in OECD, *Development Cooperation, 1982 Review*, ch. 12.
51. See in particular R. Wade, *Guiding the market: dirigism Taiwan-style*, forthcoming; R. Luedde-Neurath, *Import controls and export-oriented development: a re-examination of the South Korean case: 1962–1982*, Sussex University PhD, 1984.
52. Wade, p. 153.
53. This account comes from C. Fortin, 'The failure of repressive monetarism: Chile 1973–1983', *Third World Quarterly*, 6(2), 1984.
54. See, for example, the official British study, UK, Foreign and Commonwealth Office, *The newly industrialising countries and the adjustment problem* (London: HMSO, 1979).
55. See in particular W. R. Cline, 'Can the East Asian model of development be generalised?' *World development*, 10(2), 1982.
56. For an excellent critique of the role of Western aid in development see T. Mende, *From aid to re-colonization* (New York: Pantheon Books, 1973).
57. See in particular A. Nove, *The economics of feasible socialism* (London: Allen & Unwin, 1983).
58. For a general survey see G. White and others, *Revolutionary socialist development in the third world* (Brighton: Harvester, 1983).

Chapter 8

1. I. M. D. Little, *Economic development* (New York: Basic Books, 1983) p. 75.

2. Four Central American countries adopted Article VIII in the 1940s, and two Caribbean and one Central American country did so in the 1950s; by 1981 a total of 35 had done so. IMF, *Annual Report*, 1981, p. 130.
3. Little, p. 307.
4. G. Bird, *The international monetary system and the less developed countries*, 2nd edn (London: Macmillan, 1982) p. 16.
5. The figures in the text are taken from E. Bernstein, 'The International Monetary Fund', in R. N. Gardner and M. F. Millikan, *The global partnership* (New York: Praeger, 1968) p. 137; a critique of intervention can be found in E. Eshag and J. R. Thorp, 'Economic and social consequences of orthodox policies in Argentina in the post-war years', *Bulletin of the Oxford University Institute of Economics and Statistics*, 27(1), 1965.
6. See J. Horsefield, *The International Monetary Fund, 1945–1966* (Washington: IMF, 1969) Vol. II, pp. 378–80.
7. Details can be found in B. Tew, *The evolution of the international monetary system, 1945–1977* (London: Hutchinson, 1977) Appendix A.
8. Total lending from the Compensatory Financing Facility was only $462.6 million between 1963 and 1971 (M. de Vries, *The International Monetary Fund, 1966–1971* (Washington: IMF, 1976, p. 268), while only $12.15 million was lent to assist the International Tin Agreement in 1971 (*ibid.*, pp. 283–4).
9. The figures up to 1970, together with an account of the Bank's lending practices, can be found in E. S. Mason and R. Asher, *The World Bank since Bretton Woods* (Washington: Brookings, 1973) chs 6 and 7.
10. For details see Mason and Asher, ch. 12.
11. For details see C. Wilcox, *A charter for world trade* (New York: Macmillan, 1949); W. A. Brown, *The United States and the restoration of world trade* (Washington: Brookings, 1950); K. Dam, *Law and international economic organisation* (Chicago: University of Chicago Press, 1970); and K. Kock, *International trade policy and the GATT, 1947–1967* (Stockholm: Almquist & Wiksell, 1969).
12. Ambassador K. B. Lall, cited in J. W. Evans, 'The General Agreement on Tariffs and Trade', in Gardner and Millikan, *The global partnership*, p. 76.
13. GATT, *Trends in international trade* (Geneva: GATT, 1958); the quote is from Evans, p. 84.
14. See GATT, *Basic instruments and selected documents*, 13th Supplement, GATT, 1965.
15. K. Morton and P. Tulloch, *Trade and developing countries* (London: Croom Helm, 1977) p. 58.
16. This is the position put forward in Little, *Economic development*, ch. 14.
17. Morton and Tulloch, *ibid.* See also G. Helleiner, *Intra-firm trade and the developing countries* (London: Macmillan, 1981) for a discussion of the political influences leading to the tendency for the GATT negotia-

tions to favour exporters of capital-intensive rather than labour-intensive products (pp. 75–6).

18. R. Prebisch, *Towards a new trade policy for development* (UN E/Conf 46/3) (New York: UN, 1964).

19. UNCTAD, *Proceedings of the United Nations conference on Trade and Development* (New York, UN, 1964) Vol. 1, p. 4.

20. See R. Gardner, 'The United Nations Conference on Trade and Development', in Gardner and Millikan, *The global partnership* pp. 114–20, where he also describes the 'conciliation' machinery designed to offset Northern opposition to Southern control.

21. J. Pincus, *Trade, aid and development* (New York: McGraw-Hill, 1967) pp. 81–2.

22. IMF, *Annual Report*, 1978, p. 40.

23. *Ibid.*, p. 40.

24. GATT, *Gatt activities in 1979* (Geneva: GATT, 1980) p. 16.

25. R. E. Baldwin, *Beyond the Tokyo negotiations* (London: Trade Policy Research Centre, 1979) p. 2.

26. See Little, *Economic development* p. 368 for a list of important LDC exports affected by 'voluntary export restraints'.

27. Main documents of the Group of 77 at UNCTAD V, No. 2, 'Multilateral trade negotiations: declaration by the Group of 77', reprinted in K. P. Sauvant (ed.), *The collected documents of The Group of 77*, Vol. II (London: Oceana, 1981) pp. 525–6.

28. World Bank, *World Development Report*, 1983, p. 9.

29. GATT, *Gatt activities in 1981* (Geneva: GATT, 1982) p. 27.

30. L. Dunn *et al.*, *In the kingdom of the blind* (London: Trade Policy Research Centre, 1983) pp. 10, 13.

31. See Catholic Institute for International Relations *The renegotiation of the Lomé Convention* (London:CIIR, 1978); A. Rubin, *Lomé II*, (London: CLLI, 1978).

32. D. B. Rainford, 'Lomé II', in *The Courier*, Special Issue, 58, 1979, p. 25.

33. For example, A. J. Yeates, *Trade barriers facing developing countries*, (London: Macmillan, 1979) p. 172; Little, *Economic development*, p. 370.

34. Bienefeld and Godfrey, *The struggle for development*, p. 34.

35. Commonwealth Study Group, *Towards a new Bretton Woods* (London: Commonwealth Secretariat, 1983) p. 39.

36. Little, *Economic development*, p. 370; see also pp. 383–4.

37. OECD, *Development cooperation, 1983 Review*, p. 51.

38. *Ibid.*, 1972, p. 225; 1983, p. 188.

39. *Ibid.*, 1983, p. 51.

40. According to E. K. Y. Chen, foreign firms 'played little part in the crucial 1962–6 period, when export expansion began to replace import substitution' in Hong Kong, South Korea and Taiwan. *Multinational corporations, technology and employment* (London: Macmillan, 1983) p. 132.

41. UN Centre on Transnational Corporations, *Transnational corporations*

in world development, 3rd Survey (New York: UN, 1983) p. 28.

42. UNIDO, *World industry in 1980* (New York: UN, 1981) p. 240.
43. This growth was stimulated in particular by changes in US tariff regulations in the mid-1960s. See in particular G. Helleiner, 'Manufactured exports from less developed countries and multinational firms', *Economic Journal*, March 1983.
44. UN Centre on Transnational Corporations, p. 158.
45. UNIDO, p. 238.
46. For two relevant investigations, see S. Langdon, 'Multinational corporations, taste transfer and underdevelopment: a case study of Kenya', *Review of African Political Economy*, 2, 1975, and J. de Coninck, *Artisans and petty producers in Uganda*, Sussex University PhD, 1980, which deal with the soap and shoe industries respectively.
47. UN Centre on Transnational Corporations, p. 22.
48. Here see R. Murray, *Multinationals beyond the market* (Brighton: Harvester, 1981).
49. See T. Killick and M. Sutton, 'Global disequilibria and the non-oil developing countries', in T. Killick (ed.) *Adjustment and financing in the developing world* (Washington: IMF, 1982).
50. For an excellent examination of the problem see J. Williamson, 'The international financial system', in E. R. Fried and C. L. Schultz (eds) *Higher oil prices and the world economy* (Washington: Brookings, 1975).
51. The demands made by the LDCs can be found in the communiqués issued by the Group of 24, established to deal with this problem by the Group of 77 in 1973. They can be found in K. P. Sauvant, *The collected documents of the Group of 77*, Vol. V.
52. All the figures can be found in the IMF's 1983 annual report.
53. For an insight into the IMF's own (unpublished) thinking on both the Chile and Jamaica cases, see S. Holland and E. A. Brett, 'For a few dollars more', *The Observer*, July 1980; for a detailed critique of their role in Portugal, Jamaica and Peru, see *Development dialogue*, 1982, 2; for a recent analysis of its role in Latin America see Latin American Bureau, *The poverty brokers: the IMF and Latin America* (London: Latin America Bureau, 1983).
54. 'The Arusha Initiative', *Development dialogue*, 1982, 2; pp. 14–16.
55. M. Guitan, 'Economic management and IMF conditionality', in Killick, *Adjustment and financing*, p. 86; for a general survey of the conditionality debate, see J. Williamson (ed.) *IMF Conditionality* (Washington: Institute for International Economics, 1983).
56. Here they assert that 'the "infant industry" argument may justify some controls', but if the controls are too severe 'the resulting distortion of relative prices leads to an ineffective structure of production and investment and eventually to a lower rate of economic growth than could have been achieved otherwise'. IMF, *Annual Report*, 1983, p. 59. They also make a plea for a reduction in protectionism against LDC exports in DC markets, though without being able to exert any influence over a well established trend.

57. See D. Schydlowsky, 'Alternative approaches to short-term economic management in developing countries', in Killick, *Adjustment and financing*, p. 118; see also L. Taylor, *Macro models for developing countries* (New York: McGraw Hill, 1979) pp. 50–8.
58. Schydlowsky, p. 122.
59. *Ibid.*
60. Bienefeld and Godfrey, pp. 47–8; see also the demands put forward in 'The Arusha Initiative', *Development Dialogue*, 1980, 2.
61. These are listed and surveyed in G. Kitching, *Development and under-development in historical perspective* (London: Methuen, 1982).
62. H. Chenery *et al.*, *Redistribution with growth* (London: Oxford University Press, 1974).
63. See, for example, International Labour Office, *Employment, growth and basic needs* (Geneva: ILO, 1976).
64. See, for example, B. Belassa, *Reforming the system of incentives in developing countries*, Bank Staff Working Paper No. 203 (Washington: World Bank, 1975).
65. These reports are for restricted circulation only, available to Bank and government officials in the country concerned and in the donor countries.
66. For details see E. P. Wright, 'World Bank lending for structural adjustment', *Finance and development*, 17(3), 1980.
67. New credits agreed by IDA were $3,838 million in 1980, $3,482 million, $2,686 million in 1982 and $3,341 million in 1983. (World Bank, *Annual Report*, 1983, p. 12).
68. World Bank, *Accelerated development in sub-Saharan Africa* (Washington: IBRD, 1981) (The 'Berg Report').

Chapter 9

1. We should not overlook the contribution of the growth of bank credit in the 1920s and its collapse in the 1930s to the financial crisis and subsequent disintegration of the international economy. See H. W. Arndt, *The economic lessons of the nineteen-thirties* (London: Cass, 1972); C. Kindleberger, *Manias, panics and crashes* (London: Macmillan, 1978); M. Friedman and A. Schwartz, *The great contraction 1929–1933* (Princeton: Princeton University Press, 1965).
2. Detailed figures can be found in E. Brett, 'International banking and the crisis', *Socialist Economic Review*, 1984; the major sources of data on debt are the Bank for International Settlements, *Annual Reports*, *World financial markets*, issued by Morgan Guaranty Trust; the World Bank's *World debt tables*; IMF, *International financial statistics*; and *AMEX Bank Review*, *Special Papers*, 'International debt, banks and the LDCs', 10, 1984.
3. *Euromoney*, August 1982, p. 23.
4. According to Amex, the latest 'Current Market Estimate' put the debts

of the twenty-four largest debtors at $528.8 billion in February 1984. *Amex Bank Review*, 10, 1984, p. 30.

5. *Ibid.*, p. 16.

6. In June 1983 the nine largest US banks had lent $67 billion to the ten largest Third World borrowers representing 223 per cent of their capital assets. Exposure to Brazil was 48.8 per cent, to Mexico 48 per cent, to Korea 26.9 per cent and to Venezuela 26.8 per cent. *Amex Bank Review*, 10, 1984, p. 38.

7. US Senate Committees on Foreign Relations, Sub-Committee on Foreign Economic Policy, *International debt, the banks and US foreign policy* (Washington: Government Printing Office, 1976) p. 11.

8. IMF, *Annual Report*, 1983, p. 18.

9. See, for example, R. I. McKinnon, *The eurocurrency market* (Princeton, Princeton University Press, 1977); C. H. Stem *et al.*, *Eurocurrencies and the international monetary system* (Washington: American Enterprise Institute, 1976).

10. Bank for International Settlements, *Annual Report*, 1982/83, p. 130.

11. See various BIS Annual Reports from 1972/3 onwards; in mid-1983 GEC alone was holding £1.39 billion in short-term investments (*The Guardian*, 8 July 1983)

12. From various issues of Morgan Guaranty Trust, *World financial markets.*

13. See J. Spero, *The failure of Franklin National Bank* (New York:Columbia University Press, 1980).

14. *Amex Bank Review*, 10, 1984, p. 26. For Brazil, interest payments alone absorbed 42.6 per cent of export earnings.

15. G. Johnson with R. Adams, *Aspects of the international banking safety net*, (Washington: IMF, 1983) p. 2.

16. This issue is dealt with by the deputy governor of the Bank of England in *Bank of England Quarterly Bulletin*, June 1983, p. 222.

17. See in particular 'The maverick who yelled foul at Citibank', *Fortune*, 10 January 1983; and for a more general discussion see E. Brett, *International money and capitalist crisis* (London: Heinemann, 1983) p. 222 ff.

18. For a good analysis of the conditions under which excessive borrowing can lead to national bankruptcy, see J. Williamson, 'The international financial system', in E. Fried and C. Schultze, *Higher oil prices and the world economy* (Washington: Brookings, 1975).

19. For an early analysis of the way in which loans eventually had to be paid by an appropriation to the output of direct producers in third world countries, see R. Luxemburg, *The accumulation of capital* (London: Routledge & Kegan Paul, 1951).

20. According to the former governor of the Central Bank of Brazil, they were able to borrow 'automatically' at 'an average of $1.5 billion a month' even in the first six months of 1982. *Euromoney*, October 1983, p. 20.

21. World Bank, *World Debt Tables*, 1982–3, pp. ix–x.

22. *Euromoney*, August 1982, p. 21.

23. See in particular K. Marx, *Capital*, Vol. III (London: Lawrence & Wishart, 1972) Part V.
24. See Amex Bank Review p. 10; on Mexico BIS, *Annual Report*, 1982/3, p. 128, and personal communication, Dr Graf zu Münster, Trinkaus & Birkhardt Bank.
25. BIS, *Annual Report*, 1983/4, p. 101.
26. BIS, *Annual Report*, 1982/3, p. 182.
27. *Ibid.*, p. 183.
28. *Ibid.*, p. 188; see also *World Financial Markets*, June 1983, p. 13; *Euromoney*, June 1983, p. 7; and even some cautious support for this view at the Williamsburg Summit in 1983 (see IMF Survey, 13 June 1983).
29. See the calculations in *Euromoney*, October 1983, p. 66.
30. B. Quinn (Assistant Director, Bank of England) 'International debt: a central banker's view', *Bank of England Quarterly Bulletin*, 23(4), 1983, p. 544.
31. A rough calculation of the graphic evidence presented in Chart 2 in Quinn (see note 30) suggests that Mexico's *additional* payments will be $23 billion between 1984 and 1990; Latin American spreads widened from less than 1 per cent to 2 per cent between 1980 and 1983, while all reschedulings involve large bank charges.
32. The adverse movement in LDC terms of trade since the war is shown in the figure on page 196.
33. P.Minford, 'The effects of American policies' (mimeo) p 4
34. *Financial Times*, 21 May 1984.
35. Arndt, *The economic lessons*, pp. 281–2.
36. For a review of a powerful critique of these Latin American programmes, see 'The IMF vs. the people', *Euromoney*, October 1983, pp. 90 ff.
37. For a review of the impossible conditions being experienced in the Latin American economies in 1982/3, see *Euromoney*, March and June 1983.
38. Morgan Guaranty Trust, *World Financial Markets*, October 1983, p. 4.
39. *Guardian*, 24 July 1984.
40. Brett, *International money and capitalist crisis*, pp. 223–6.
41. US Senate, *International debt*, made the case in 1976.

Conclusion

1. V. I. Lenin, *Imperialism* (Moscow, Progress Publishers, 1970, p. 178/9.
2. According to Hans Singer, about 0.5 per cent of global industrial production was located in the Third World in 1949 (personal communication).
3. W. A. Brown, *The United States and the restoration of world trade* (Washington: Brookings, 1950) p. 45.

4. M. Kostecki, *East-west trade and the GATT system* (London: Macmillan, 1979) p. 3.
5. J. S. Mill's words, *Principles of political economy* (London: Longmans 1980) p. 352.
6. H. W. Arndt, *The economic lessons of the nineteen-thirties* (London: Cass, 1972, first issued in 1944) p. 296. This view did not meet general approval in the Chatham House group and was opposed by Sir Andrew McFadyean and Professor A. G. Fisher.
7. *Ibid.*, pp. 297–8.
8. See, for example, J. Williamson, *A new SDR allocation?* (Washington: Institute for International Economics, 1984).
9. Independent Commission on International Development Issues, *North-South* (London: Pan, 1980); *Common crisis* (London: Pan, 1983).
10. I have developed this argument at length in E. A. Brett, *International money and capitalist crisis* (London: Heinemann, 1983) chs 3 and 4.
11. See in particular R. Kaplinsky, 'The new international division of labour and the Transnational Corporation', 1984, manuscript; within three to four years we can apparently expect the capital-labour ratio in the textile industry to move from 20:80 to 80:20, thus decisively ending the advantages now enjoyed by Third World producers. Dr H.-S. Graf Zu Münster, personal communication.
12. For Bull, the current system exists as an 'anarchical society' (p. 51) governed by a high degree of self-regulation and therefore capable of order (H. Bull, *The anarchical society* (London: Macmillan, 1977) especially pp. 47–51). By excluding the problem of uneven development from the analysis he is also able to ignore the fact that anarchy leads to uncontrolled disorder unless it is based upon an equitable structure of distribution and democratic political regulation.
13. G. Lukács, *History and class consciousness* (London: Merlin, 1971) p. 63.
14. See the Labour Party, *Labour's programme, 1982* (London: The Labour Party, 1982).
15. Arndt, *The economic lessons*, p. 300; See also H. Laski, *A grammar of politics* (London: Allen & Unwin, 1925) p. 587.
16. J. M. Keynes, 'Proposals for an International Union', in H. G. Grubel, *World monetary reform* (London: Oxford University Press, 1964) p. 66.
17. Independent Commission on International Development Issues, *North-South* (London: Pan, 1980) p. 244.
18. Cited in Brown, *The United States and the restoration of world trade*, p. 406.
19. From 'The Arusha Initiative', *Development Dialogue*, 1980, 2, p. 19.
20. H. Chenery *et al.*, *Redistribution with growth* (London: Oxford University Press, 1974); C. Thomas, *Dependence and transformation* (New York: Monthly Review Press, 1974).
21. An important exception is A. Nove, *The economics of feasible socialism*

(London: Allen & Unwin, 1983) together with Thomas, *Dependence and transformation*, and Chenery *et al.*, *Redistribution with growth*.
22. Here we might include the Brandt Report's demand for a new World Development Fund, Independent Commission, *North-South*, pp. 252–3.
23. A useful discussion of these issues can be found in H. Radice, 'The national economy – a Keynesian myth?', *Capital and class*, 22, 1984.
24. In A. Gorz, *Strategy for labour* (Boston: Beacon, 1967) Part 2.
25. Published in S. Holland (ed.), *Out of crisis* (Nottingham: Spokesman, 1983).

Index